MENTAL HEALTH HOMICIDE AND SOCIETY

A homicide committed by a mentally disordered person who is under the care of health service professionals is a shocking event. Otherwise known as a 'patient homicide', these incidents are followed by an investigation into the care and treatment received by the perpetrator. These investigations are often regarded as a way to 'learn lessons', establish accountability and provide catharsis to families and the public. The book argues however that patient homicide events and the circumstances in which they occur are communicated about within closed systems of life (eg law, medicine). These systems operate according to unique internal logics. The communications produced by these systems, nevertheless, resonate in society and enable a diverse and complex space of governance to emerge – a space of governance in which universal understandings about patient homicides, health care, public safety and risk are unachievable.

The Scottish Government initiated reform of their patient homicide investigation procedures in 2017 and plans to reform patient homicide investigations in England are slowly germinating. This original and compelling book is therefore a timely and important contribution. It concludes that health policy makers should re-evaluate their normative commitments to patient homicide risk reduction in a world of disharmony, objection and resistance.

Mental Health Homicide and Society

Understanding Health Care Governance

David P Horton

•HART•
OXFORD • LONDON • NEW YORK • NEW DELHI • SYDNEY

HART PUBLISHING

Bloomsbury Publishing Plc

Kemp House, Chawley Park, Cumnor Hill, Oxford, OX2 9PH, UK

HART PUBLISHING, the Hart/Stag logo, BLOOMSBURY and the Diana logo are trademarks of Bloomsbury Publishing Plc

First published in Great Britain 2019

A catalogue record for this book is available from the British Library.

A catalogue record for this book is available from the Library of Congress.

ISBN: HB: 978-1-50991-214-8
ePDF: 978-1-50991-215-5
ePub: 978-1-50991-213-1

Typeset by Compuscript Ltd, Shannon

PREFACE

The relationship between homicide and health care is often discussed in the context of patient deaths caused by medical errors during health care treatment. The author, however, focuses on an overlooked, yet important, relationship between homicide and health care in a completely different context: homicides committed by mentally disordered persons in receipt of care and treatment (ie, otherwise known as 'patient homicides'). Patient homicides are less discussed. They occupy, however, a central focus of the patient homicide governance space. The patient homicide governance space is a phrase used at many points throughout the book. It refers to an investigatory domain constituted by diverse communications (eg, medical communications, legal communications, political communications) about patient homicide. These communications have immense social significance.

In general, the patient homicide governance space involves a unique marriage of two issues that resonate in society and call for rigorous, original examination: the adequacy of health care services and public safety. The adequacy of health care services and public safety are issues of seismic importance. Yet, they are accompanied by a series of challenges that make their management difficult: the deterioration of mental health in populations; the ineffective measures taken by health services and politicians to address mental illness; resource limitations; and limited understanding in policy-making circles of mental illness, victim support and adverse event investigation. These challenges appear in the patient homicide governance space as focal points of anger, frustration and concern. The families of patient homicide victims are especially vocal. Local and national media dig for stories and provide coverage. Politicians, police officers and health care providers issue statements at press conferences. Government agencies and health care professionals are expected to provide answers, improve safety and reassure the public. Reputations and jobs are at stake. Technical experts examine the facts of individual cases and deliver recommendations for service change. These experts are uniquely placed to make judgements about other technical experts (eg, clinicians) involved in the delivery of the services in question. They are tasked to carry out close scrutiny of those responsible for the perpetrator's care and treatment, although the difficulty of the investigatory task is compounded in cases where the decisions identified for scrutiny were made a long time ago.

Patient homicide and health care is a unique area of health care governance with huge implications that deserve rigorous examination. *Mental Health*

Homicide and Society: Understanding Health Care Governance provides the scrutiny required. Not only does it conduct an original exploration of a complex area of life fraught with tension and high expectations, the novel theoretical design of the book supports a call for health care policy makers and decision-making elites to re-evaluate their commitments to effecting change in public services when responding to patient homicide.

ACKNOWLEDGEMENTS

I am indebted to Ms Kirsty Keywood and Professor Toby Seddon of the University of Manchester's School of Law for their guidance and years of solid support. I also give warm thanks to Professor Jill Peay of the London School of Economics for her invaluable comments and suggestions.

I give special thanks to those who were interviewed for the book. In particular, I thank Julian Hendy, the founder of Hundred Families. Julian tirelessly promotes learning and awareness about mental health homicides and provides vital support to families affected by patient homicide incidents. He shared his unique views during an interview and kindly consented to his name being used in the book.

I thank colleagues and students at the University of Liverpool. In particular, I thank Kieran Fahey and Mandana Khajehnouri for their help with interview transcription. I also express sincere gratitude for the assistance received from the production team at Hart Publishing.

I deeply thank my Dad, my sisters Lisa and Kate, my Brother-in-Law Darren, my nieces Caitlin and Pheobe, my nephews Dermot, Flynn and Gunnar and Auntie Viv. I am eternally indebted to my wife, Karen, for her patience and support over the past six years. She continues to understand the arduous task of living with a scholar.

The book is dedicated to the memory of Karen's parents, Avtar Singh Heer and Balwinder Kaur Heer. Both Avtar and Balwinder embodied the virtues of care, respect and discipline. Their memory continues to inspire me when life's challenges become great.

David Paul Horton
Liverpool, England
25 December 2018

CONTENTS

TABLE OF CASES

TABLE OF LEGISLATION

Statutory Instruments

Hansard

Introduction

According to official figures, homicides committed by mentally disordered individuals are rare. Yet, these events resonate in society. They resonate in society's legal system, political system, economic system and mass media system. It is unusual to see an area of health care governance resonate in society to such a scale. A small crop of issues relating to patient homicide governance have, thus far, occupied academic attention however; hindsight bias, counterfactual reasoning and blaming are issues that form epicentres of focus for scholars. These are important issues but there is more to patient homicide governance. It is an area of immense social significance that the author unpacks using novel theoretical design. In doing so, the book advances a whole new understanding of patient homicide and health care services. Furthermore, it provides an original theoretical model for research conducted in areas beyond the patient homicide governance space because it embarks on a deep questioning of conventional policy-making orthodoxies.

A central and far-reaching message of the book is that responses to patient homicide are carried out in a chaotic space of health care governance. Further still, the book argues that implementing service change in accordance with predefined goals is fraught with conflict and uncertainty. Implementing change is not, contrary to conventional orthodoxy, a linear process of exacting improvements in services and learning lessons. Rather, the predefined efforts to implement change often meet resistance and unexpected outcomes. The patient homicide governance space is a maelstrom of different values and logics that read from different communicative scripts. The book, accordingly, prompts policy makers within the patient homicide governance space to re-evaluate their conventional approaches towards change and policy implementation.

The author uses systems theory – and more specifically the work of Niklas Luhmann – to carry out the study. A number of reasons underpin the book's theoretical preference. On the one hand, Luhmann's work – unlike other social theories – provides a precise view of society that helps readers reliably understand events and relationships in the world. His work is notable for insisting that society is differentiated into functional spheres of closed autonomous communication; each functional sphere (eg, law, politics, the economy) is impervious to direct influence, control and domination by other functional spheres. Luhmann's theory enables a radical, original, picture of society's most recognisable roles (eg, clinicians, health care managers, politicians) and organisations (eg, health care providers, non-departmental public bodies, media organisations) to emerge. Furthermore, Luhmann's theory helps to frame these roles and organisations as crucial to societal functioning in a host of different ways. These roles and organisations are meaningful for the functions of, say, law (eg, as 'litigants', as 'courts') and medicine (ie, as 'patients', as 'hospitals'). As *closed* communication spheres in society, the conclusion is that exacting precise social change and control from a particular perspective (eg, a legal perspective, an administrative perspective) over complex areas of life (eg, medicine) is impossible. A novel and comprehensive research contribution that captures these dynamics and examines their implications for patient homicide policy making and scholarship has yet to be conducted. The book, however, fills the gap. Luhmann's work is identified as an ideal theoretical place holder for these purposes.

Luhmann's work is notable for many other reasons but its divergence from mainstream intellectual scholarship stands out above all. Conventional social theories – chiefly those of the Anglo-American tradition – tend to view society as stratified (ie, differentiated according to a hierarchy), amenable to direct influence and adequately represented in one single perspective (eg, think Marx's historical materialism or Hegel's dialectical materialism). Traditional academic enquiry is, furthermore, confined to commenting on specific cause-and-effect relationships (eg, between economics and health services). Luhmann's work stresses, however, that traditional intellectual approaches oversimplify their focus of study (eg, society). It stresses that social and political theory must acknowledge the imprecision of cause-and-effect reasoning. Notable theories (eg, Marxism) are, according to Luhmann, imprecise in their diagnosis; after diagnosing the chief problems afflicting society (eg, capitalist inequality), conventional theories of the Anglo-American tradition go on to advocate social steering in accordance with a predetermined set of aims (ie, cause and effect) as a solution. Luhmann's work is sceptical of these attempts to socially steer. It reminds readers that society is too complex to be steered by any one perspective. An attempt to implement social steering will result in unintended consequences.

The author takes Luhmann's message seriously by using it to develop an original theoretical basis for the book. The book argues that the patient homicide governance space is constituted by moments of observation created within functionally differentiated spheres of communication. The book's argument enables a creative tapestry of patient homicide governance to emerge. From law to politics and the mass media, Luhmann's work provides the navigational tools required to provide a comprehensive map of the governance terrain in a way that has not been done before. Furthermore, it argues that exacting precise and predictable change in health care services in response to these dreadful incidents is far more challenging than is often realised.

An additional reason underlines the book's theoretical commitment. Luhmann is considered to be one of the most important thinkers of the twentieth century. A sociologist by trade, his work has informed swathes of legal, political, economic and regulatory scholarship. Despite Luhmann's profile, his work is abstract, controversial and viewed with scepticism in Anglo-American intellectual circles because of how it conceptualises the individual. The Western intellectual tradition has long regarded the individual as having a complete essence (eg, a soul that exercises mastery over the body, as a holder of inalienable rights). The tradition is committed to the belief that humanity possesses an ability to set predefined goals, determine its destiny and take the action necessary to achieve it. Luhmann, however, questions these commitments by breaking the individual down into 'systems' that operate on different premises.

Luhmann conceptualises the individual as consisting of two separate, polycentric systems: psychic systems (ie, consciousness) and biological systems (ie, organic matter, such as cells). Individuals think using their minds only and, at the same time but in a completely separate process, operate organically as physical entities. For example, thinking produces thoughts only rather than biological material (eg, lungs inflate, not by thinking about lung inflation, but through cellular and gaseous processes). Biological and psychic systems, as autonomous and separate processes, are thus unable to merge or directly instruct each other. It is generally assumed in mainstream intellectual life, however, that these systems are able to merge or undergo direct instruction from the 'outside'. For instance, it is commonly accepted that individuals have free will. The exercise of free will over, say, the body is a commonly held belief. In fact, from head to foot, the individual is commonly regarded as an entity embodied with a complete essence (eg, a soul, Reason) that exercises mastery over the body and the world in general. Individuals self-determine their destiny, so the story goes.

The story, however, is questioned by Luhmann on the basis that it overlooks the existence of wholly separate psychic and biological systems that do completely different things. Luhmann argues that studies of society have been led astray by being underpinned by the modern concept of 'the individual'. He charges the concept with wrongly conflating biological and psychic systems (ie, by allowing for direct influence of one over the other). A theory that recognises biological and psychic systems, however, and accounts for their autonomy and closure provides a vital entry point for a new sociology. Luhmann's theory of social systems is advanced by its creator as the entry point. It is held out by Luhmann as a new sociological paradigm that the present work holds up as an ideal theoretical framework upon which an original study of the patient homicide governance space can be mounted.

A crucial aspect of Luhmann's work is the argument that psychic and biological systems are inadequately placed to produce the 'material' required to constitute society. Thoughts are the 'material' of psychic systems although we are unable to see these systems with our own eyes. Organic processes (ie, cells) are the 'material' of biological systems. Mental and biological 'materials' are crucial to human existence but they have nothing whatsoever to do with the production of meanings that are available to everyone (ie, socially available meanings). Socially available meanings are the meanings that we are all able to share for the purposes of going about our business. We all know what it means to obtain goods that improve our lives. It means that we pay for those goods (although a minority may choose not to) and increase our resources. We all know what it means when we are accused of a crime. It means that we are accused of acting illegally and we contact a lawyer for advice and representation. We all know what it means when we are stricken with a serious illness. It means that we fear for our health and call a doctor. Going about our business in the world involves the production of specific meanings that are, somehow, accessible to us all. We do not have to speak to anyone in order to find out what these meanings are but we are somehow able to read from the same page. Socially available meanings are, therefore, unlike the meanings produced in our thoughts. Our thoughts are inaccessible to the world at large, but the socially available meanings we are all able to share (eg, economic meanings, legal meanings, medical meanings) are accessible to everyone.

A central element of Luhmann's work involves explaining how socially available meanings are produced. His work raises a crucial question that he supplied an answer for: how does meaning become socially available? Luhmann's answer is captured in an important concept: communication. Communication is the basic building block of socially available meaning. Thoughts are the basic building block of psychic systems, and cellular processes are the basic building block of biological systems. Communication, however, is the basic building block of *society*.

Unless 'the individual' is conceived as a plurality of wholly separate systems (biological and psychic systems), it becomes difficult to precisely account for how socially available meanings emerge. Things become easier, however, if the individual is conceived as a divisible set of psychic and biological systems on the one hand and as a construct of meaning produced within society's social subsystems of communication on the other. The thoughts inside people's heads and the biological processes inside their bodies are unable to take us very far in describing how socially available meaning emerges. Something else must account for the emergence of, say, law, politics, medicine and the economy. Luhmann's answer identifies social (ie, communication) systems as a third separate and autonomous type of system responsible for the emergence of these important functions in society. Social systems are wholly separate from the human minds and bodies typically associated with the human experience.

Society is a specific type of social system identified by Luhmann because it is constituted with communications that are accessible to everyone. There are, however, other types of social system identified by Luhmann that are not accessible to everyone. These are personal *interactions* and *organisations*. These two types of social system are differentiated from society because of their form and limited accessibility. For instance, personal interactions are face-to-face communications and have no relevance beyond the interaction. It is important to note that personal interactions involve communications between two psychic systems whereas communications that are accessible to everyone have relevance for society. These social communications have functional relevance for society whereas personal interactions between people, ordinarily, do not (unless and until they acquire relevance in society). Organisations, on the other hand, are made up of *decisions* to select between certain possibilities. The decisions of organisations admit certain members to the organisation and establish its agendas, goals and physical locations. Social communication (ie, society), however, is the 'material' (albeit a non-physical 'material') out of which socially available meaning is produced. These communications are unable to directly 'speak' to each other, but they are recognisable by everyone and serve an essential social function.

The implication of these theoretical arguments is that 'the individual', as a psychic system on the one hand and a biological system on the other, is not part of society. Similarly, the personal interactions between these 'individuals' and the organisations that they may be a member of are not part of society. Rather, the individual, their personal interactions and the organisations that they may be members of are always *communicated about in society*. They are all socially meaningful constructs produced in normatively sealed communication systems.

The dynamics of health care governance, particularly in the context of homicide and health care, are elusive – especially if conventional theoretical models are used to unfold them. The book, however, harnesses Luhmann's theoretical fleet with rigour and conviction. It engages his general theory of social systems and positions it in specific contexts, some of which Luhmann himself explored. For example, Luhmann's systems theory – ossified in 1984 – provides the theoretical groundwork for his 1993 monograph about law and a 1995 monograph about the mass media. The present work draws on these diverse works, among others, to capture the dynamics of the patient homicide governance space, its significance in society, its capabilities and what policy makers can learn from it. It takes advantage of Luhmann's radical theoretical portrayal of how the individual, as traditionally conceived, may be reliably understood and how change properly accounted for in society. The portrayal offers an impressive and original theoretical account of society that the present book utilises to inform its novel analysis. For some readers of the book, however (especially readers new to Luhmann) his theory may appear odd, inappropriate and insensitive because of the way it conceptualises the individual. As a consequence, the book restates and clarifies its theoretical design on a small number of occasions and the risk of sounding mildly repetitive while doing so is voluntarily assumed. However, given the unique theoretical position adopted in Luhmann's work and the abstract level at which it sits, restatements and clarifications of the book's theoretical design will help readers fully engage with the content.

In drawing on Luhmann's theory, the book argues that the patient homicide governance space is constituted with moments of socially significant observations produced within closed social systems of communication. The book challenges the assumption held by policy makers and some investigators that health care provision is viewable from a privileged vantage point and successful change to health services pursuant to predefined goals (ie, improving services) is possible. The purpose of challenging these assumptions is to moderate what can be expected from the patient homicide governance space and to draw attention to the 'blind spots' of the policy and practices behind them; systems theory is about observing systems that observe rather than observing the world a priori. The book, therefore, draws attention to the limitations of conventional normative approaches within the patient homicide governance space by carrying out a novel, yet unpopular, theoretical manoeuvre: the observation of observing systems and what they are unable to see.

The author draws from two main empirical sources to support the analysis undertaken: documents and face-to-face interviews. In particular, a series of sub-sources are covered: conventions, legislation, inquiry reports, government circulars, NHS (National Health Service) policy documents and academic material (eg, journal articles, monographs).

Most of the interviews conducted were carried out with investigators of patient homicides. These investigators comprise a relatively small community of experts who enter into special commissioning arrangements with NHS England to carry out their work, but they have conducted hundreds of investigations between them. One interview, however, was conducted with Julian Hendy. As a charity leader and television producer, Julian Hendy represents families affected by mental health homicide.

It is worth drawing attention to the scope and apparent limitations of the author's study. First, a principal focus of the book is on independent investigations conducted in England. A narrow focus may raise the concern that the research conducted is insignificant. However, the NHS in England treats thousands of mental health patients every day. It is therefore vital to examine how services are investigated after a homicide incident. It is crucial that the challenges associated with these investigations are explored because these services touch thousands of lives. Second, it may be argued that the book is irrelevant to the experience of other countries. The book focuses on how publicly funded health care services in England are investigated and their significance for society. A further question may therefore be posed: how can a book about the English patient homicide governance space speak to the experience of other countries that have different institutional arrangements? The public health and safety concerns that patient homicide incidents arouse in England are similar to the public health and safety concerns aroused in other jurisdictions, such as the United States. US authorities are often the focus of critique and response when a mentally disordered individual commits a homicide. The critique and response that usually surface in these situations are especially acute if the homicide is carried out using a firearm; US citizens have a constitutional right to own and, in some circumstances, carry a gun and some mentally disordered individuals have used firearms to kill. The lofty ambitions that underscore responses to these incidents (eg, 'reducing risk', 'improving public safety') are, nonetheless, universal experiences that cut across jurisdictional lines. Similarly, Luhmann's theory of social systems recognises no political boundaries. Communication is everywhere and the utilisation of Luhmann's theory in academic study enables light to be shed on the entrenched Anglo-American philosophies (eg, cause-and-effect reasoning) that drive policy responses to crises. In particular, independent investigations are part of a broader effort by law enforcement agencies, the legal system and policy makers everywhere to manage risks in public life posed by dangerous individuals. The book is, therefore, perceptive to a modern, universal, problem. It is dedicated to stimulating ideas around how complex responses to devastating incidents may become while examining the finer details within established patterns of scholarship (eg, the regulatory state literature) that only a study of this kind can reveal.

Chapter 1 provides a contextual overview of patient homicide governance. The legal, administrative and regulatory terrain is broadly mapped with a view to demonstrating the complex environment in which patient homicide governance is located. The chapter then carefully adjoins a tranche of important theoretical content which informs subsequent chapters. In particular, the chapter introduces systems theory and, specifically, Luhmann's brand of it, to frame a series of questions about how to analyse the complex space of patient homicide governance.

Chapter 2 provides a brief historical overview of the investigations that animate the patient homicide governance space, followed by their current configuration and underlying policy rationale. The changing form of the inquiry is then explained; it was a process led by lawyers but it is now led by other areas of expertise. These areas of expertise are primarily clinical (eg, psychiatry) but they also include other types of expertise (eg, managerial and commercial). Chapter 2 shows that the patient homicide governance space has become more sophisticated. It argues inquiries are opportunities for health services to be communicated about, expanded or changed. They resemble an industry that reproduces expertise when a homicide incident occurs. The values of cost and competition (ie, economics) in particular are communicated about, with investigator companies seeking out contracts with NHS commissioners to conduct investigations and to generate economic gains.

Chapter 3 sets out Luhmann's systems theory, a vital part of the book's conceptual framework. It identifies and explains the concepts that underpin the theory. Chapter 3 also explains the relevance of these concepts to the patient homicide governance space. The chapter explains that Luhmann draws on the theory of distinction in mathematics to argue that systems of meaning are differences, drawn by an observer, between a designated form and an unmarked space. Luhmann uses the concept of difference to describe what systems of meaning are; they are the difference between an observing system and its environment. Social systems like law and the mass media, observe their environment through drawing distinctions. Law, he argues, observes its environment (eg, other social systems, psychic systems) in purely legal terms – by distinguishing legality and illegality through the legal code. The legal code embodies the legal system's function and identity. The mass media observes its environment by distinguishing between information and non-information using the code of the mass media. Again, the code of the mass media embodies the function and identity of the mass media. In both systems, however, people are communicational constructs (eg, 'defendants' in law, 'stories' in the mass media). Chapter 3 explains that independent investigations are relevant to these social systems (eg, in the form of legal actions, news reports), among many others (eg, medicine, morality, politics, economics), and this is followed by an assessment of the implications of Luhmann's theory regarding how change in society is to be reliably understood.

The relevance of social systems theory to the patient homicide governance space is developed in Chapter 4. Chapter 4 builds on Chapter 3 by developing the argument that the patient homicide governance space is constituted with social systemic observation, conducted within society's communication systems. The chapter examines, in detail, the different communicational realities that constitute the patient homicide governance space. A central message of Chapter 4 is that the processes referred to as 'inquiries' and 'investigations' are imprecise labels that obscure social systems observing their specific environments. A critical tone is adopted, where necessary, because systems theory is open to criticism. Prominent systems theorists, however, accept that all social and political theories cannot lay claim to possessing a foundation of unambiguous evidence. The test of reliability for such theories should be that they provide 'a convincing way of understanding some of the complexities of modern societies and the relationships of people to these societies'.[1] Chapter 4 considers that Luhmann's systems theory appears to meet the test.

Chapter 5 situates Luhmann's theory in the context of two, more familiar, elements of the patient homicide governance space: time and accountability. It argues that investigations, as moments of communicative observation within social function systems, self-construct distinct versions of time and accountability. Social systems self-construct their past and future in the present: 'If society is regarded as being functionally differentiated into spheres of different communications, it can be argued that there are several times'.[2] Inquiries, as moments of observation within different functional spheres, construct time (eg, the medical past, the psychiatric past) on their own terms. Traditional concepts of accountability often describe the giving of an account to another and explaining past conduct. These traditional concepts are unsatisfactory from the perspective of Luhmann's systems theory because they assume that persons have purchase in the world. They assume that humans are able to transmit explanations of the past to others, unchanged. Chapter 5 appeals to Luhmann's work in order to rehabilitate the concept of accountability; accountability is a relation, but it is a relation that is self-constructed within society's social function systems of communication. These systems are structures of life in which closed communications are made about events that are typically associated with accountability relationships. In other words, they communicate about their environment (ie, biological, psychic and

[1] M King, 'The "Truth" About Autopoiesis" (1993) 20 *Journal of Law and Society* 218 at 222 222.

[2] N Luhmann, 'The Future Cannot Begin: Temporal Structures in Modern Society' (1976) 43 *Social Research* 130, 134–35.

other social systems) and the past (eg, past medical decisions, past legal decisions). People play no part. Bodies, thoughts and events (eg, a fatal stabbing, a hallucination, a decision to administer treatment) – time even – are constructed as meaningful within social systems before, during and after an investigation. For example, these elements become relevant to the work of 'psychiatrists', 'lawyers' and 'investigators' in medicine and law. Chapter 5 seeks to overcome popular, yet reductionist, conceptions of accountability which assume that direct information exchange between individuals is possible. As part of the chapter's argument, it refers to Luhmann's theory of politics. It argues that the patient homicide governance space is constructed politically; the political system communicates about power, has a tendency to assume accountability for society's welfare problems as a way to generate further power, and directs greater levels of government bureaucracy to managing its assumption of accountability for welfare problems. Chapter 5 argues that the patient homicide investigators are enlisted to investigate wider swathes of health care administration, beyond their usual remits, because the political system constructs the investigatory domain as a resource through which political performances are enabled. The outcome is an expansion of accountability for welfare (ie, health-related) problems through the investigation process.

Chapter 6 introduces the concepts of risk, danger and protest. Luhmann's theory posits that communications about risk reduce the complexity of an unknown future. Risk communications specifically are communications about time (ie, the future). Policy and investigative responses to patient homicides are focused around minimising risk and increasing safety. However, these responses are the focus of conflict between different groups; there is an insoluble opposition between those who make decisions (eg, NHS Trusts, independent investigators) and those who are affected by those decisions (eg, the families of homicide victims). Those affected observe danger (ie, the effects of decisions made by others), thus precipitating opposition to the extent that conflicts about certain issues (eg, safety) become morally charged, are protested and stymie ambitions to establish conditions of safety. Chapter 6 therefore calls for moderating certain expectations around what patient homicide governance can achieve when it comes to minimising risk and maximising public safety.

Chapter 7 concludes the book. It summarises the argument that the patient homicide governance space is constituted by moments of observation carried out within society's social communication systems. Acts of killing, health care services, decisions, events and people are communicated about within operationally closed social subsystems of communication, such as medicine, politics and law. There is, consequently, no shared understanding between these social subsystems; the concept of learning universal lessons after patient homicides is impossible, contrary to what is often assumed in the policy domain. Learning does occur, but at the level of society as opposed to learning a priori. If learning lessons universally is possible, absolute safety would be realisable as a condition and homicides would not occur. Yet, homicides continue to occur. In a functionally differentiated society, safety – absolute or partial – is unrealisable as a condition. Rather, there is risk, uncertainty and further complexity. Crucially, in the light of the book's theoretical claims, Chapter 7 encourages policy makers to re-evaluate their normative commitments to exacting change in health services pursuant to predefined goals. A series of points are raised thereafter in relation to the role systems theory may play in health care regulation and governance scholarship generally.

1

Homicide and Health Care: Context and Complexity

I. Introduction

Health care services treat thousands of mentally disordered individuals every day. Many of these individuals are considered to be a public danger by the professionals they are treated by because they behave violently or show indications of future violent behaviour. A minority of these individuals have gone on to commit homicide. These events are dreadful. They severely impact the families of the victim and the perpetrator. They unsettle the local communities in which they occur. They are sensationally reported in the media. They jolt important legal and governance mechanisms into action. An important governance mechanism is an independent investigation (or inquiry) into health care services. These investigations animate what the author refers to as the patient homicide governance space. The patient homicide governance space refers to an investigatory domain constituted by diverse communications systems (eg, medicine, law, politics, morality, mass media) about patient homicide. The author rigorously examines the space through a novel appeal to social theory and empirical methods.

The author's focus, however, is a process of 'looking through'. It is concerned with looking through common descriptors like 'investigation' and 'inquiry' and embarks on an original, yet demanding, analysis of how patient homicide and health care resonate through the patient homicide governance space and indeed how they resonate throughout society. These descriptors indicate, rightly, that there is a procedure through which health care services are placed under scrutiny, accountability established and truth seeking carried out. These terms, however, provide only a partial description of what these investigations are. They are much more than these descriptors suggest. A fuller, more comprehensive and original, account of these investigations requires conceptualising them as moments of observation and sense making about a range of different 'events' by different observers. Put another way, independent investigations into patient homicide are more reliably understood as being constituted by moments of observation and sense making in society about homicide and health care services.

These moments of observation and sense making assume different forms. For example, an observation about a homicide incident may be carried out by an investigator or a health care professional merely through thinking about it; it is the minds of these actors that observe. The 'stuff' out of which these observations are made is consciousness (or cognition). Consciousness is invisible to others. We are unable to look into someone else's mind and observe what their mind observes. We are, however, able to observe the utterances of information by others (eg, a spoken word, a hand gesture) and form an understanding of what the information means. For example, an investigator commissioned to investigate health services after a patient homicide may observe the 'facts' of the incident by uttering information that is understood in one or more senses in society. The investigator may use a specific investigatory technique, accredited by science and recognised by others as such, because it serves the purpose of establishing truth about the case. On the other hand, an investigator's finding might later be referred to by a judge or a lawyer in a legal action for judicial review. Consciousness, albeit crucial to the operation, ceases to play a direct role in producing the scientific and legal meanings in these scenarios. These meanings are observable and accessible throughout society generally; persons could be hundreds of miles apart and not interact with each other in any way, but they may all engage or step into science and appreciate the scientific 'truth' of a patient homicide event. In similar fashion, everyone may step into law to understand the same event. Scientific and legal meanings are produced within overarching, yet distinct, structures of life that everyone is familiar with and may step into, despite the physical barriers that may exist between persons. In short, science and law have social significance. Both have distinct, widely recognisable functions and they are accessible to everyone.

The book's core argument is that the patient homicide governance space produces a range of socially available, yet highly distinct, meanings through a specific form of observation: social communication. The book's argument is developed through the lens of Niklas Luhmann's general systems theory. Systems theory will be fully explained in later chapters. For now, it is sufficient to comment that Luhmann's theory provides the important conceptual material required for making the book's argument come to life and say something original about how patient homicides are addressed and understood in society.

Luhmann's work helps illuminate a diverse range of social phenomena that other, more conventional approaches, are unable to do. Conventional approaches, such as looking at investigations from an ideological perspective or from a legal-political perspective (eg, as forms of public accountability) are unable to capture the level of detail behind these processes that systems theory is able to capture. Systems theory, moreover, avoids the assumptions adopted by conventional theoretical approaches. Conventional approaches focus on whether governance procedures are well positioned to establish 'the facts' or 'the truth' whereas the theoretical approach adopted here refrains from assuming that 'the facts' or 'the truth' are out there waiting to be discovered. Rather, 'the facts' and 'the truth' are constructed within closed-function systems of social communication. For example, 'the facts' and 'the truth' are internally constructed within each system as an event of significance. 'Facts' and 'truth' have economic significance in the function system of the economy, legal significance in the function system of law and so on. Each instance of significance is a construction within a closed structure of communication that is unable to directly communicate with other structures of communication for the purpose of deriving an objective understanding about events in the world.

The widespread assumption, then, that predefined change to health services after patient homicide through the implementation of policy techniques and decision making is possible is open to question. Indeed, the book's contribution radically questions contemporary policy approaches to patient homicide using the novel theoretical approach summarised thus far. In particular, it seeks to moderate the expectations that are formed around patient homicide governance. The book is therefore important for policy makers and academic scholars. It showcases an ambitious approach to a controversial area that is often loaded with the expectation that truth can be gleaned and lessons can be learned. The author, however, suggests that these expectations oversimplify the governance arena.

II. Patient Homicide and Health Care

In March 2013 Christina Edkins was randomly stabbed to death on a bus by Phillip Simelane. Phillip was known to local health authorities prior to the incident. He had been receiving mental health care and treatment for his schizophrenia and an independent inquiry was set up after the killing. Its panel judged that those responsible for Phillip's care and treatment had not properly diagnosed his condition. The incident raised important questions: if Phillip's condition had been properly diagnosed, would Christina still be alive today? If his condition had been managed differently, would the hallucinations that commanded him to commit the crime that day have occurred? Would better management have enabled staff to recognise his deteriorating condition much earlier and take timely action? Similar questions were raised in relation to a double homicide committed in 2015. The perpetrator killed his mother and sister. Like Phillip Simelane, the perpetrator was well known to the authorities. He had previous convictions for robbery, assault and drug possession and received an official diagnosis of paranoid schizophrenia and personality disorder in 2014. He was imprisoned for a period of time and was scheduled to attend an outpatient appointment on his release to ensure that his condition could be properly managed. An independent investigation set up in response to the killings found that the perpetrator failed to attend his appointment and that he did not experience any contact with mental health services between the time of his release from prison and the incident.[1] In the same year, a patient in

[1] See D Hunter and P Cheeseman, *Domestic Homicide Review Incorporating an NHS Independent Investigation [Mental Health]: 'Nina' and 'Jenny'*, Overview Report Post Quality Assurance Panel (Sefton Safer Communities Partnership, November 2017).

receipt of mental health services in Greater Manchester punched a man in a public house, causing fatal brain injuries. The patient had a long history of contact with the police and mental health services. The incident raised a familiar set of questions about the care and treatment received prior to the attack. An independent investigation found that the patient's actions were 'predictable'.[2] In more recent times, in an event that made national news, a man was stabbed to death outside his home. The man had briefly left his house to post letters announcing the birth of his new baby daughter. He encountered the perpetrator shortly after leaving his home and was fatally stabbed. The perpetrator was not known to local health authorities, although he was known to the police and had a history of receiving mental health care in Nigeria.[3] Again, questions surfaced over whether public authorities could have done more to address the perpetrator's condition prior to the killing.

According to the National Confidential Inquiry into Suicide and Homicide by People with Mental Illness (NCISH), 11 per cent of all homicide convictions in the United Kingdom between 2005 and 2015 were committed by mental health patients.[4] There were, according to the report, 835 patient homicides over the NCISH's report period and an average of 76 homicides per year.[5] Patient suicides are far more common: 1,538 occurred in 2015.[6] Unlike mental health suicides, however, mental health homicides resonate in society more acutely. The rate of patient homicides in England since 2009 has declined but they are still reported widely in the media because they prompt questions of public safety in ways that suicides do not. Local communities are gripped by the realisation that an individual treated by health professionals for his or her mental disorder subsequently goes on to commit acts of violence. The relatives of the deceased express anger, disbelief and frustration at the authorities: how could an individual, known to the authorities, go on to commit a dreadful act leading to loss of life? What care and treatment did the perpetrator receive and was it adequate? Who is to blame? These questions often get asked. An inquiry is set up. The learning of lessons is made a priority. The same questions and concerns are voiced when new incidents happen. The procedural and emotional cycle starts over: anger, disbelief and frustration are expressed. A slew of familiar questions are asked that the authorities are called upon to answer.

The author goes behind the process of investigation and questioning around homicides committed by mental health patients. The book rigorously examines the

[2] C Rooney, *An Independent Investigation into the Care and Treatment of a Mental Health Service User (B) in Greater Manchester: Executive Summary* (Niche Health & Social Care Consulting Ltd, March 2017) 8.

[3] See G Jenkins and N Moor, *An Independent Investigation into the Care and Treatment of P in the West Midlands* (Niche Health & Social Care Consulting Ltd, June 2017).

[4] 'Mental health patients' refers to individuals who receive NHS care and treatment for a mental disorder. Independent investigations are triggered if perpetrators of homicide are mental health patients up to six months prior to the crime.

[5] L Appleby et al, *National Confidential Inquiry into Suicide and Homicide by People with Mental Illness, Annual Report 2017: England, Northern Ireland, Scotland and Wales* (Manchester, University of Manchester, 2017) 4.

[6] ibid.

investigation's dynamics as a governance space replete with ambitions, conflicts, tensions and challenges. It forges a new understanding of the complexities within, drawing attention to a neglected area of concern. The purpose of the present chapter, in particular, is to provide essential context for the book. It describes the wider context in which these investigations are situated and identifies relevant theoretical issues, followed by a short list of central research questions.

III. Background and Context

The killing of a human being by another is known in law as a homicide. Homicide is a criminal offence and two forms of the offence exist. The first is murder and it requires an intention to kill or commit grievous bodily harm.[7] The second is manslaughter. Manslaughter does not require an intention to kill or commit grievous bodily harm. If any of these two offences are committed, a series of other legal and quasi-legal measures and responses are triggered. On the one hand, the perpetrator is arrested, charged, sent to trial and is usually given a custodial sentence if found guilty. On the other hand, a coroner's inquest will be held. A death certificate will be signed. The family of the deceased may initiate legal action in the civil courts. If the perpetrator was receiving care and treatment for a mental disorder at the time of the offence, an independent investigation or inquiry[8] into that care and treatment must be conducted.[9]

Mental health care and treatment in the United Kingdom is delivered by health professionals employed by the National Health Service (NHS). As a publicly funded institution, the NHS is an arm of the state.[10] It employs clinicians and nurses to make important decisions about the physical and mental health of individuals. These employees also make important decisions about individuals who present public safety concerns. Many individuals treated by the NHS exhibit violent behaviour or tendencies because they have serious mental health problems. These patients are treated in spaces of legal, regulatory and administrative activity. It is apposite to provide an overview of these spaces with a view to adding context to the governance landscape.

A. The General Legal Context

All EU Member States have a legal duty to respect citizens' right to life under Article 2 of the European Convention on Human Rights (ECHR). A Member

[7] See *Attorney-General's Reference (No 3 of 1994)* [1998] AC 245 (HL).

[8] The terms 'investigation' and 'inquiry' are used interchangeably throughout the book.

[9] Department of Health, *Guidance on the discharge of mentally disordered people and their continuing care in the community*, NHS Executive, HSG(94)27.

[10] See National Health Service Act 1948.

State's duty to respect Article 2 is prima facie breached if a citizen is unlawfully killed.[11] The European Court of Human Rights (ECtHR) has accepted that the obligation is activated in 'a variety of situations where an individual has sustained life-threatening injuries, died or has disappeared in violent or suspicious circumstances, irrespective of whether those allegedly responsible are state agents or private persons' in violation of Article 2.[12] These investigations must have special qualities: independence, effectiveness, speed, transparency and next-of-kin involvement.[13] Homicides committed by mentally disordered individuals who, at the time of the offence, were under the care of NHS professionals activate the Article 2 duty to investigate.

Article 2 jurisprudence relating to the duty to investigate germinated in challenges to the quality of investigations into loss of life caused by the state's use of force.[14] The ECtHR heard a series of cases and reasoned that there exists an implicit procedural requirement to hold an official investigation in such circumstances.[15] It was argued in *Ergi v Turkey* that the Article 2 investigatory requirement was confined to cases where the state had, in fact, caused loss of life. The ECtHR, however, rejected the argument. The court, furthermore, did not specify the situations which could activate the implicit requirement, thus creating broad scope for the duty to be etched into a range of situations involving loss of life.

The ECtHR's early jurisprudence set the stage for later judicial developments in the area of hospital fatalities. It was successfully argued in *Powell v United Kingdom* that the duty to investigate was triggered where a surgical or medical procedure led to the loss of life. The reason that the argument succeeded was founded on the view that the state must 'take appropriate steps to safeguard the lives of those within its jurisdiction'.[16] The ECtHR therefore interpreted Article 2 broadly, albeit with the caveat that it was a procedural right. It referred to previous case law relating to the use of force and ruled that the state must create an effective investigation framework into losses of life in hospitals.

The NHS is an agent of the state for Article 2 purposes and the duty to conduct an official investigation is therefore a compelling one for public health authorities in the United Kingdom. The Court in *Powell* held that where a Member State makes adequate provision for securing high professional standards and affords adequate protection for lives, matters such as medical judgement errors or negligent coordination between professionals are sufficient, of themselves, to trigger

[11] See European Convention on Human Rights, Article 2.

[12] See *Osman v United Kingdom* (1998) 29 EHRR 245; *McCann v United Kingdom* Series A no 324 (1995) 21 EHRR 97; European Court of Human Rights, *Guide on Article 2 of the European Convention on Human Rights*, 1st edition (Council of Europe, 2018) 28.

[13] *R (Amin) v Secretary of State for the Home Department* [2003] UKHL 51.

[14] See generally J Chevalier-Watts, 'Effective Investigations under Article 2 of the European Convention on Human Rights: Securing the Right to Life or an Onerous Burden on a State? (2010) 21(3) *European Journal of International Law* 701.

[15] *McCann v United Kingdom* Series A no 324 (1995) 21 EHRR 97; *Ergi v Turkey* [1998] 32 ECHR 18.

[16] *Powell v United Kingdom* (2000) 30 EHRR 362.

the duty to investigate in the event that life is lost.[17] Governments must therefore create the conditions for these events to be effectively investigated and the causes identified.

Different types of investigation (eg, a police investigation, a coroner's investigation) may fulfil the Article 2 obligation. Investigations assume different forms, do different things and have different purposes depending on the circumstances. The investigation conducted by the police is different to that conducted by the coroner, for instance. All investigations, however, must be effective if they are to comply with Article 2. It is crucial that an effective investigation of any type must establish and examine the relevant facts. If a patient in the care of health professionals commits a homicide, then an investigation into the health services provided prior to the incident must occur if it is to be effective under Article 2. The services provided are, after all, fundamental to the relevant factual background. Establishing the relevant facts, however, requires special knowledge and skill. Clinical experts, knowledgeable about health care services, are regarded as best placed to effectively establish these facts.

B. Regulatory and Administrative Context

The regulatory and administrative context of investigations is equally crucial. The NHS is expanding in size and complexity. Investigators must investigate it or at least a part of it when things go wrong. One million patients are treated by the NHS every 36 hours.[18] It employs almost 1 million people. For the 2016/17 financial year, the Department of Health allocated £117.6 billion in revenue funding,[19] with approximately £110 million allocated to commissioning expenditure alone.[20] Mental health services represent a smaller fraction of NHS activity but thousands of health professionals are involved in it; hundreds of hospitals, clinics and agencies around the country underpin these services. They manage patients with complex mental disorders, chaotic histories, drug problems, nomadic behaviour patterns and violent tendencies.[21] The hundreds of decision-making sites that manage these individuals form complex networks of responsibility. The investigation of health services after a patient homicide is therefore challenging.

[17] ibid.

[18] Department of Health, 'Chief Executive's Report to the NHS' (London, Department of Health, December 2005).

[19] Department of Health, *Department of Health: Annual Report and Accounts 2016–17* (London, HMSO, 2017) 2.

[20] HM Treasury, *Public Expenditure: Statistical Analyses 2018* (London, HMSO, Cmnd 9648, 2018) 15.

[21] See generally J Shaw et al, 'The Role of Alcohol and Drugs in Homicides in England and Wales' (2006) 101(8) *Addiction* 1117; PJ Taylor, 'Psychosis and Violence: Stories, Fears, and Reality' (2008) 53(10) *The Canadian Journal of Psychiatry* 647; M McGrath and F Oyebode 'Characteristics of Perpetrators of Homicide in Independent Inquiries' (2005) 45(3) *Medicine, Science and the Law* 233, 243.

Ethical controversies emerge out of these incidents.[22] Perpetrators are sometimes shown to have experienced contact with public services outside traditional health services. The police, probation services, courts, prisons and social housing agencies may have been involved with the perpetrator at any one time. It is common for investigations to focus on a number of different sites of decision making that appear separated out from each other and differentiated along functional lines. For instance, investigations focus on decision makers in medicine primarily, but also engage decision makers in politics, law and regulation. Investigations are compelled to understand these spheres of operation. They examine an environment of different technical disciplines, administrative procedures, governance mechanisms and market-based practices.

The regulatory and administrative environment of independent investigations into health services after patient homicide is hard to define but the 'regulatory state' is a well-known conceptual tool which may be used to produce a useful sketch. The 'regulatory state' – at its core – is an analytical construct that depicts complex changes in how the state is configured.[23] These changes are varied but they include elaborate governance practices: the privatisation of state-owned assets, the 'contracting out' of state functions to the private sector,[24] the growth of independent regulatory agencies, the separation of policy-making and service-delivery functions, the increasing reliance on rules and standards and new forms of economic organisation (eg, incentives).[25] The regulatory state refers to a 'style of governance away from the direct provision of public services associated with the welfare state and towards oversight of public services by others'.[26]

These developments have been accompanied by the growing concern that governments are incapable of addressing social problems. Governments are publicly distrusted even. A variety of forums (eg, interest groups, the media) have become the vehicles for the expression of doubt about the competency of government to manage services for the greater good. Administrations are often perceived

[22] See H Packer, *The Limits of the Criminal Sanction* (Stanford, Stanford University Press, 1968/1999) 74. See also SJ Pfohl, 'Predicting Dangerousness: A Social Deconstruction of Psychiatric Reality' in LA Teplin (ed), *Mental Health and Criminal Justice* (California, Sage, 1984) 201.

[23] K Yeung, 'The Regulatory State' in R Baldwin et al (eds), *The Oxford Handbook of Regulation* (Oxford, Oxford University Press, 2010) 65.

[24] Examples include the creation of contractual agreements, with built-in incentives, between mental health professionals, law enforcers and the state (see generally N Wolff, 'Interactions Between Mental Health and Law Enforcement Systems: Problems and prospects for Cooperation' (1998) 23(1) *Journal of Health Politics, Policy and Law* 133, 152–54).

[25] ibid. See also GD Majone, 'From the Positive to the Regulatory State: Causes and Consequences of Changes in the Mode of Governance' (1997) 17(2) *Journal of Public Policy* 139; J Black, 'Tensions in the Regulatory State' (2007) (Spring) *Public Law* 58; M Lodge and L Stirton, 'Accountability and the Regulatory State' in Baldwin et al, *Oxford Handbook* (n 23) 349–70; D Campbell, 'Luhmann Without Tears: Complex Economic Regulation and the Erosion of the Market Sphere' (2013) 33(1) *Legal Studies* 162, 162; DP Horton and G Lynch-Wood, 'Rhetoric and Reality: User Engagement and Health Care Reform in England' (2018) 26(1) *Medical Law Review* 27.

[26] C Scott, 'Accountability in the Regulatory State' (2000) 27(1) *Journal of Law and Society* 38 (footnote omitted).

as failing to achieve their aims and objectives.[27] Scandal, disaster and incompetence all contribute to the negative perception of governmental competence. A distrust of those traditionally considered to be best placed to resolve these problems (ie, politicians) has set in.[28]

Governments increasingly delegate more important tasks to external agencies and expert bodies, however, as a way to manage complexity in society more reliably. For example, independent regulators and non-departmental public bodies exercise authority over vital areas of life that were once the sole province of governmental authority.[29] Governments, traditionally, have relied on cumbersome procedures of the legislature, courts and policy domain to solve society's problems. The advent of the regulatory state, loosely defined, however, has meant that independent expertise now wields greater power and authority. It involves the exercise of power and authority in highly flexible ways for the purpose of becoming more responsive to society's problems. It operates on an ad hoc rule-making basis and applies special skills designed to address complex problems quickly and effectively.[30]

There has also been a noticeable shift towards delegating responsibility over public services from the policy domain to independent experts versed in managing and cultivating market conditions. The progressive marketisation of the NHS is a salient example.[31] In 1990 health care providers were required – for the first time – to compete with each other for contracts with health service commissioners. These requirements prepared the ground for subsequent measures to be implemented that made it easier for private firms to enter the health care-provider market. The most recent round of significant reform that further crystallised market-based conditions in the NHS was instituted by the Health and Social Care Act 2012. The 2012 Act marked a return to the efficiency-inspired reforms of the 1980s.[32] The 2012 Act also signalled a heightened emphasis on arms-length economic regulation, independent regulatory power and competition between market players.[33]

NHS regulation, governance and administration are therefore typified by developments that underline the emergence of what may be described as the regulatory state. Traditional lines of hierarchical accountability in the NHS have been altered. The NHS, once known for being an iron cage of 'top-down' bureaucracy,

[27] AJ Wistrich, 'The Evolving Temporality of Lawmaking' (2012) 44 *Connecticut Law Review* 757, 784.

[28] ibid 784. See also S Prasser, 'Public Inquiries in Australia: An Overview' (1985) 44(1) *Australian Journal of Public Administration* 1, 1.

[29] See F Vibert, *Rise of the Unelected* (Cambridge, Cambridge University Press, 2007).

[30] ibid.

[31] See A Pollock, *NHS Plc* (London, Verso Books, 2004); DP Horton and G Lynch-Wood, 'Technocracy, the Market and the Governance of England's National Health Service' (2018) *Regulation & Governance* (forthcoming).

[32] L Stirton, 'Back to the Future? Lessons on the Pro-competitive Regulation of Health Services' (2014) 22(2) *Medical Law Review* 180.

[33] ibid; ACL Davies, 'This Time It's For Real: The Health and Social Care Act 2012' (2013) 76(3) *Modern Law Review* 564; Horton and Lynch-Wood, 'Technocracy' (n 31).

is now a fragmented edifice of independent agencies, expert bodies, public and private providers, ministerial involvement, consumer champions and local patient groups. These sites of activity interconnect with each other, coexist on a complex regulatory terrain and administrate the practice of medicine and psychiatry in particular.[34]

The regulatory state concept is not uncontested however. Scholars disagree on how best to capture the changes described above and they advance a variety of conceptual formulations.[35] It is beyond the scope of the book to conduct a detailed examination of the regulatory state concept and the debate over its cogency. The concept simply helps provide initial context for beginning an appreciation of the complex conditions in which patient homicide and health care occur. Despite its imprecision,[36] the regulatory state concept helps to indicate the broader governance arrangements underpinning patient homicide investigations. There is much complexity and fragmentation which the author takes as a vital cue for further theoretical development.

Independent investigations of health services after patient homicide, like the NHS generally, are market based and technocratic. NHS England is the independent expert body responsible for overseeing the commissioning of health care services in England and regulations enable it to procure tenders from investigators and contract out the Article 2 investigative function to private companies.[37] Furthermore, independent investigators interact with dozens of expert agencies and organisations. They also regularly connect with affected families who are not experts, which is a marked contrast to what investigations are usually expected to do. They are expected to engage with experts and market-based practices but they are also compelled to engage with bereaved families and tenacious journalists. It is important that these dynamics are acknowledged and examined for the purpose of providing an original and reliable account of their complexity. After all, these dynamics constitute important terrain in the patient homicide governance space.

On the other hand, different disciplines and rationalities operate in and around health services, which investigators are expected to understand and judge at times of crisis and uncertainty. These disciplines and rationalities inform conflicting aims and goals. For example, the aim of medicine is completely different to the aim of politics. Regulatory actors may not see eye to eye. Some actors may not even realise what others are doing. Things go wrong. Lawyers,

[34] See N Rose, 'Psychiatry as a Political Science: Advanced Liberalism and the Administration of Risk' (1996) 9(2) *History of the Human Sciences* 1, 5.

[35] See generally G Lawson, 'The Rise and Rise of the Administrative State' (1994) 107(6) *Harvard Law Review* 1231; P Tucker, *Unelected Power: The Quest for Legitimacy in Central Banking and the Regulatory State* (Princeton, NJ, Princeton University Press, 2018).

[36] Yeung, 'The Regulatory State' (n 23) 68.

[37] See generally Health and Social Care Act 2012, s 75; Health Service (Procurement, Patient Choice and Competition) (No 2) Regulations 2013.

policy makers, interest groups and the media respond by making sense of such difficulties. The risk, however, is that they may disagree with each other and engage in conflict.

Independent investigators of health services after mental health homicide are unique because they are commissioned to make sense of these uncertainties. They are expected to untangle the wild entanglement of reeds that make up health services.[38] They are, furthermore, expected to do so in a convincing and rigorous manner by engaging in a series of complex tasks: the questioning of health care professionals, the scrutiny of medical documentation, the establishment of facts, the compilation of a report demonstrating their findings and the forwarding of recommendations. These are difficult tasks because the NHS is a complex institution. There are surprises around its every corner. Medical treatment is carried out by legions of personnel. Decisions may have unintended consequences. Lines of communication may fail. Budgets may become strained. Journalists may dig too deeply. Patients may become violent.

Again, health service complexity is relevant here because it may intimidate. The author interviewed an investigator who commented that some cases are beyond her resource capabilities:

> Most of the cases I've worked on are cases where you're looking at management … there are cases where you need to rummage around in the commissioning arms of what's going on, big companies rather than I are better off at doing that because they have a longer reach, bigger resources at their disposal. It's not the sort of stuff that floats my boat. I much prefer to work with incidents where I'm working with a cluster of organisations or local agencies and looking at it with them. Things like judicial reviews … I just wouldn't put myself in the line for those, even if I was doing it in partnership with one of my competitors, which I could do; I get on very well with my competitors and I could co-work with them on a case if I wanted to, but I prefer to work at ground level with staff. **Investigator 2**

The issue of resources is therefore important. The investigator's comment suggests that there is a division of labour between investigators. Some investigators are more comfortable with cases involving small groups of individuals and agencies and some are more comfortable with large, demanding investigations.

The issue of change is crucial to health care policy and practice also. The NHS is a moving target for investigators because it frequently undergoes politically driven change and relies on continuous decision making. Investigators must investigate the past, identify decisions made in it and compare these decisions to how decisions in health services are made in the present. There is always a prima facie case

[38] 'We have given this report the title of 'Looking Through the Reeds' as this phrase was used to us by a sister of John West to describe the inherent difficulty of reconstructing events prior to the homicide' (Lady Wall et al, *'Looking Through the Reeds': The Report of the Independent Inquiry into the Care and Treatment of Richard King*, NHS East of England SHA (June 2008).

for arguing that inadequate mental health care was provided to a mentally disordered patient perpetrator of homicide.[39] If care failings are found, it is important for investigators to establish whether these failings are happening in the present because it enables them to advance reliable recommendations for changes in practice. Health services cannot, however, stand still while investigators prepare their inquiry and do their work. Indeed, health services are unique because they carry on, even after the most serious failures.[40] Services are constantly engaged by health care users before, during and after an investigation. Employees come and go. Teams and agencies are disbanded and created, sometimes over brief periods of time. What is more, investigations are completed four years after a homicide incident has occurred, on average. Significant change in services is likely to occur during the intervening period. Investigators face the prospect of investigating services that bear little resemblance to the arrangements in place at the time of the homicide.

Investigating services provided to a perpetrator before the Health and Social Care Act 2012 came into force is particularly demanding because the legislation brought about a radical reorganisation of services. Commissioning authorities were abolished and replaced with bodies staffed with different personnel, competition between providers was strengthened and new legal obligations were imposed on regulatory actors. It is almost impossible for (some) investigators of mental health services provided to patient perpetrators prior to 2013 to conduct a straightforward investigation because services have undergone change. Yet, investigators are expected to chase shadows and make judgements on services then and now which policy makers and health care providers are expected to use to procure change.

These points raise a curious question: if past care and treatment arrangements do not resemble current arrangements, can reliable findings be produced by investigators and logical change implemented? An investigator interviewed by the author commented that suggesting and implementing change in services should be approached with caution:

> [The NHS] is a very complex environment to be dictating change [to]. **Investigator 2**

The investigator's comment is understandable. Health care systems are a collection of fragmented and ambiguous disciplines that conflict with each other.[41]

[39] A Buchanan, 'Independent Inquiries into Homicide: Should Share Common Methods and Be Integrated into New Quality Systems' (1999) 318 *British Medical Journal* 1089, 1089.

[40] K Walshe and SM Shortell, 'When Things Go Wrong: How Health Care Organizations Deal with Major Failures' (2004) 23(3) *Health Affairs* 103, 109.

[41] See N Eastman and J Peay, 'Law without Enforcement: Theory and Practice' in N Eastman and J Peay (eds), *Law without Enforcement: Integrating Mental Health and Justice* (Oxford, Hart Publishing, 1999) 8–9. See also A Perron et al, 'Citizen Minds, Citizen Bodies: The Citizenship Experience and the Government of Mentally Ill Persons' (2010) 11(2) *Nursing Philosophy* 100, 107. Perron et al claim that psychiatric risk assessment techniques arose out of the increasing need to assess mental disorders using jargon gleaned from other disciplines from the eighteenth century onwards.

Services change. Investigations are yet another source of change. Investigators tread cautiously. At the same time, they must re-inspire trust and confidence in services. However, the anxiety surrounding investigations makes for a difficult experience. Health professionals identified for questioning have been known to feel witch-hunted. The media publish attention-grabbing headlines. NHS Trust directors may await investigation findings with trepidation. Families grieve and want answers.

C. Sites of Resistance

The fierce criticism often levelled at health services poses an additional challenge for investigators to overcome. In particular, the families of mental health homicide victims often question whether health authorities take public safety seriously. Family questioning is often extended towards those tasked with investigating the perpetrator's care and treatment. An investigator who was interviewed for the research described the relationship between inquiries and families as tumultuous. He commented further that these relationships work better when investigators take their mandate from the victim's relatives:

> I think the most powerful thing I learned from doing one of the inquiries was meeting the mother of the daughter who was killed one evening and really trying to get my remit from her. In other words, what were the questions she wanted to know, pretty obvious ones. We would have done that anyway. But her believing, which I think was right, that we were acting much more on her behalf than on the organisation that commissioned us I think was really important. It was really important to her. And, I use phrases like the 'mandate coming from the family'. That's my authority, as much, if not more so, than the people actually paying me. **Investigator 6**

The investigator went onto agree that the mandate he refers to is a form of 'moral authority'. Inquiries, then, are not just a procedure. They mean something. To the investigator above, investigating has a strong moral component.

Moral components are not always visible on the surface of an investigator's final inquiry report. These reports are rarely explicit about the moral status investigators afford families. All inquiry reports express sympathy towards families and describe them as important to the investigation process. The interviews conducted by the author with investigators, however, show differences between investigators in how the role of families is regarded. Some investigators, like the one above, think that input from families is a good thing. Families are reported to be a source of moral authority for the investigation. Others, however, think that family input is a problem (eg, interfering, costly). It is extremely unlikely that an opinion of family involvement in investigations as being 'interfering' and 'costly' would be publicised in an inquiry report. One investigator commented during interview that his opinions on family involvement would be 'career-limiting' if they were made public. He acknowledged that the victims' families have a story to tell about their experience but opined that their value to an investigation is minimal because they were not at the scene of the crime, they did not know the perpetrator and have no knowledge about the treatment provided to him or her. The investigator expressed criticism of what he regarded as a growing expectation that the experiences of families are made relevant to a difficult investigation, despite the existence of separate processes that cater to families and their experience as victims (eg, victim impact statements in court, police liaison officers). He emphasised that investigations are not designed to provide 'succour' to victims of crime, but that requirements imposed by NHS England South that an investigation panel member be appointed to oversee family-related issues was burdensome.[42] The interviews conducted by the author therefore show a mixed picture about how investigators regard families. Inquiry reports are perceptive but they are coy about how investigators frame the role of families.

The author refers to inquiry reports, on occasion, at different points throughout the book however. These reports are still a valuable resource. The interview data is nevertheless more important because, when combined with the book's rigorous theoretical design, it helps produce a detailed and more accurate picture of the patient homicide governance space. The monograph is supported by data from interviews with 14 independent investigators who collectively have conducted hundreds of investigations between them. These investigators enter into contractual arrangements with NHS England after submitting a bid in response to a tender. They form a relatively small community. As one investigator remarked:

> There's not a huge number of people who've got the expertise really to comment on others when there's been such a tragedy. **Investigator 6**

An interview was also conducted with Julian Hendy, the trustee of the charity Hundred Families. Julian has represented hundreds of family members involved in independent investigations and he also sits as a lay member on NHS England South's Independent Investigations Governance Committee. The Committee's aim is to ensure quality and learning after independent investigations.

IV. Thinking About Complexity

The author casts extensive light through the patient homicide investigative process and its wider context in order to provoke further discussion about its dynamics and what it is capable of. Policy makers are increasingly asking whether these investigations need to be reformed; a public consultation in 2018 was completed

[42] Cf MJ Gregory, 'Managing the Homicide-suicide Inquest the Practices of Coroners in One Region of England and Wales' (2014) 42(3) *International Journal of Law, Crime and Justice* 237, 249. Gregory's study found that coroners, when conducting inquests, demonstrate awareness of family bereavement, although a coronial lack of expertise in these matters was apparent.

on the need to reform the mental health homicide investigation procedure in Scotland.[43] The author has also received personal communications from a non-executive NHS Trust director who has been tasked to review a series of investigations in England as part of a wider process of change planned in England. In writing the book, however, the author avoids taking sides in normative debates about how best to conduct investigations, although policy makers and scholars may indeed use the book contents to evaluate their normative claims. The book draws attention to the limitations of normative arguments in policy making by advancing a theoretically distinct account of the dynamics that work in and around investigations. For example, the economic cost of investigations is relevant to the issue of what these investigations are (ie, economic observations) and what their purpose is. Similarly, the moral components of investigations or their relevance to law in the form of judicial review applications is relevant to the issue of what these investigations are also (ie, moral and legal observations).

An investigation framed in moral terms is bound to jar with an investigation framed as a news item with informational value or as an endeavour constrained by economic costs. Families may want moral vindication or justice in the courts but morality and justice are a far cry from the media's construction of the incident and subsequent investigation as a 'story'. The intentions of investigators remain noble throughout (eg, that 'lessons must be learned'). Yet, these intentions arguably downplay the complexity of health services and the varied interests of those relevant parties connected to them. What is more, certain actors (eg, investigators, families) claim to occupy a privileged vantage point from which the issues raised during an investigation may be accurately appraised. The scholarship is clear however: 'no single actor has all the knowledge required to solve complex, diverse and dynamic problems'.[44] It is questionable whether there is a supreme vantage point from which social and regulatory complexity can be viewed and wholly appreciated.[45] It is impossible to get a comprehensive picture of what goes on in the NHS. Taking action on issues that relate to health and public safety is also difficult. Mental health homicides vividly demonstrate the point.

The issue of complexity in public health services provides an appropriate entry point to begin thinking about these matters theoretically. Many theories of complexity have been advanced over the years. Systems theory in particular offers a reliable and precise way of thinking about modern legal, political and administrative complexity. When used, it creates a degree of theoretical manoeuvrability that other theories are unable to achieve. It illuminates a diverse range of social relationships and events and the couplings between them. As a highly influential contribution to a range of studies of society, law, regulation and governance, Niklas Luhmann's theory of social systems is of particular interest here.

[43] Scottish Government, *Review of homicides by people with recent contact with NHS Scotland mental health and learning disability services: A Consultation on the Mental Welfare Commission for Scotland's proposal* (Edinburgh, Scottish Government, 2017).

[44] J Black, 'Critical Reflections on Regulation' (2002) 27 *Australian Journal of Legal Philosophy* 1, 5.

[45] See N Luhmann, *Risk: A Sociological Theory* (New Brunswick, Aldine Transaction, 1993/2008) 22.

A. Luhmann's Systems Theory

Luhmann's work is uniquely sceptical of the long-standing assumption that our efforts to understand society's complexity and organise our affairs are achievable through cause-and-effect reasoning. The procedural and emotional cycles that typify the experiences of those connected to mental health homicides involve relentless pursuits to minimise future homicides, create conditions of public safety and provide adequate support for bereaved families. Yet, these aspirations are made the subject of initiatives that are predicated on a cause-and-effect model; something awful has happened and measures must be put in place to fix the harm caused and make society a better place. That has failed to happen because, occasionally, patient homicides continue to occur. The emotional and procedural cycle therefore continues. In addition to providing a reliable account of the investigatory governance space after patient homicide, the author questions why the tumultuous investigatory cycle occurs and whether there is scope for policy makers to re-evaluate their normative commitments. Niklas Luhmann's general theory of social systems provides the tools for such a novel and far-reaching examination.

Niklas Luhmann developed an influential, albeit unorthodox, understanding of complexity. He claims that there is no privileged perspective from which society can be viewed and objectively understood. Neither the policy maker in Whitehall who seeks to implement reforms for the purposes of improving social cohesion nor the economist at the World Bank who seeks to eradicate poverty can – contrary to common assumption – occupy such a privileged position. Rather, Luhmann questions whether ontological or anthropocentric approaches to the study of society can provide an adequate explanation for how society works. Ontological questions seek to define the world or an aspect of it, a priori (eg, Kant's concept of Reason). Anthropocentric questions consider humankind to be the most significant aspect of the world and that the most reliable interpretations of the world can be reached using human values. Ontological and anthropocentric approaches dominate academic and political life. They share one thing in common: they are both humanist in design. According to Luhmann, both approaches are questionable as starting points for understanding society. Luhmann advances a functional analysis of society that removes human beings, as traditionally conceived, from the equation.

Luhmann heads into novel philosophical territory with his approach because it goes against intellectual custom; his theory has been compellingly described as the fourth major insult to Western intellectual vanity.[46] Luhmann's theory, however,

[46] See HG Moeller, *The Radical Luhmann* (New York, Columbia University Press, 2011) 28. Freud outlined three major insults: the Copernican revolution, Darwin's theory of evolution and his own theory of the unconscious. Moeller writes that 'Luhmann now adds another insult to this list – one that could be called the *sociological insult*'.

consists of concepts unfamiliar to students and scholars steeped in the 'Old European' tradition. Luhmann's dense, abstract and soporific writing style does not help matters. Scholars admit that his writings have sent them to sleep.[47] Luhmann's writings have much to offer, however, because they provide the tools for identifying social phenomena previously unrecognised by the reductionist categories advanced thus far in Western intellectual thought. A price is nonetheless payable for these benefits. Students and readers new to Luhmann are asked to jettison all of the theories, concepts and assumptions that they commonly use to understand society; a huge demand by anyone's standards.

Luhmann's theory relates to how meaning in society is produced. It argues that meaning is produced by communication and that communication constitutes society. For something to be meaningful to everyone it must be communicated about and made socially available to everyone. A bottle of milk may be communicated economically by referring to its price, but it may be communicated about medically if its spoiled contents have been consumed. Such communications, therefore, are significant for society's function systems (eg, the economy and medicine). That which lacks social significance meaning (ie, the thoughts inside someone's head, the biological material in their bodies) is outside of society.

Organic matter and mental processes are the two 'systems' that Luhmann contends are outside of communication and hence outside of society; these things can be communicated about within society but they do not form part of society because they do not *directly* produce socially relevant meanings. Systems of organic life (eg, our circulatory system) produce biological reactions (eg, oxygen supply) and our psychological systems produce cognition (eg, the way we feel about life). Oxygen supply and human cognition have no *direct* purchase in society, according to Luhmann. The point may be rephrased by positing two questions: is it wholly logical to conclude that our circulatory systems play a direct role in how economic transactions are made? Is it wholly logical to conclude that our (invisible) thoughts can perturb someone else's behaviour from across the room? The answer to these questions is a resounding no. Blood circulation and consciousness are the primary movers responsible for oxygenation and cognition respectively but they have nothing directly to do with making monetary payments. Something else must occur if making these payments is to have (economic) significance for others involved in the transaction. What is the 'something else'? Luhmann's answer is *communication*.

There are, then, three separate systems of observation for Luhmann: biological, psychic and communication (or social) systems. Luhmann's tripartite distinction between these systems is a cornerstone of his sociology. Furthermore, Luhmann describes these systems as operationally closed; they operate autonomously, lack a direct mutual connection and involve no overlap. Thoughts can only produce more thoughts. Biological matter, such as cells, can only produce more biological

[47] ibid.

matter (ie, cell reproduction). Communications (ie, socially available meaning) produce communication only. There is, thus, no direct relationship of influence or causality between thoughts and cells. People cannot reproduce a cell by thinking about one and the thoughts in a person's head cannot reproduce cells in the thinker's body. Communication, as socially available meaning, is unable to directly access human thoughts or biological cells. Rather, communication structures life independently of the bodies, intentions and motivations of persons.[48] Communication provides a structure of life whereby organic matter and thoughts may be communicated about by individuals who step into these structures. 'As organisms, "persons" use "life", and as minds, they use "consciousness" to persist'.[49] The third element of the tripartite distinction is communication; persons – as biological and psychic systems – persist *in society* as communicative constructs.

Yet, each of these systems operates because the others do. For example, psychic systems function to produce thoughts only, but an oxygen supply guaranteed by our circulatory (biological) system is necessary for thinking to happen. A person with the relevant qualifications may be regarded by everyone as a 'doctor' because the role has a distinct meaning provided by a communicative structure we call medicine, but the existence of a psychic system socialised into recognising why a doctor is a doctor is essential for a doctor to be recognised as such. A person's biological and psychic systems are necessary for constructing roles in society but at the same time they are not responsible for the construction. For Luhmann, human beings are constituted by separate systems (eg, biological, psychic) that are outside of society. They are an environment for society that society communicates about. It is more precise, therefore, to argue that human beings participate in society as incomplete persons.[50] The physical bodies of humans and their minds are outside of society. Persons have nothing whatsoever to do with the structures already in place (ie, communication) that produce socially available meanings *about* the world.

B. Society's Function Systems

It is more logical, according to Luhmann, to claim that human beings – as physical bodies and psychological entities – are rendered into socially meaningful constructs in society's systems. These constructions are formed in different ways and they correlate to society's function systems. These systems (eg, law, medicine, politics) construct 'persons' as having roles that pertain to a subsystem's function.

[48] M King and C Thornhill, *Niklas Luhmann's Theory of Politics and Law* (Basingstoke, Palgrave Macmillan, 2005) 163; J Jalava, *Trust as a Decision: The Problems and Functions of Trust in Luhmannian Systems Theory* (Helsinki, University of Helsinki, 2006) 71.

[49] S Fuchs, 'Niklas Luhmann' (1999) 17(1) *Sociological Theory* 117, 119.

[50] See M King, 'Child Welfare within Law: The Emergence of a Hybrid Discourse' (1991) 18(3) *Journal of Law and Society* 303, 304.

Persons are 'lawyers' in law, 'doctors' in medicine, 'politicians' in politics and 'stories' in the media. The entities that we refer to as human beings are, for Luhmann, *communicated about* in the system of society and within society's social systems of communication.

There are many social systems. They are distinct from one another in the same manner that biological, psychic and communication systems are distinct from one another. The non-replicability and non-substitutability of social systems may be compared to the non-replicability of biological and psychic systems. For example, scientific communications produce truthful scientific facts about their environment (eg, biological systems, psychic systems) in the form of disciplines like biology and psychology. Science may, furthermore, communicate about other social systems (eg, religion) in its environment, albeit scientifically (eg, rejecting religion on scientific grounds). Scientific knowledge is produced through an appeal to scientifically accredited methods. Scientifically truthful statements about other social function systems are the province of science only. For instance, if the world's scientists were replaced by priests and an attempt was made by these priests to establish truthful facts about the world using religious doctrines, the result would be unconvincing. The results would be rejected as unscientific and false.

It is tempting to regard social systems as interpreters of objective facts that exist 'out there'. Luhmann's argument, however, is that systems of life, thought and communication are wholly distinct and closed off from each other; the social systems that make up society construct reality from within and not without. They produce meaning about the world on their own terms.[51] Meaning, so the argument goes, is produced through a self-validating network of communication within each of society's communication systems. For example, law is law because legal communications determine what law is. The question of what law is (ie, distinguishing between legality and illegality) cannot be answered by appealing to what law is not (eg, religion). To argue otherwise would be to assume that social systems of meaning are hierarchical, replaceable and amenable to direct manipulation through a particular perspective; a misleading assumption according to Luhmann's theory because it fails to stand up to close scrutiny, ignores systemic complexity and represents too imprecise a starting point for reliably analysing society.

The theoretical design advanced thus far shows that social systems, like science, produce facts by referring to the same type of communications on subsequent occasions. A condition of self-reference is created for that system alone and by it, to the point where it becomes autopoietic. In other words, the meanings produced by that system are wholly derived from its own communicational elements. Science refers to *scientific* concepts and theories, verified by *scientific* methods, in order to establish *scientific* truth. The system of psychiatry constructs

[51] See M King, 'The "Truth" about Autopoiesis' (1993) 20(2) *Journal of Law and Society* 218, 220.

reality on the basis of what kind of *psychiatric* disorder a patient is suffering from and what treatment they should receive; identifying *psychiatric* disorders and appropriate treatment is only possible by appealing to communications accredited by *psychiatric* experts about what *psychiatric* health and ill-health is and what *psychiatric* medications are appropriate. *Legal* communications are produced by a *legally* constituted court tasked to refer to previous *legal* communications in order to produce *legal* facts in cases recognised as *legally* relevant. Social systems, then, operate self-referentially rather than appealing to other social systems and extracting information from them in order to operate as if they were grabbing something 'off the rack'.[52]

Social systems are distinguishable from each other according to the meaning that they produce about events recognised as part of their environment (ie, other social systems, biological systems, psychic systems). Social events acquire meaning within social systemic communications and these communications structure life for the human participants who step into them. Law, economics, education and politics are communication systems that are differentiated from each other because they produce distinct functional meanings about their environments. Law communicates about its environment by distinguishing legality from illegality and, by extension, law from non-law. Medicine communicates about its environment, distinguishes health from illness and, by extension, distinguishes itself from non-medical systems of communication. Law and medicine are able to communicate about each other (both are environments for each other) but it is impossible for both systems to replicate each other's communications. Law is always law. Medicine is always medicine. Law and medicine are unable to assume each other's meaning. For example, a court battle is fought not by demonstrating first aid skills, but by making legal arguments. In similar fashion, demonstrating legal skills will not get a person very far in a medical emergency.

One of the implications of social autopoiesis is misunderstanding between two or more social subsystems. By way of illustration, psychiatric expert witnesses in court often experience difficulty understanding the legal defence of insanity. The defence has no meaning in the world of psychiatry; psychiatrists did not contribute to the defence's establishment and they do not refer to its rules in their practice. The rules, theories, taxonomies, processes and procedures of psychiatry have no direct bearing on law and vice versa.[53] The legal system may communicate *about* psychiatric communications but only insofar as they are relevant to legal system operations (eg, as evidence to prove the defendant's guilt).

Luhmann's systems theory represents a radical reformulation of the individual. Each social subsystem constructs the individual in accordance with what previous

[52] N Luhmann, *Social Systems* (Stanford, Stanford University Press, 1984/1995) 140.

[53] See Eastman and Peay, 'Law without Enforcement' (n 41) 21; T Ward, 'The Sad Subject of Infanticide: Law, Medicine and Child Murder, 1860–1938' (1999) 8(2) *Social & Legal Studies* 163, 174; M King and C Piper, *How the Law Thinks About Children*, 2nd edn (Aldershot, Arena/Ashgate Publishing, 1995) 49.

communications have been validated as meaningful by that system alone. Humans, in their systemic plurality, participate in these systems of meaning as constructs only and not as essential beings with Reason or a soul. Luhmann therefore renounces an objective concept of the human being. An objective concept of the human being is, for him, the stuff of Enlightenment philosophy and should be rejected for being too imprecise. Enlightenment philosophy inadequately describes reality. It wrongly conflates the three systemic realms (ie, biological, psychic and communication systems) that make up the human being.

Individuals remain important in Luhmann's theory, however, because their systemic dimensions enable society to exist. To describe human beings as having a body and soul, however, with the soul defining the essence of human reality, is criticised by Luhmann as too much of a stretch. There is no evidence available upon which the body (ie, biological systems) is subservient to any other system.[54] A serious study of society must, therefore, involve the construction of a 'supertheory' that is able to account for the systems that operate biologically, psychically and socially. The tripartite distinction between biological, psychic and social systems forms the basis of Luhmann's 'supertheory'. It reappraises the status of the human being in society and enables the concept of communication to be articulated as a central reference point for describing how society functions.[55] Biological and psychic systems have, as we have seen, no direct influence on or connection to communication systems. To argue otherwise would suggest that the biological and psychic systems that make up human beings can directly produce communication. Under Luhmann's theory, human beings (as traditionally conceived) are unable to directly produce communication.

C. Homicide, Health Care and Society

The unusual theoretical arguments postulated thus far may seem alien to the context of mental health patient homicides. A brief demonstration, however, is apposite to show the link. When a patient's thoughts of killing another person (ie, psychic systems) are accompanied by the muscular movements required to pick up a knife and cause physical injury to another (ie, biological systems), the social subsystem of law will communicate about these events legally (eg, that a crime has been committed, that the perpetrator intended to commit murder). The social subsystem of economics will communicate about these events economically (eg, legal costs, compensation for the victim's families). The social subsystem of politics may communicate about these events politically (eg, opposition parties blaming government for policy failures in the area of mental health care, for electoral purposes).

[54] See generally HG Moeller, *Luhmann Explained: From Souls to Systems* (Chicago, Open Court, 2006) 81.

[55] See generally D Baecker, 'Why Systems?' (2001) 18(1) *Theory, Culture & Society* 59, 59.

Luhmann's theory, however, is quite open to the idea that there are penetrable barriers between function systems.[56] Luhmann is, indeed, adamant that social systems of communication are too different to be directly controlled by other social systems but he argues that they may *perturb* or *irritate* each other's communications. Perturbation or irritation involves inadvertent coupling relationships known as 'interpenetration'. Interpenetration may occur between wholly different systems. Biological and psychic systems may interpenetrate. Social systems and biological systems may interpenetrate. Social systems may interpenetrate. Interpenetration may be demonstrated by returning to the illustration above relating to homicide and health care. An event in the biological system (eg, the muscular movements and organic reactions respectively involved in picking up a knife and plunging it into the chest of another person) and the psychic system (ie, the thoughts produced in someone's mind about stabbing another person) are environments for each other. Each system is wholly separate. Each is unable to directly influence the other's operation (ie, thoughts do not directly produce the relevant muscular movements involved in the stabbing). Each system, however, is *dependent on the existence of the other to operate and continue their functioning*. Biological and psychic systems are environments for each other and, in the process, are mutually necessary for the purposes of their operation. Biological and psychic systems are also environments for the social subsystems of law (the crime of homicide) and medicine (treatment and diagnosis). Each system – social and otherwise – is a point of perturbation for the other. They are coupled and function in those moments because other systems function in those moments but they all remain distinct as autopoietic systems. In systems-theoretical parlance, social systems are normatively closed, but cognitively open to their environment. These observations are unorthodox but they revolutionise how society may be understood and, in particular, help articulate the unexplored relationship between patient homicide, health care and society.

The attempts, by philosophers, to provide supreme explanations of society are a familiar tradition. The primacy given to law or politics in situations of crisis, despite the reported lack of trust that has bedded in in societies, is a common habit that remains unbroken in modern times, particularly in the context of vital public services. If something goes wrong, the politicians and the lawyers must fix it. Western societies have conditioned themselves to follow a predictable routine. It is a routine of identifying problems, implementing solutions, recognising new unforeseen problems and proposing – once more – to finally bring about a better society with another solution. For Luhmann, it is a routine that is *the* problem. Moeller puts it best when he writes that rather than looking for better solutions to problems, Luhmann asks what the problem is in the first place.[57] The problem is how Western philosophical thought conceptualises society.

[56] See R Nobles and D Schiff, *Observing Law Through Systems Theory* (London, Hart Publishing, 2012) 132.

[57] Moeller (n 46) ix.

Western conceptualisations of society consider society to be directly amenable to steering by individuals. Moreover, they continue to have major influence on the problem-solving approaches taken by society's elites (eg, economists, regulators, judges, politicians). Elites often reduce society's problems to simple categories (eg, political incompetence, class divisions) and propose solutions (eg, regulation, law reform) for them. These practices are supported by well-intentioned ambitions (eg, making society a better place). These ambitions are perceived by some as realised to some degree. For Luhmann, however, society is far from being a preordained configuration of affairs amenable to control. Successes are merely constructed. Society is typified by different forms of communication that do not read from the same script. Society is contingent and unpredictable. Solutions forged in one area (eg, politics) are known to raise unforeseen problems in another (eg, the economy). For instance, medicine is generally considered to be a well-intentioned discipline that avoids harm but it has been criticised for unwittingly doing harm to human bodies and interests.[58] Indeed, medicine and psychiatry have complex and controversial histories.[59] At the same, medicine and psychiatry have been described as facilitating inclusion.[60]

Luhmann's systems theory provides a framework for understanding the complex maelstrom of contingency in society. The author has, thus far, sought to craft an early summary of Luhmann's sociology with two aims in mind. First, the summary situates Luhmann's work against established theoretical orthodoxy. Second, the summary prepares those readers who are unfamiliar with Luhmann's position. The summary is rounded off here by emphasising Luhmann's non-normative posture; it avoids commitment to ideology or morality. Luhmann criticises the Western intellectual tradition for naïvely making these types of commitments however. For him, such commitments are unreliable because they are too reductionist. The author similarly adopts a non-normative position. The book's analysis avoids questions regarding what is right and wrong in the context of homicide investigations. Rather, it explores the significance of complexity surrounding independent inquiries, reframes what it means to explore adverse

[58] See generally I Illich, *Limits to Medicine: Medical Nemesis, the Expropriation of Health* (London: Penguin, 1990); JP Davies et al, 'The Problems of Offenders with Mental Disorders: A Plurality of Perspectives within a Single Mental Health Care Organisation' (2006) 63 *Social Science and Medicine* 1097, 1097.

[59] See M Foucault, *Madness and Civilisation* (London, Routledge, 1971/2008); R Porter, *A Social History of Madness* (London, Weidenfeld and Nicholson, 1987); A Scull, 'The Domestication of Madness' (1983) 27(3) *Medical History* 233; I Hacking, *Mad Travelers: Reflections on Transient Mental Illness* (Richmond, VA, University of Virginia Press, 1998).

[60] EJ Novella, 'Mental Health Care and the Politics of Inclusion: A Social Systems Account of Psychiatric Deinstutionalization' (2010) 31 *Theoretical Medicine and Bioethics* 411, 421–22. Novella argues that the shift from asylum-based psychiatry to community-based psychiatry necessitates the inclusion of patients in society's function systems. For example, she points out that as part of community care-based initiatives, patients are encouraged to participate in social activities as a way of improving their mental health.

events in public health services and urges policy-making elites to re-evaluate their normative commitments. Luhmann's theory of social systems is, understandably, controversial and the details of the controversy will be explored in later chapters.

V. Central Questions and Themes

A central focus for the author is to examine whether the objectives set by independent inquiries are achievable. These objectives generally comprise the following series: the learning of lessons from patient homicides; the investigation of their causes; and the subsequent improvement of mental health services. Independent inquiries are, however, controversial because they are regarded as invasive and humiliating.[61] They are described as having little value because they are expensive, time-consuming, biased and incapable of answering basic questions about what happened.[62] The author's reliance on systems theory to organise the book's focus raises the question of whether a non-normative position that rejects the possibilities of reaching privileged observational vantage points and societal steering excludes itself as a privileged seat of observation. Luhmann claims that there is no privileged seat of observation, his own theory included: 'the epistemologist becomes him/herself a rat in the labyrinth and has to reflect on the position from which he/she observes the other rats'.[63] He writes that systems theory appears in the real world as one of its own objects: 'Because it [systems theory] claims universal validity for everything that is a system, the theory also encompasses systems of analytic and epistemic behavior. It therefore itself appears within the real world as one of its own objects, among many others'.[64] It is 'part of the reality it attempts to describe'.[65] King describes Luhmann's theory as a vision of 'contingency, unpredictability of social events, explicable only in retrospect and then only by using one or other of the available social systems'.[66]

The author, in similar fashion, does not claim a privileged seat of truth or observation. Rather, attention is drawn to an area that has been forgotten, neglected and criticised for the approach policy makers have taken in relation to patient homicides. It attempts to perturb academic and policy custom around what it means

[61] G Szmukler, 'Homicide Inquiries: What Sense Do They Make? (2000) 24 *Psychiatric Bulletin* 6, 9.

[62] ibid, 7 and 8.

[63] See N Luhmann, 'Cognition as Construction' in Moeller, *Luhmann Explained* (n 54) 250.

[64] Luhmann, *Social Systems* (n 52) 11. See also P Barbesino and SA Salvaggio, 'How Is a Sociology of Sociological Knowledge Possible?' (1996) 35 *Social Science Information* 341. Luhmann's theory of social systems has been regarded as 'a sociology of sociological knowledge'.

[65] M Brans and S Rossbach, 'The Autopoiesis of Administrative Systems: Niklas Luhmann on Public Administration and Public Policy (2002) 75(3) *Public Administration* 417, 418.

[66] M King, 'What's the Use of Luhmann's Theory?' in M King and C Thornhill (eds), *Luhmann and Law and Politics: Critical Appraisals and Applications* (Oxford, Hart Publishing, 2006), 41.

to investigate the overlooked space of patient homicide governance. An empirical examination of the patient homicide governance space in England is conducted for these purposes. Fourteen patient homicide investigators and one family representative were interviewed. The data from those interviewed provides a supplementary, yet vital and original, mechanism of support for the book when combined with the novel theoretical design built in throughout. The data combines with the book's unique theoretical direction for the purposes of producing a comprehensive and novel understanding of the patient homicide governance space.

A. Subsidiary Themes

A group of important subsidiary themes emerge throughout the author's work. The vexed debate over whether promulgating desired change in spheres of public life pursuant to predefined goals can be made through decision making is one of these themes. It underscores thinking across a range of academic schools; Teubner's concept of reflexive law,[67] governmentality[68] and Giddens' structuration theory.[69] The book engages generally with the aforementioned theme in its analysis and discussion, further enhancing the book's originality and rigour.

The book is also a timely contribution. A series of investigators interviewed for the research stated that their investigations aim to deconstruct lapses in care and establish a better perspective. There is ambition on the part of investigators to occupy a specific vantage point in order to procure desired change in accordance with predefined goals. These goals and the change that follows are informed by the knowledge, skills, expertise and experience of investigators that cohere into a vantage point that Luhmann's theory of social systems would regard as unable to represent the complexity of the problems at hand.

Social systems theory is an important theoretical framework for the book but three additional conceptual elements of the book's approach are placed within the framework: the concepts of accountability, time and risk. These concepts help establish a novel look into the finer dynamics and challenges within the patient homicide governance space. These concepts are familiar to the Western intellectual tradition. One of the author's tasks, however, is to revise the concept of accountability in particular within a systems-theoretical framework.[70]

[67] G Teubner, 'Substantive and Reflexive Elements in Modern Law' (1983) 17(2) *Law and Society Review* 239–85.

[68] M Foucault, *The Order of Things: An Archaeology of the Human Sciences* (London, Routledge, 2004); G Burchell et al (eds), *The Foucault Effect: Studies in Governmentality* (Chicago, IL, University of Chicago Press, 1991).

[69] A Giddens, *The Constitution of Society: Outline of the Structuration Theory* (Cambridge, Polity, 1984).

[70] The concepts of time and risk receive close attention in Luhmann's writings.

At a general level, time is relevant because inquiries are mainly retrospective. Accountability is relevant because inquiries elicit information from health professionals (among others) about past decisions. Risk, too, is relevant because inquiries attempt to reduce the risk of future mental health homicides through the learning of lessons. These concepts, in various ways, are familiar to the Western philosophical tradition. They are often channelled into narrowly focused understandings about how problems in society should be understood and resolved. For example, time is often regarded as a universal experience for everyone. Accountability is commonly regarded as a process of direct information transmission between individuals. Risk is famously associated with the destructive potential of technology.[71] Luhmann's work raises questions over all of these claims.

The present book draws on Luhmann's work in order to examine the aforementioned concepts and apply them for the purposes of advancing a comprehensive understanding of the patient homicide governance space. In doing so, the book inspires theoretical enquiry in other spaces of governance that share conventional policy-making orthodoxies. A short overview of how the book engages the concepts of accountability, time and risk is apposite for introductory purposes.

Establishing accountability for past conduct involves selecting persons from whom an account is to be elicited. An account will be meaningful to the relevant parties, as determined by a particular set of communications; independent investigations into patient homicides will, primarily, involve persons giving accounts about medical treatment and diagnosis given to the perpetrator (ie, medical communications).

Time is important also because accountability is concerned with producing communications about the past. It also entails making sense of the accounts given in the present and minimising the occurrence of an adverse event. Communications take time to be triggered, thus raising yet another dimension of time; an adverse event may be registered by a social subsystem, culminating in reactions from the medical and legal professions at different speeds. Law is notoriously slow to communicate. Litigation on a legal issue may take up to a decade to reach a conclusion.

Risk is important to time because it relates to possible future loss. Furthermore, risk has different meanings.[72] *Legal* risks (eg, the risk of litigation) are wholly different from *medical* risks (eg, risks to the physical body posed by medication). The risk of a mental health homicide occurring in the future may invite diverse interpretations from different experts[73] and create a gulf between them over how they understand it.[74] Independent investigators instigate processes of decision

[71] U Beck, *Risk Society: Towards a New Modernity* (London, Sage Publications, 1992).

[72] Luhmann, *Risk* (n 45).

[73] J Peay, 'Working with Concepts of "Dangerousness" in the Context of Mental Health Law' (2003) 51(1) *Criminal Justice Matters* 18, 19.

[74] See generally J Peay, *Decisions and Dilemmas: Working with Mental Health Law* (Oxford, Hart Publishing, 2003) 29.

making through their findings and through their recommendations. Their recommendations may lead to change for the purposes of minimising the likelihood of an adverse event happening again. Recommendations are made with an eye on their future consequences. An inquiry might also engage a specific form of communication when forging a set of recommendations for change to health care provision. For instance, they may recommend the creation of new clinical posts (ie, a medical communication). In turn, health service personnel may construct the same recommendation as an issue about having the resources to create these posts (ie, economic communication). The future consequences of adopting recommendations may, furthermore, involve a clash of meanings with other closed spheres of communication produced elsewhere about the homicide incident or the health care services connected to the incident. Recommendations, if implemented, may therefore lead to error, objection, rejection and regret. They are a risk to make.

VI. Conclusions

The present chapter sets a general context for the rest of the book. On the one hand, it appraises the legal, administrative and regulatory environment of the patient homicide governance space. Patient homicides trigger legal obligations under Article 2 of the ECHR to conduct an independent and effective investigation. These investigations occur within a complex labyrinth of NHS administrative activity, decision making and competing rationalities. There are thousands of decision makers who make decisions. These decisions affect thousands of vulnerable individuals. These decisions are, furthermore, informed by medical rationalities, political rationalities and economic rationalities, among others. These rationalities inform different aims and objectives for decision makers. There is conflict and disagreement between decision makers informed by different values and logics. There is conflict between staff and between organisations. Decision-making elites (eg, regulators, politicians) are reported to be widely distrusted by patients, citizens and other decision makers. Elites are often criticised for failing to recognise the diversity of interests that occupy the legal and regulatory space of the NHS and patient homicide governance.

In particular, market conditions, the logic of competition and technocratic decision making have become dominant forces in NHS provision, commissioning and patient homicide governance. Important regulatory actors (eg, hospitals, NHS Trusts, commissioners) are increasingly required to behave in ways that are consistent with the rhythms of a dynamic health care market. There is, now, an emphasis on speed, efficiency, contracting and cost. As subsequent chapters will allude to, patient homicide investigators are clinically trained specialists. They are required to enter into contracts with commissioners to conduct their investigations. Furthermore, they must compete with other investigators for these contracts and remain within strict budgets if they are commissioned. Investigators are continually pressured to complete their investigations in shorter time frames too, despite being required to investigate swathes of health service activity that previously were not part of the investigatory remit. The voice of families affected by patient homicide is increasingly vociferous also and investigators are increasingly expected to engage with them during their investigations.

In the light of the competing rationalities that ventilate the NHS governance space, patient homicide investigators encounter the difficulty of managing a variety of situations (eg, engagement with commissioners, engagement with family members) that are very different from each other. These situations are informed by different values. They set a stage for conflict, disagreement, resistance and complexity to flourish.

Modern society is typified by complexity. A major task assumed by scholars since the twentieth century has been to form adequate understandings of society and to evaluate the extent to which existing approaches sufficiently enable precise, accurate and reliable studies. Luhmann's systems theory is unique as an understanding of society. It questions the dominant conceptual underpinnings of Anglo-American scholarship: the 'Old European' Enlightenment concept of the individual. Luhmann argues that the individual is a fragmented entity of psychic and biological systems that exist in society as a self-construction in one of society's social communication systems. As the book will later explain, Luhmann's thesis challenges conventional ways of understanding how change in society occurs, especially in the context of elite practices (ie, decision makers and policy making). These practices are known for their diversity, unpredictability, failures and unintended consequences. Luhmann's work provides a conceptually rigorous framework for understanding why such practices are questionable. In particular, patient homicide governance – despite being overlooked – is an area typified by unpredictability, failure and unintended consequences. It is punctuated with conflict, disagreement and new patient homicide incidents. The present book utilises Luhmann's theory of social systems with a view to formulating a novel, yet reliable, understanding of the patient homicide governance space. It explains that patient homicides resonate throughout society in different ways (eg, politically, medically, legally). It draws a series of novel conclusions on why conflict, disagreement and resistance between decision makers and affected parties occur within the space. In supporting the book's central task, the present chapter summarises Luhmann's theory and prefaces subsequent chapters that engage it closely. In doing so, it provides an essential introduction for readers who are unfamiliar with Luhmann's work; Luhmann's theory of social systems is abstract and challenging because it requires readers to abandon the conventional theoretical tools they use to understand society.

2

The Investigatory Domain

I. Introduction

Independent inquiries (or investigations) into health care services after patient homicide are, in general, retrospective examinations of the past decisions and conduct of health professionals. They are situated on a broad landscape of inquiries; there are different types of inquiries and each has a different status under the law. Different types of inquiry have distinct policy backgrounds and histories but it is not the task of the present chapter to examine their different forms in detail. The chapter proceeds by briefly outlining the diverse investigatory landscape. It then provides a historical and policy overview of inquiries after mental health homicide. The key elements of the inquiry process are explained and a description of its basic components set out. The chapter, furthermore, develops essential themes and questions referred to in the previous chapter and examined later in the book. In doing so, the chapter clears the ground. It provides a contextual description of how inquiries are set up and the common challenges they are considered to face.

Independent investigations were once led by a judge or senior lawyer. They are now contracted out by NHS commissioners to private companies, primarily, and carried out by investigators who have expertise and skill sets in a number of distinct fields (eg, psychiatry, social work). Investigators, furthermore, use analytical tools to carry out their tasks, amplifying their specialist role.[1] Investigators are, loosely speaking, scientific in their approach. They apply accredited knowledge and skills. They gather evidence. They review the evidence. They forge understandings of health care services. They promote the learning of lessons. They seek to make services safer after a patient homicide. Their aims and objectives, however, relate to a diverse range of issues. These inquiries raise economic concerns (eg, they incur costs) and they are relevant to the demand for answers expressed by grief-stricken relatives of the deceased. Investigations are fraught with tension.[2]

[1] LA Neal et al, 'Root Cause Analysis Applied to the Investigation of Serious Untoward Incidents in Mental Health Services' (2004) 28 *Psychiatric Bulletin* 75, 75.

[2] See generally J Rumgay and E Munro, 'The Lion's Den: Professional Defences in the Treatment of Dangerous Patients' (2001) 12(2) *The Journal of Forensic Psychiatry* 357, 357.

The present chapter signposts these important aspects of the independent inquiry after homicide because they are relevant to the theoretical appraisal carried out in all subsequent chapters.

The present chapter begins by outlining the general landscape of inquiries, followed by a review of independent investigations into health care services after homicide. The background will facilitate later discussion, particularly in relation to the growing complexity of governance in the overlooked area of patient homicide. The present chapter goes on to frame a series of important questions regarding how best to frame the patient homicide governance space in subsequent chapters.

II. The Inquiry

Inquiries, generally, are set up by the state or its agents in response to an event, a series of events or an area of public concern deserving of investigation.[3] They assume different forms however. These forms, furthermore, have different purposes. Inquiries used to have different statutory bases in areas ranging from aviation to railways. Some functioned as a tribunal authorised by Parliament. These tribunals were equipped with judicial powers under the Tribunals of Inquiry (Evidence) Act 1921. It is only since the passing of the Inquiries Act 2005 that all forms of statutory inquiry were brought together under one inquiry system. Other forms of inquiry have operated on – and continue to operate on – a non-statutory basis. Statutory inquiries, on the one hand, provide a series of procedural safeguards.[4] Non-statutory inquiries, however, are limited in the procedural safeguards they guarantee; at most, they must conform to the principles of natural justice.

Despite the differences between the two forms of inquiry (statutory and non-statutory), both aim to realise a series of ambitions: establishment of the facts; accountability; the learning of lessons; recommendations; dispelling public disquiet; reconciling those affected by the event with those who caused or failed to prevent it; the development of public policy; and the discharge of state obligations to satisfy the requirement under Articles 2 and 3 of the ECHR (ie, to investigate alleged breaches by state agents).[5]

Independent non-statutory inquiries must be carried out where an adverse event of public concern relating to the delivery of publicly owned health care

[3] See generally J Beer, *Public Inquiries* (Oxford, Oxford University Press, 2006).

[4] J Peay, 'Themes and Questions' in J Peay (ed), *Inquiries after Homicide* (London, Duckworth & Co, 1996) 16.

[5] See House of Lords Select Committee on the Inquiries Act 2005, *The Inquiries Act 2005: Post-legislative scrutiny* (House of Lords, HMSO, 2014) 9, para 9. See also L Blom-Cooper, 'Public Inquiries' in M Freeman and B Hepple (eds), *Current Legal Problems, Vol 46, Part II, Collected Papers* (Oxford, Oxford University Press, 1993) 206.

services occurs. They are an independent 'retrospective examination of events or circumstances surrounding a service failure or problem'.[6] These inquiries are set up specifically in response to a mental health homicide event and are referred to as a sub-species of the non-statutory inquiry.[7] Government guidance (hereafter referred to as 'the Guidance') issued in 1994 sets out the circumstances in which these inquiries should be held. The Guidance stipulates that 'in cases of homicide, it will always be necessary to hold an inquiry which is independent of the providers involved'.[8] It also sets out the scope of an inquiry. It states that inquiry terms of reference should encompass the care the patient was receiving at the time of the incident and the suitability of that care in view of the patient's history and assessed health and social care needs. The Guidance requires inquiries to examine the extent to which the care provided corresponded with statutory obligations, relevant guidance from the Department of Health, local operational policies, the exercise of professional judgement and the adequacy of the care plan and its monitoring by the key worker.[9]

The Guidance was amended in 2005 to reflect changing medical, social and legal conditions.[10] The amendments added the requirement that inquiries must be set up if the perpetrator was receiving care from specialist mental health services in the six months prior to the event or where commissioners are concerned that an adverse event represents a serious systemic service failure. The amendments also removed the requirement that inquiries be chaired by a legal member (a judge or senior lawyer was usually tasked to chair inquiries).[11] Legal members were regarded as elite specialists. They were considered to possess skills that could, when applied, improve the quality of independent inquiries.[12] The 2005 amendments to the Guidance, however, reflect a change of policy posture.[13] The rationale behind the change was to bridge the gap between inquiry panel members and the technical issues raised in an investigation. Health services are technical and

[6] K Walshe and J Higgins, 'The Use and Impact of Inquiries in the NHS' (2002) 325 *British Medical Journal* 895, 895. See also A Buchanan, 'Independent Inquiries into Homicide: Should Share Common Methods and Be Integrated into New Quality Systems' (1999) 318 *British Medical Journal* 1089, 1089.

[7] Peay, 'Themes and Questions' (n 4) 17.

[8] Department of Health, *Guidance on the Discharge of Mentally Disordered People and Their Continuing Care in the Community*, NHS Executive, HSG(94)27, 11, para 34.

[9] ibid, para 36.

[10] Department of Health, *Independent investigation into adverse events in mental health services* (Department of Health, 2005).

[11] ibid.

[12] See D Carson, 'Structural Problems, Perspectives and Solutions' in Peay, *Inquiries After Homicide* (n 4) 141.

[13] G Szmukler, 'Homicide Inquiries: What Sense Do They Make? (2000) 24 *Psychiatric Bulletin* 6, 9. Szmukler illustrates a double standard: 'What if a psychiatrist chairman of the inquiry panel were giving an account at a press conference of a report, years in the preparation, to be presented to the Bar Council of, for example, evidence not adequately uncovered, poor communication between members of the prosecution team, arguments poorly presented, and so on, all in the presence of the victim's family and the sensationalist-seeking gaze of the media? Would this be reasonable?'.

panel members equipped with the knowledge and skills necessary to understand how these services operate was eventually considered to be an important element that inquiries could benefit from. Of particular importance was the perceived need to sharpen the ability of panels to identify lessons that could be learned for future practice. For example, a perpetrator who experienced considerable levels of contact with social services will raise a host of nuanced issues that only a chair with a background in social work is best placed to navigate.

Legal experts, on the other hand, are good at establishing cause and effect through persuasive argument but they are 'poor at checking the reliability of their inferences'.[14] Furthermore, the independent investigations conducted during the 1990s and before were focused on issues that investigators today would not be preoccupied with as much. An investigator, interviewed as part of the research for the book, described in hypothetical terms how the presence of a legally qualified chair on inquiry panels would influence an investigation today and concluded that legal expertise is incompatible with investigative priorities:

> If I'm doing an investigation from a legal framework point of view, you're looking for causality, you're looking for duty of care, you might be looking for negligence, but also in the legal field you may be giving too much attention to detail. That is the nature of their work. If you're going to defend or prosecute a case, every line matters … You'd have reports that were hundreds of pages long that were dense and not particularly readable or engaging, not particularly learning-oriented. Blame orientation in the NHS was a big thing back then. It's not now. **Investigator 2**

The relevance of legal expertise to independent investigations after homicide has diminished over time. There is now a reduced emphasis on blaming in their investigations. Bread-and-butter lawyering, however, is different. Lawyers, generally, are experts at taking up an adversarial posture in their line of work. They are well trained in certain cases to locate individual blame by advancing 'a case to be placed before the court for the court's consideration'.[15] Lawyers in courtrooms rigorously argue their case on behalf of their clients, with the aim of proving the case beyond a reasonable doubt or on the balance of probabilities. There is no 'investigation' as such. Inquiries after homicide, however, are inquisitorial.[16] The parties involved do not promote arguments.[17] These processes are unbound by case law and the strict rules of evidence typical of the courts. They enjoy broad investigatory scope. They may 'produce a mushrooming of observations and recommendations few could have anticipated in the preparatory stages'.[18] In similar fashion to legal processes, independent inquiries gather evidence and interview witnesses. At their core,

[14] Carson, 'Structural Problems' (n 12) 143.

[15] R Scott, 'Procedures at Inquiries – the Duty To Be Fair' (1995) 111 *Law Quarterly Review* 596, 596.

[16] ibid, at 596–97; J Beatson, 'Should Judges Conduct Public Inquiries?' (2005) 121 *Law Quarterly Review* 221, 224.

[17] Scott, 'Procedures at Inquiries' (n 15) 597.

[18] J Peay, 'Introduction' in Peay, *Inquiries After Homicide* (n 4) 2.

however, they are unconcerned with winners and losers. In fact, an investigator interviewed for the book expressed her dislike for adversarial information gathering within these types of investigation:

> I don't think I've ever had an interview since I've been working as an independent reviewer where I've felt it's been uncomfortable in the room, except one occasion when a colleague was interviewing. He was a specialist advisor. When I say he was really pushing the interviewee in a corner with their back against the wall, he was. I don't like that interview style. So, we did take time-out. So, that wasn't the interviewee bit being difficult. It was a member of my team being bloody-minded and I won't have it. I will not have an adversarial interview style. **Investigator 2**

Other investigators attached less significance to whether inquiries were influenced by an adversarial approach. An investigator commented that adversarial approaches to evidence gathering (ie, legal knowledge and skills) are a crucial part of a good investigation:

> Conventionally, it was a legal member chairing ... a bit like a Mental Health Review Tribunal. A doctor and a lay person who was often a social services person. That has changed dramatically. Not necessarily for the better. **Investigator 6**

Independent inquiries after mental health homicide have undergone a shift in composition, skill set and overall approach in recent decades. Investigators now prefer different ways of communicating about certain issues and express dislike for certain practices that at one time were stock-in-trade. Further still, a series of values, concerns and ways of doing things have become dominant within investigations that were irrelevant 10 years ago. The chapter goes on to provide an overview of these values, concerns and ways of doing things in more detail. Before doing so, however, the chapter will now explore some common concerns and developments that have influenced understandings of what independent investigations into health care after patient homicide are, what can be expected from them and what their purpose in society has hitherto been.

A. Central Issues and Influential Developments

Independent investigations after patient homicides are considered to contain weak procedural safeguards. Proceedings may be held in secret, eschew the public disclosure of evidence and involve non-publication of a final report.[19] Whether stronger procedural safeguards would facilitate an inquiry's pursuit of the truth is a question that has already been considered.[20] The author disagrees with the claim that these safeguards enhance the pursuit for truth, *objectively conceived.*

[19] Peay, 'Introduction' (n 4) 17.
[20] See generally Peay, *Inquiries After Homicide* (n 4).

The patient homicide governance space is framed as a closed social communication system that produces many 'truths'. These 'truths' exist in a non-hierarchical relationship with each other. In other words, there is no privileged truth capable a providing a supreme vantage point from which a homicide, health care services – the world even – can be occupied. The stated objectives of inquiries (eg, seeking truth, learning lessons, improving safety) suggest otherwise, but the theoretical framework adopted by the author supports the argument that these objectives overlook a series of crucial questions. Who is expected to pursue truth and learn lessons? Are these pursuits and lessons for lawyers and politicians? Are they for psychiatrists and probation services? Or, are they pursuits of truth and learning that everyone can follow and understand? As one investigator explained during an interview:

> I've done a lot of training with people who do their own investigations. People don't really know what it [learning lessons] means. **Investigator 1**

The author argues that truth and learning are constructed within structures of meaning made up of distinct forms of communication. These forms are varied. For example, they have legal form and they have medical form. Crucially, these forms of communications are the building blocks that constitute unique structures of life in society that we, as individuals with bodies and minds, step into in order to make sense of the world. An act of killing and its surrounding circumstances are, therefore, meaningful in different ways, depending on the structure of life in which these events are being observed. A legal observer is bound to frame an act of killing as an illegal act (ie, as a crime of homicide) whereas a medical observer is bound to see the same event as a medical emergency (ie, as an occasion to keep the victim alive). The questioning of witnesses by an independent panel after patient homicide will be informed by the observational standpoint of investigators also. These standpoints are informed by, but not limited to, the disciplines of medicine and psychiatry. As the book will demonstrate in subsequent chapters, investigators step into other observational standpoints that construct reality for an inquiry, such as economics and politics.

The book's argument showcases the complexity of the patient homicide governance space. Independent investigations, in particular, are typified by a host of further complexities, which the book examines closely. Recalling actions and events, especially those dating back years, may be difficult for witnesses. An inquiry's judgement about the evidence may be influenced by its knowledge of the adverse outcome (ie, hindsight bias). Inquiries conducted in recent years now avoid references to terms like 'hindsight' altogether. All reports published after 2013 are devoid of such references. Prior to 2013, these terms would sometimes be used in reports to embody the investigator's observations and designate the corrupting, albeit potential, influence of hindsight bias.[21] What these points tell

[21] B Ward and C Brougham, *An independent investigation into the care and treatment of Mr G* (Verita, January 2012) 4, 45, 101, 117, 130; M Clay et al, *An Independent Investigation into the Care and Treatment*

us is that among the complexity of meaning that an investigation may produce about certain events through its different observations, establishing answers (ie, accountability) and looking back into the past (ie, time) are pressing issues also. The book explores these issues in later chapters.

A series of developments have influenced the way independent mental health inquiries have evolved and are understood. Three high-profile investigations stand out: *The Case of Jason Mitchell*,[22] the Ritchie Report[23] and *The Falling Shadow*.[24] Others may be cited also,[25] but those aforementioned are notable for their unique style, impact and ambition to learn lessons.

The Case of Jason Mitchell investigated the care and treatment received by an individual who had been a restricted patient[26] and thereafter was released into the community. He subsequently killed three people. Jason Mitchell had been well known to health authorities. He had a history of violence and communicated homicidal fantasies to an occupational therapist prior to the killing. The inquiry reported that there was a lack of communication between relevant agencies and an understatement of important information about Jason's psychological health. *The Case of Jason Mitchell* was considered to be an unpleasant experience for many of those involved, such as Jason's doctor and the victim's families.[27] All wanted to find out what happened and for reoccurrences to be prevented. The inquiry was held in public in the interests of serving truth and openness.[28] The proceedings therefore attracted media attention, placing the professionals involved under broad scrutiny.

of a service-user at South Essex Partnership University NHS Foundation Trust (SEPT), formerly known as Bedfordshire and Luton Mental Health and Social Care Partnership NHS Trust (Health & Safety Laboratory, June 2011) ix; M Dineen et al, *An independent investigation into the care and treatment of a person using the services of the former Norfolk and Waveney Mental Health Partnership NHS Trust* (Consequence UK, July 2011) 30; M Rae et al, *Report of the independent investigation into the circumstances surrounding the care and treatment of Mr A* (Caring Solutions UK, February 2012) 10 and 36; M Dineen et al, *An Independent Investigation into the Care and Treatment of a person using the services of Nottinghamshire Healthcare NHS Trust, NHS East Midlands* (Consequence UK, October 2011) 21, 22, 40, 62, 63 and 72; LA Rowland et al, *Independent Investigation into the Care and Treatment provided to Mr AT* (Health and Social Care Advisory Service, November 2009) 30.

[22] L Blom-Cooper et al, *The Case of Jason Mitchell: Report of the Independent Panel of Inquiry* (London, Duckworth, 1996).

[23] J Ritchie et al, *The Report of the Inquiry into the Care and Treatment of Christopher Clunis* (London, HMSO, 1994).

[24] L Blom-Cooper and H Hally, *The Falling Shadow: One Patient's Mental Health Care 1978–1993* (London, Duckworth, 1995).

[25] R Francis et al, *Report of the independent inquiry into the care and treatment of Michael Stone*, South East Coast Strategic Health Authority, Kent County Council, Kent Probation Area (September 2006).

[26] Patients are 'restricted' when an order of the Crown Court is made to detain a mentally disordered offender in hospital for treatment because he or she poses a risk to the public (see Mental Health Act 1983, s 41(1)). Restricted patients are subject to special controls exercised by the Secretary of State for Justice.

[27] See H Prins, 'Mental Health Inquiries – "Cui Bono"'? in N Stanley and J Manthorpe (eds), *The Age of the Inquiry: Learning and Blaming in Health and Social Care* (London, Routledge, 2004) 22.

[28] L Blom-Cooper, 'Public Inquiries in Mental Health (with Particular Reference to the Blackwood case at Broadmoor and the Patient-complaints of Ashworth Hospital) in D Webb and R Harris (eds), *Mentally Disordered Offenders: Managing People Nobody Owns* (London, Routledge, 1999) 34–35.

The Ritchie Report, on the other hand, was published following the killing of Jonathan Zito by Christopher Clunis in 1992. Christopher had a long history of contact with mental health services. He had been diagnosed with schizophrenia and had been receiving care in the community at the time of the killing. He was known for living a nomadic lifestyle. He regularly failed to take medication for his condition right up to his fatal attack on Jonathan. The inquiry report into Christopher's care and treatment was published in 1994. It described the fragmented provision of mental health services in East London at the time of the killing. The report, furthermore, acquired subsequent political significance.[29] The wife of the deceased was very prominent in proceedings. She gave dignified evidence to the panel and was praised for her participation. She later went on to found the Zito Trust, an organisation instrumental in bringing about reform of mental health legislation.

The Falling Shadow was published following the killing of Georgina Robinson by Andrew Robinson. Georgina was employed as an occupational therapist at a psychiatric unit located in Torbay General Hospital. She was fatally stabbed by Andrew while on duty in September 1993. Andrew had been detained at the unit under section 3 of the Mental Health Act 1983. Prior to the killing, he was diagnosed with paranoid schizophrenia several years earlier, experienced periods of time in hospital and had convictions for firearm possession and assault. *The Falling Shadow* catalogued a series of failures. In particular, notable breakdowns in communication were indirectly linked to the homicide incident. The detail and analysis of the inquiry's final report is impressive but it has been criticised as unhelpful.[30] Maden criticises the report for 'creating a sense of inexorable progress towards tragedy, exemplified by the metaphor of the falling shadow, which runs throughout the book'.[31] It could be argued that the inquiry's report inappropriately made it appear that the events leading up to the killing occurred in a linear sequence. Bynoe praises the report's lucidity but he too draws on the report's inclusion of literary quotations at the beginning of each chapter as 'awkwardly ornamental'.[32] Its literary style is questionable. Bynoe also criticises the inquiry's view that it was – in its words – 'unnecessary either to apportion blame to any individual or to spell out what needs to be done in the form of specific recommendations'. Bynoe analyses the inquiry's position by drawing on the inquiry's commitment to deliver suitable recommendations. He claims that the panel's reluctance to apportion blame or spell out what needed to be done was inconsistent with these terms.[33] The tone set by *The Falling Shadow* was, in

[29] HL Deb, 20 June 1995, vol 262, col 159: 'We have in particular taken very full account of the recommendations of the inquiry into the treatment and care of Christopher Clunis'.

[30] See T Maden, 'The Falling Shadow' (1995) 167(6) *The British Journal of Psychiatry* 827–28; I Bynoe, 'The Falling Shadow: A Lawyer's View (1995) 6(3) *The Journal of Forensic Psychiatry* 588, 589–90.

[31] See Maden, 'The Falling Shadow' (n 30) 827.

[32] Bynoe, 'The Falling Shadow' (n 30) 590.

[33] ibid.

general, received uncomfortably.[34] It does, however, evidence an approach (ie, a reluctance to apportion blame) which in subsequent decades has achieved wider currency.

Influential developments occurred in 1996 when the Zito Trust commissioned the publication of *Learning the Lessons*.[35] *Learning the Lessons* is a compilation of over 700 inquiry recommendations advanced between 1969 and 1994. Its author, Sheppard, sought to provide an accessible and concise summary of the lessons learned. A common criticism of inquiries is that it is difficult to learn lessons from them, partly because a central repository containing all published reports is lacking. Some reports are, in fact, difficult to obtain. Sheppard's work attempts to address these problems tenaciously but it has been criticised for failing to place its compilation into sufficient context.[36] However, calls for better systems of reporting and investigating failures continue to be made.[37]

A one-day seminar was held in 1996 and attended by a range of academics, professionals and lawyers who exchanged views about what inquiries after homicide do, the benefits they bring and whether they are able to facilitate the learning of lessons. The outcome of the exchange was an edited collection that draws on a range of perspectives about inquiries after homicide.[38] *Inquiries After Homicide* emphasised a number of important themes: an expectation for those staging an inquiry to be publicly accountable; that proceedings are held in public, unless there are clear and demonstrable reasons for not doing so; that access to reports is granted and learning facilitated; that resource and management issues are often neglected during inquiry proceedings; the role of the individual and systems; and the argument that inquiries after homicide are damaging to the psychiatric profession.

Subsequent tranches of research into inquiries explore a further range of themes and issues: the difficulty of conducting retrospective investigation;[39] the problems associated with engagement in counterfactual reasoning;[40] the

[34] ibid. See also D Chiswick, 'The Falling Shadow: A Psychiatrist's View' (1995) 6(3) *The Journal of Forensic Psychiatry* 594; A Maden, *Treating Violence: A Guide to Risk Management in Mental Health* (Oxford, Oxford University Press, 2008) 52.

[35] D Sheppard, *Learning the Lessons: Mental Health Inquiry Reports Published in England and Wales Between 1969–1994 and Their Recommendations for Improving Practice* (London, Zito Trust, 1996).

[36] E Petch and C Bradley, 'Learning the Lessons from Homicide Tragedies: Adding Insult to Injury?' (1997) 8(1) *The Journal of Forensic Psychiatry* 161, 163.

[37] K Walshe and SM Shortell, 'When Things Go Wrong: How Health Care Organizations Deal with Major Failures' (2004) 23(3) *Health Affairs* 103, 108.

[38] See Peay, *Inquiries After Homicide* (n 4).

[39] D Reiss, 'Counterfactuals and Inquiries After Homicide' (2001) 12(1) *The Journal of Forensic Psychiatry* 177. See also Szmukler, 'Homicide Inquiries' (n 13) 8; A Grounds, 'Commentary on "Inquiries: Who Needs Them?"' (1997) 21 *Psychiatric Bulletin* 134, 134; J Peay, 'Thinking Horses, Not Zebras' in Webb and Harris *Mentally Disordered Offenders* (n 28) 142.

[40] Reiss, 'Counterfactuals' (n 39) 177. Reiss argues that inquiries 'mutate' past actions that could have easily been done differently, prompting a dysfunctional causal analysis to occur that does not reflect reality; a cause may be imputed to a homicide on the basis that an event simply could have been done differently, as opposed to it being judged as fundamentally causative.

accessibility of findings;[41] the issue of evidential awareness;[42] diminishing professional trust and confidence;[43] the potential for inquiries to reinforce clinical blaming cultures;[44] the shift in emphasis away from blaming;[45] the problems of defensive medical practices;[46] the possibility of their replacement;[47] and the complexities posed by selective media reporting.[48] Furthermore, recent research has highlighted that a significant number of families of mental health patients have not received adequate support from health services.[49]

The Age of the Inquiry appeared in 2004.[50] It examines inquiries across a range of health and social services. The book devotes attention to mental health homicide inquiries in a number of contributions. Prins, for instance, examines their various benefits and argues that despite their limitations and the need for their improvement these inquiries offer necessary criticism and provide public catharsis.[51] McCulloch and Parker, on the other hand, summarise the strengths and weaknesses of inquiries and conclude that they have rarely influenced policy relating to assertive outreach and compliance; they are just one aspect of a complex political landscape.[52] Recent studies indicate that inquiries achieve very little; rather than focusing on the outcome of recommendations, inquiries overemphasise the production of recommendations.[53]

The aforementioned contributions contrast with arguments that describe independent inquiries after homicide as a crucial aspect of generating change. Health care scandal and crisis are acknowledged to have an important role in shaping

[41] H Prins, 'Half a Century of Madness and Badness: Some Diverse Recollections (2008) 19(4) *The Journal of Forensic Psychiatry and Psychology* 431, 436.

[42] Scott, 'Procedures at Inquiries' (n 15) 602. Scott argues that 'witnesses of whose existence and of whose evidence the Inquiry has no knowledge cannot be asked to give evidence'.

[43] Szmukler, 'Homicide Inquiries' (n 13) 8.

[44] J Peay, 'Clinicians and Inquiries: Demons, Drones and Demigods? (1997) 9 *International Review of Psychiatry* 171, 171; P Munro, 'Privacy v. Publication: Homicide Inquiries in the Balance' (2007) 15(1) *Medical Law Review* 109, 113; J Warner, 'Inquiry Reports as Active Texts and Their Function in Relation to Professional Practice in Mental Health' (2006) 8(3) *Health, Risk & Society* 223, 231. See also Walshe and Higgins, 'Inquiries in the NHS' (n 6) 897. See generally Peay, 'Introduction' (n 4) 26; Szmukler, 'Homicide Inquiries' (n 13) 8.

[45] D Tidmarsh, 'Psychiatric Risk, Safety Cultures and Homicide Inquiries' (1997) 8(1) *The Journal of Forensic Psychiatry* 138.

[46] Warner, 'Inquiry Reports'. (n 44) 234.

[47] N Eastman, 'Inquiries into Homicides by Psychiatric Patients: Systematic Audit Should Replace Mandatory Inquiries' (1996) 313(7064) *British Medical Journal* 1069.

[48] A Hallam, 'Media Influences on Mental Health Policy: Long-term Effects of the Clunis and Silcock Cases' (2002) 14(1) *International Review of Psychiatry* 26, 31.

[49] AL Pitman et al, 'Support for Relatives Bereaved by Psychiatric Patient Suicide: National Confidential Inquiry into Suicide and Homicide Findings' (2016) 68(4) *Psychiatric Services* 33, 34.

[50] Stanley and Manthorpe, *The Age of the Inquiry* (n 27).

[51] Prins, 'Mental Health Inquiries' in Stanley and Manthorpe, *The Age of the Inquiry* (n 27) 29.

[52] A McCulloch and C Parker, 'Mental Health Inquiries, Assertive Outreach and Compliance: Is There a Relationship?' in Stanley and Manthorpe, *The Age of the Inquiry* (n 27) 136, 145, 147.

[53] M Williams and P Kevern, 'The Role and Impact of Recommendations from NHS Inquiries: A Critical Discourse Analysis' (2016) 2(2) *Journal of New Writing in Health and Social Care* 1, 9. See also PJ Taylor, 'Decline of the English Inquiry?' (2007) 17(2) *Criminal Behaviour and Mental Health* 69.

health care policy and they are prone to political response.[54] Inquiries, in particular, have been used to support efforts to shift the burden of responsibility from systems to individuals in the context of negligence cases.[55] And in line with his previous important work, Sheppard reviews a range of inquiries conducted into mental health services following accidental deaths and homicide.[56] In more recent work, Stanley argues that inquiry reports are social documents that reveal how services interact with users. She draws on service interactions with women in particular and contends that reports reveal stereotyping within services.[57]

The author of the present work adds to the field of enquiry by placing independent investigations after patient homicide under rigorous theoretical scrutiny. The work provides a novel account of how these processes understand and manage complexity, within health services and without. It also examines the relationship between homicide, health care and society. It examines how these dreadful incidents are communicated about in society. It depicts a rich tapestry of communications that are commonly produced about patient homicides and health services. It captures how these processes involve communications about a range of 'events', including the economic costs of investigations, the political implications of homicides committed close to Parliament and the protests of the media and families.

B. Accountability and Truth Seeking

It is prescient to explain in more detail what inquiries after patient homicide are commonly expected to do and what ambitions are often attached to them. The establishment of truth through accountability is particularly notable. Inquiries induce the expectation that someone will produce an account to an authority, the authority being appointed to elicit the account for the purposes of getting to a truthful version of the past. Furthermore, versions of the past are then used as a basis for taking action in the present. Lawyers are tasked to elicit accounts and get to the truth in the law courts, after which a binding legal judgment will be delivered by the judge. Inquiries, however, involve clinically trained investigators eliciting accounts from health professionals and other persons, after which a report is compiled and a series of non-binding recommendations advanced.

Accountability is a term of traditional and historic pedigree. It is only recently that the concept has been revisited because of the seismic changes in the way society's institutions are organised. Chapter 5, in similar fashion, revisits the

[54] JS Hutchison, 'Scandals in Health-care: Their Impact on Health Policy and Nursing' (2016) 23(1) *Nursing Inquiry* 32, 39.

[55] Peay, 'Thinking Horses, Not Zebras' (n 39) 142.

[56] D Sheppard, 'Mental Health Inquiries 1985–2003' in Stanley and Manthorpe, *The Age of the Inquiry* (n 27) 165–212.

[57] N Stanley, 'Women and Mental Health Inquiries' in Stanley and Manthorpe, *The Age of the Inquiry* (n 27) 151–164.

concept of accountability. It develops the argument that accountability should be understood as an observation structured by distinct systems of communication. In contrast to traditional concepts of accountability, Chapter 5 avoids attributing the creation of accountability relationships to human agency. First and foremost, Chapter 5 contends that accountability relationships are constructed within systems of meaning that human beings do not have direct influence over. It is sufficient, however, at the moment, to proceed by outlining how the accountability concept has developed and its relevance to health care services. The scene will henceforth be set for subsequent chapters, particularly Chapter 5. An outline of the accountability concept, as traditionally understood, will provide an essential contrast between traditional understandings of the concept and the author's novel conceptualisation of it.

Accountability may mean different things in different contexts. At its core, accountability relates to answerability. Bovens defines it as follows: 'a relationship between an actor and a forum, in which the actor has an obligation to explain and justify his or her conduct, the forum can pose questions and pass judgement, and the actor may face consequences'.[58] Accountability has been used to denote a dry image of bookkeeping and financial administration but it is now shorthand for fair, equitable and transparent governance over asymmetric authority relationships.[59] Its 'core' is rather straightforward but accountability as a concept has been developed considerably. It has been defined as a 'liability to reveal, to explain, and to justify what one does; how one discharges responsibilities, financial or otherwise, whose several origins may be political, constitutional, hierarchical or contractual'.[60] Generally, accountability is about answerability.[61] Public accountability is a type of accountability that refers to those mechanisms that make governmental institutions responsive to citizens.[62] Accountability, however, is an elusive term. It resembles a collection of loosely defined concepts and vague images of good governance.[63] Accountability is interchanged with responsibility, responsiveness and control.[64] The concept, generally, is not straightforward.[65]

[58] M Bovens, 'Analysing and Assessing Accountability: A Conceptual Framework' (2007) 13(4) *European Law Journal* 447, 450. Core accountability is traditionally associated with the relationship between citizens and the holders of public office. See also Mulgan, '"Accountability": An Ever-expanding Concept?' (2000) 78(3) *Public Administration* 555, 555.

[59] R Mulgan, 'The Processes of Accountability' (1997) 56(1) *Australian Journal of Public Administration* 25, 27; Bovens, 'Analysing and Assessing Accountability' (n 58) 449.

[60] EL Normanton, 'Public Accountability and Audit: A Reconnaissance' in B Smith and DC Hague (eds), *The Dilemma of Accountability in Modern Government: Independence Versus Control* (London, Macmillan, 1971) 311.

[61] See BS Romzek and MJ Dubnik, 'Accountability in the Public Sector: Lessons from the Challenger Tragedy' (1987) 47 *Public Administration Review* 227, 228.

[62] Normanton, 'Public Accountability and Audit' (n 60) 311.

[63] Bovens, 'Analysing and Assessing Accountability' (n 58) 449; Mulgan, 'The Processes of Accountability' (n 59) 26.

[64] Mulgan, 'The Processes of Accountability' (n 59) 26; Bovens, 'Analysing and Assessing Accountability' (n 58) 449.

[65] Mulgan, '"Accountability"' (n 58) 555. Mulgan comments that the 'concept of "accountability" has lost some of its former straightforwardness and has come to require constant clarification and increasingly complex categorization'.

It is compared to a chameleon.[66] It is described as multi-directional; accountability may be upwards,[67] downwards,[68] horizontal[69] and hierarchical.[70] The meaning and significance of accountability has constantly changed over time. It is often determined by the context in which it is practised too.[71] The delegation of duties and the growth of discretionary power in modern societies have challenged our core definitions of it.[72] More complex structures have been created that 'devolve more authority downwards, reduce the number of layers (and hence the capacity for close supervision), and which recognize and encourage a more diverse range of relationships with actors outside the traditional hierarchy'.[73] Decision making in society now occurs in a regulatory space[74] of activity involving two-way, three-way and four-way relationships.[75] Diversity in accountability relationships is the rule rather than the exception.[76] Furthermore, accounting occurs along networked nodes of governance in which 'knowledge, capacity and resources are mobilized to manage a course of events' and establish information flows and communication.[77] Inquiries after homicide may be likened to a governance node because they engage resources (eg, expenditure), technologies

[66] A Sinclair, 'The Chameleon of Accountability: Forms and Discourses' (1995) 20(2/3) *Accounting, Organizations and Society* 219, 219. Sinclair writes that accountability 'exists in many forms and is sustained and given extra dimensions of meaning by its context'.

[67] C Scott, 'Accountability in the Regulatory State' (2000) 27(1) *Journal of Law and Society* 38, 42. 'Upwards' accountability is rendered to a higher authority (such as a junior minister accounting to a cabinet minister).

[68] ibid. 'Downwards' accountability involves rendering an account to lower-level institutions and groups (such as consumers).

[69] ibid. 'Horizontal' accountability involves rendering an account to a parallel institution, for instance between contracting agencies.

[70] Bovens, 'Analysing and Assessing Accountability' (n 58) 458. Bovens describes hierarchical accountability as a 'pyramidal image of organisations'. He writes that accountability starts 'at the top, with the highest official', with the 'rank and file' hiding 'behind the broad shoulders' of whoever is in charge. See also J Roberts, 'The Possibilities of Accountability' (1991) 16(4) *Accounting, Organizations and Society* 355, 356.

[71] Sinclair, 'The Chameleon of Accountability' (n 66) 219.

[72] Scott, 'Accountability' (n 67) 38.

[73] B Stone, 'Administrative Accountability in the "Westminster" Democracies: Towards a New Conceptual Framework' (1995) 8(4) *Governance* 505, 511.

[74] L Hancher and M Moran, 'Organising Regulatory Space' in L Hancher and M Moran (eds), *Capitalism, Culture and Regulation* (Oxford, Clarendon Press, 1989) 277. Hancher and Moran use the notion of a 'regulatory space' as an analytical device. They contend that the term denotes a space which is occupied unevenly by actors in a regulatory process that is typified by competition, contestation, struggle and power over resources.

[75] J Black, 'Decentering Regulation: Understanding the Role of Regulation and Self-Regulation in a "Post-Regulatory World"' (2002) 54 *Current Legal Problems* 103, 109; Hancher and Moran, 'Organising Regulatory Space' (n 74) 276. Hancher and Moran write that 'organizational alliances are constantly forming and reforming without any reference to a conventional public-private divide, parties bargain, co-operate, threaten, or act according to semi-articulated customary assumptions'.

[76] Stone, 'Administrative Accountability' (n 73) 511. For example, Parliamentary control (supervision/command), managerialism (fiduciary/contract), judicial review or quasi-judicial review (individual rights/procedural obligations), constituency relations (representation/responsiveness) and the market (competition/sovereignty) are in abundance.

[77] See generally S Burris et al, 'Nodal Governance' (2005) 30 *Australian Journal of Legal Philosophy* 30, 36, 37.

(eg, health services experts), mentalities (eg, the ways of thinking about homicide, for instance through causal analysis and references to standards of care) and institutions (eg, the NHS Trust). Moreover, with the range of values being accounted for in governance extending,[78] social norms and aspirations play an increasingly important role in how accountability is understood.[79] Bodies and organisations, each with their own distinct objectives, values and agendas, have been specifically created to elicit accounts from others.[80]

Accountability is, therefore, an expansive and changeable concept.[81] The classic Leviathan state is no longer the sole orchestrator of accountability.[82] Accountability is increasingly framed as a relationship that exists outside of quintessential state officialdom.[83] It clarifies 'focus into the lived reality of everyday life'.[84] It disciplines the self, socialising individuals into a 'fictitious atom of an "ideological" representation of society'.[85] Inquiries, hospitals, courts, tribunals all involve combinations of resource, technology, norms and values that produce informational outcomes and new conceptual explanations.

Accountability in a health care service context is especially elusive. It has been described as those 'procedures and processes by which one party justifies and takes responsibility for its activities'.[86] Emanuel and Emanuel identify three essential components to it: the 'loci of accountability' (ie, the relevant parties that can be held accountable or hold others accountable); the 'domains of accountability' (ie, the domains where parties can be held accountable for professional competence, legal and ethical conduct, financial performance, adequacy of access, public health promotion and community benefit); and the 'procedures of accountability' that evaluate compliance and disseminate the evaluation and responses by the accountable parties.[87] Others point out that these types of accountability relationships have emerged because of the growing involvement of health ministries, insurance agencies, private health care providers, legislatures, regulatory agencies and service facility boards in health service organisation and management.[88] These parties are connected to each other in networks of control, oversight,

[78] ibid, 33.

[79] Sinclair, 'The Chameleon of Accountability' (n 66) 221.

[80] Scott, 'Accountability' (n 67) 48. See also Mulgan, '"Accountability"' (n 58) 558. Mulgan discusses how accountability has been widened to include the area of administrative discretion.

[81] Mulgan, '"Accountability"' (n 58) 556.

[82] See N Rose, *Governing the Soul* (London, Free Association Books, 1989/1999) 10. Rose posits that the state might formally delegate power and responsibility and expand accountability relationships between individuals and create the space for a host of informal, unobserved interactions to take place.

[83] Roberts, 'The Possibilities of Accountability' (n 70) 363.

[84] ibid, 357.

[85] M Foucault, *Discipline and Punish* (London, Penguin, 1977/1991) 194.

[86] EJ Emanuel and LL Emanuel, 'What is Accountability in Health Care?' (1996) 124(2) *Annals of Internal Medicine* 229, 229.

[87] ibid.

[88] DW Brinkerhoff, 'Accountability and Health Systems: Toward Conceptual Clarity and Policy Relevance' (2004) 19(6) *Health Policy and Planning* 371, 371.

cooperation and reporting.[89] Accountability relationships in health care services are established for different reasons also, be they financial (eg, health care budgeting), performance (eg, service quality) or political (eg, transparency).[90]

The patient homicide governance space resonates with all of these descriptions of accountability. Independent investigations are part of a network. They are commissioned by NHS England and they enter into relationships with clinicians to investigate cases. They engage in relationships with clinicians and other health care personnel in order to question them, elicit information from them, conduct the investigation and manage the governance space. Witnesses may face consequences in these circumstances but these consequences are somewhat different from those seen in court cases. Inquiries are inquisitorial and they do not have formal powers to punish or impose sanctions for errors discovered. They may, however, instigate a series of negative, albeit unintended, consequences for those called upon to answer its questions (eg, public humiliation).[91] They also attempt to understand other accountability relationships – formed in the past – between different professionals at the time care was provided to the perpetrator. They must make sense of their accountability relationship with agencies and organisations (eg, the police) in the present who, for one reason or another, are engaged in discussions about how homicide investigations should be conducted. Certain parties (eg, families, clinicians, health care providers, commissioners) utilise their respective knowledge and experience when making judgements about the outcome of the investigation. It is a complex affair; 'Health care is currently too complicated, with too many parties consisting of diverse relationships, to be encompassed in only one model [of accountability]'.[92]

It is unsurprising that, in the light of health service complexity, inquiries produce more questions than they do answers.[93] They attract objection and are subjected to extensive criticism.[94] Subsequent chapters explain that these criticisms may be grounded in politics (ie, NHS managers exerting power and influence over an investigation to preserve their jobs and reputations), morality (eg, witnesses volunteering to account for their actions because it is the right thing to do) or clinical knowledge (ie, justifying a clinical judgement made in the past). The outcome of a particular decision made about a homicidal patient might well be disputed at an inquiry by affected parties (eg, relatives of the victim). These past decisions might be selected for their information value by the mass media and later used to

[89] ibid.

[90] ibid, 373–75.

[91] P Hobbs, 'Inquiries – High Costs, Unacceptable Side Effects and Low Effectiveness: Time for Revision' (2001) 9(2) *Australasian Psychiatry* 156, 159. See also Szmukler, 'Homicide Inquiries' (n 13) 9 who reports that the professionals who provide mental health services are unnecessarily humiliated by inquiries. Members of staff have been known to hand in resignations, suffer drops in confidence and deteriorating morale. Inquiries have, consequently, proved to be very unpopular among professionals, with their repetitive findings militating against the aim of learning lessons (see also Maden, *Treating Violence* (n 34) 39, 40).

[92] Emanuel and Emanuel, 'What is Accountability' (n 86) 237.

[93] See Szmukler, 'Homicide Inquiries' (n 13) 9.

[94] ibid.

elicit accounts from health care organisations. Yet, despite these different readings of accountability in inquiries, the latter have been considered to embody a supreme ideal of accountability and truth seeking.[95] Things were much simpler in the past. Inquiries used to focus more on human error, for the most part as a cause and not a symptom of the unwanted event.[96] They were closely associated with discourses of blame. They all shared a focus on assigning blame and taking measures to control individuals judged to be dangerous.[97] The 2005 Guidance amendments, however, signalled a shift in how mental health homicides are communicated about. Recent inquiries into health care failings in hospitals reflect a shift away from blame and more towards systems.[98] Scientifically accredited analytical techniques (eg, root cause analysis) began to be utilised and human error began to be understood in an organisational context.[99] The perceived relationship human beings have with the world around them after disaster occurs has changed.

Bovens' 'problem of many hands' demonstrates well the complexity constituted by these issues.[100] Modern governance struggles to untie 'who has contributed in what way to the conduct of [an] agency or to the implementation of a policy and who, and to what degree, can be brought to account for it'.[101] Changing landscapes of health law and policy have been typified by a burgeoning of new disciplines, professions, decision makers and social relations. These changes have turned the tide of accountability from individuals to systems and processes.[102] A conceptual reappraisal of what it means to hold individuals to account after adverse health care events has therefore become a natural focus for academics and policy makers. Observers have come round to the view that 'Treatment decisions do not take place independently of the system'.[103] The individual's influence in complex public services is debatable. Decision makers influence each other.[104] There is connectivity

[95] See Blom-Cooper, 'Public Inquiries' (n 28) 206 cited in Peay, *Inquiries after Homicide* (n 4) 2; E Munro, 'Mental Health Tragedies: Investigating Beyond Human Error' (2004) 15(3) *Journal of Forensic Psychiatry & Psychology* 475, 477.

[96] Munro, 'Mental Health Tragedies' (n 95) 476.

[97] ibid, 477–78.

[98] See Francis, *Michael Stone* (n 25) 36. The high-profile inquiry into Stafford Hospital over failings in care that resulted in a number of patient deaths noted that determining individual responsibility did not come within its capability. It stated that individuals and organisations may be called to provide evidence accompanied by legal representation and may have the opportunity to respond in accordance with the Inquiry Rules 2006 and procedure to potential criticisms, but they could not defend themselves as they could in adversarial proceedings (eg, by cross-examination of witnesses). Furthermore, the inquiry stated that individuals and organisations have only a limited right to make representations.

[99] E Munro and A Hubbard, 'A Systems Approach to Evaluating Organisational Change in Children's Social Care' (2011) 41 *British Journal of Social Work* 726, 727.

[100] Bovens, 'Analysing and Assessing Accountability' (n 58) 457.

[101] ibid.

[102] See N Eastman and J Peay, 'Law without Enforcement: Theory and Practice' in N Eastman and J Peay (eds), *Law without Enforcement: Integrating Mental Health and Justice* (Oxford, Hart Publishing, 1999) 9 and 21. 'Indeed, the manifest forms and ways in which the domination and subjugation are exercised within social relations probably best capture the realities of day-to-day mental health practice'.

[103] ibid.

[104] J Peay, *Decisions and Dilemmas: Working with Mental Health Law* (Oxford, Hart Publishing, 2003) 264–65.

between them. As one independent inquiry after homicide reported, investigating is complex because of 'the number of agencies that had contact with [the patient] at any one time'.[105]

The author acknowledges that accountability is an important concept for understanding health care services. It is a theme of the book, however, that the accountability concept, traditionally conceived and more recently developed, provides only a partial understanding of health care services, particularly in the aftermath of adverse incidents. Chapter 5 draws on systems theory to posit the novel argument that accountability is a communicative construction.

III. The Inquiry Industry

The previous chapter referred to inquiries today as more commercialised, managerial and technocratic compared to those set up in the 1990s and before. Peay observed in 1999 that an inquiry 'industry' was created following the implementation of the Guidance.[106] An inquiry became mandatory after every killing committed by a patient who had contact with mental health services.[107] A steady stream of inquiries after 1994 was guaranteed; an expectation was created that investigators would become busier and more industrious than before. Someone had to conduct inquiries now that a mandatory requirement was imposed for them to be carried out.

An investigator interviewed for the present book was asked whether independent inquiries have become similar to an industry. His reply suggests a slick 'cut-and-paste' way of doing things and a desire to obtain lots of work:

> [T]hey [investigations] have become quite sanitized, a lot of cut and paste … The problem is … more commercial organisations … will be presumably wanting a lot of work. **Investigator 6**

An 'industry' typically refers to economic activity. Inquiries set up during the 1990s and before were not in any way affiliated to economic processes beyond those used to resource them from public funds. They were led by a senior lawyer appointed by the relevant health authority and they did not have an overt commercial imperative. Profit seeking was completely off the agenda, with investigators conducting investigations around their main source of employment:

> [P]eople [were] doing it in addition to their normal job. And there were quite a few people doing it as a bridge between retirement from the NHS and whether they were going to do more of this or more self-employed work. **Investigator 4**

[105] See Ward and Brougham, *Mr G* (n 21) 8.
[106] Peay, 'Thinking Horses' (n 39) 142.
[107] ibid.

The independent inquiry, however, has become more of an industry. Most investigators today are dedicated to the full-time occupation of investigating.

Reinforcing these themes are the commercial imperatives that now drive all investigations. Those managing investigations today harbour incentives to pursue more investigatory work. Over the past decade, inquiries have been increasingly managed and carried out by investigators employed by private companies. Company directors owe special duties to the company's shareholders. They must manage the organisation in the most profitable way. The 'business' of independent investigation provides a neat complement to broader regulatory trends. As explained in the previous chapter, the Health and Social Care Act 2012 introduced a stronger and more 'real' NHS market.[108] Competition and marketisation in the NHS have been gradually emboldened. Investigators have adapted to these reforms. They compete for contracts with other investigator companies to conduct investigations. These contracts are eventually awarded to a 'winner' by a central commissioning body (ie, NHS England). An investigator interviewed for the book described the competitive and cost-driven nature of the process:

> We're invited to tender. So, we get a brief. We're part of a network of people who get sent these tenders and we'll be invited to send it to tender, which means we're in a competitive process and there's a factor of cost that needs to be considered. I could, say, look at an incident and have ten of the top experts say 'no chance, that's hugely expensive'. So, you have to cut the cloth to what you think is competitive as well. **Investigator 3**

Another investigator pointed to money as the biggest driver of change. The ability of investigations to 'pay' has become more important:

> I think there are a lot of drivers changing the old school. The biggest one was money. The biggest driver was money, not learning. These reviews needed to be done faster. Some of them were taking a couple of years. They needed to be done cheaper … [h]aving to wade through an awful lot of data and an awful lot of time … and the trouble with local authority work and this is going to sound callous, is that it doesn't pay. **Investigator 2**

It may be argued that the inquiry industry Peay referred to in 1999 has developed into a more sophisticated and commercialised form. Contracts have become an important tool for organising the relationship between commissioners and investigators. Cost and competition are crucial elements in commissioning decisions to award contracts. They are also elements that are vital to the profitability of investigator companies; if the contracts are not awarded, then companies do not fare as well within the investigation market. Economic values and competition are more relevant to inquiries than in the past. All actors within the NHS regulatory space, especially commissioners and investigators, behave more like market players.

[108] See ACL Davies, 'This Time, It's for Real: the Health and Social Care Act 2012' (2013) 76(3) *Modern Law Review* 564.

There is a commercial imperative at play, which, according to some investigators, drives the need for more and more work.

Independent inquiries after homicide also exhibit a stronger managerial imperative. Investigator companies compartmentalise the inquiry process and sometimes assign a manager to delegate tasks to other investigators and exercise operational oversight until the process is completed. An investigator interviewed by the author described the process in detail:

> I'm the investigation manager. I'm involved in the bidding and doing the proposals that we get through. I keep the operational process together, so I keep track of everything, when things should be done, what everybody is doing, that sort of stuff. And I keep in touch with the people who are carrying out the investigations. Not in a supervisory way, but keeping in touch about any problems and so on. **Investigator 9**

The author also interviewed a consultant psychiatrist with considerable experience investigating patient homicides. He commented that inquiries are managerially led by those with clinical governance backgrounds:

> They're [inquiries] led by a manager-type person … they have people and workers who lead the investigations. They tend to have governance-type backgrounds. They tend to draft external experts for advice or consultancy or to do interviews. You don't tend to lead the investigations. It's more that you provide the medical input. Which is partly, I suspect, for reasons of cost. **Investigator 7**

Some investigation firms pride themselves on values that are highly regarded in market-driven environments. One of these values is flexibility:

> [I]n terms of mental health investigators we've got a core group of four. We've got a wider group of associates who we can pull in. That's the great strength, for an individual project we can pull someone in for a few days. And that someone, a nurse working in a clinic or way up to a … we pull people in, we call them and we ask them: 'do you want to be involved in this project?' Nine times out of ten they will say yes. If they can fit it in, they will. But in terms of core members, there are four. **Investigator 1**

Independent inquiries held in the 1990s and before were much simpler. They did not involve contract procurement issues and they were led by a panel of three throughout all stages of the investigation, from interviewing witnesses to compiling the final report.

Other market-based values that investigators subscribe to include networking, opening up opportunities for themselves and their firm and developing relationships with health care providers with a view to helping them manage services after adverse incidents have occurred:

> We train people in NHS and social care about the basic rudiments of conduct and investigations where the outcomes for patients or for clients is less than we hoped for and to help them with a proportionate approach to help them realise where case management met the acceptable standard; if there are any reflective opportunities for learning and if what I call 'howlers', 'monumental cock-ups' … I also support individual NHS Trusts with difficult adverse event reviews where the incident is too hot for them to handle

> on their own. My style and the company's style is that we don't tend to take those cases away from Trusts. We tend to co-work with them. **Investigator 2**

The investigator continued by describing the importance of exhibiting behaviours (eg, networking) that are conducive to market-based environments:

> I pick up professionals the way I choose my specialist advisors and this is where my training work and my investigatory work sit quite nicely together. If I'm doing a training programme … and I think there's a couple of clinicians who have got the right mind-set, I like their thinking, I think they've got the right attitude, I'll get their CVs [Curriculum Vitae] and put them in my persons of interest list. So, if a case comes along where I need an a, b or c and I go to my persons of interest list, I'll contact them and say 'this case has come in, I'm quite interested in it, do you fancy giving me a hand?'. Then we see how they're going to do that. So I will always try and make sure that the professionals I use are case appropriate. **Investigator 2**

The same investigator expressed the concern that inquiries continue to be carried out by those without sufficient skill. She suggested that training and accreditation processes similar to those developed by the Social Care Institute for Excellence (SCIE) for serious case reviews should be devised to give commissioners confidence of a better outcome:

> We have lots of people investigating in health who are untrained, but what the SCIE have done is set up an accredited training programme. You go through their training programme, you get accredited and they provide a professional support network, provide mentorship and local authorities will go to them and say 'who has been on your training in our area and who we can approach to do a review?' … We should have something similar in health really. **Investigator 2**

The investigator's comments show that she considers that there is more to investigating. For her, investigating involves opening up avenues to apply knowledge and skills in other areas of health services, such as training. Investigating appears to be just one industry among a possible range of industries which may be developed as part of the adverse event governance space more generally.

The use of clinical knowledge and skills for the purpose of conducting investigations is said to reduce scope for ambiguity, uncertainty or contradiction.[109] Investigations relate to technical aspects of health care (eg, prescribing medication) that only experts in prescribing (ie, psychiatrists) can authoritatively comment on. Some of the investigators interviewed by the author commented that they benefited from having co-panel members versed in scientific expertise sitting beside them, particularly expertise in psychology. Inquiries have, therefore, become more informed by technical (clinical) expertise over the years. Inquiries of previous decades demonstrated technical ability in other ways however. They were led by lawyers who brought a range of technical skills to the inquiry table.

[109] Warner, 'Inquiry Reports' (n 44) 231.

An increased emphasis has, however, emerged on technical disciplines such as medicine and science because investigations now have to make sense of *medical* services provided to the perpetrator and make sense of the different causal factors (ie, root and contributory causes) that arguably led up to the homicide incident. The issue of bridging the gap between an investigation and health services has become paramount:

> [I]n order to criticise a member of the medical profession or aspects of their care, you probably have to have another medical professional on the team. I think the credibility is otherwise not there. **Investigator 2**

The points discussed in the present section cohere into an original argument that frames independent inquiries after patient homicides as more commercialised, managerially focused and clinically technocratic when compared to previous years. The need to conduct inquiries, however, has remained constant yet paradoxical; despite the efforts made to learn lessons, reform services and improve practices, the need to conduct inquiries continually re-emerges when a homicide incident occurs. One of the book's unique purposes is to provide a greater understanding of the paradox.

IV. Conclusions

The purpose of the present chapter continues the task performed in Chapter 1: to set out a general context for the rest of the book and to identify central themes of enduring interest that are ripe for further original development. In particular, the present chapter shows that independent inquiries after patient homicide link up with vital areas of societal functioning (eg, law, economics, psychiatry). The present chapter also shows that inquiries after mental health homicide are considered by investigators and policy makers to be truth-seeking processes that occupy a privileged vantage point from which to assess health care services and make judgements about their adequacy. Investigators are regarded as skilled operators who confront the complexity of health care services, formulate an understanding of problems within them and recommend actions that purport to minimise or eliminate these problems.

These points share a theme: inquiries are complex processes of high ambition. Yet, despite their ambitions and the measures they take to address problems within services after a patient homicide has been committed, homicides still occur and inquiries are almost always conducted as a response. The purpose of the book is to explore the impulse to investigate more closely and to develop an accurate and original nuanced picture of why the impulse emerges.

The central thesis of the book is that independent inquiries are better understood not as truth-seeking procedures of accountability, but as moments of observation formed in different systems of communication (eg, the economy, medicine, law). The minds and bodies of investigators, and those associated with investigations (eg, families, health care commissioners, lawyers), step into these systems of communication to form a socially relevant observation about homicide and health care. These systems of communication make up society and they provide structures of life in which meanings about homicide and health care are produced. Crucially, these different observations are, it is argued, unable to speak directly to each other. The prevailing intellectual orthodoxy that regulation and governance spaces are able to produce aims and objectives capable of implementation and directed change is thus challenged by the present book.

The following chapter provides the conceptual framework underpinning the book's approach. Chapter 1 outlined Luhmann's theory of social systems but the next chapter explains it in more detail. Luhmann's work is important because it reminds its readers that events in society cannot be separated out and studied in isolation from the broader social environment around which those events occur. In similar fashion, independent investigations after patient homicide are more complicated than the depictions of accountability theorists and policy makers would lead us to believe. Studying these processes requires adopting a theory that is up to the task of situating them against society's complexity. Systems theory is ideal because it embraces the uncertainty, disagreement, objection, failure and unintended consequences that beleaguer governance processes. The following chapter sets out the main components of Luhmann's theory of social systems and discusses their relevance. From there, the conceptual components of systems theory are used to inform the tasks of subsequent chapters. These tasks include the application of Luhmann's theory to the patient homicide governance space and to demonstrate how the space may be more reliably understood.

3

Social Systems

I. Introduction

The present chapter constructs the theoretical lens for the rest of the book. It draws on Luhmann's general theory of social systems. Luhmann's theory was outlined in Chapter 1 but it is apposite now to engage it closely and to explain why its central concepts are relevant to the patient homicide governance space. The present chapter begins by drawing on a range of works published by Luhmann – from his fundamental introduction of his theory in 1984 to other works, published subsequently – that applied his theory in specific areas (eg, politics, law, risk). It outlines the general background to Luhmann's ideas, followed by an examination of the central concepts holding his theory together. Luhmann's relationship with academic convention is a peculiar one. The present chapter is an ideal opportunity to explain the relationship and understand the paradigm change that Luhmann introduces. Chapter 1 explained that readers new to Luhmann must jettison their conventional theoretical and ideological commitments in order to understand his theory. Luhmann's anti-humanism led him to devise a series of original concepts (eg, autopoiesis, structural coupling) that readers new to his work may find alien and eccentric. It is therefore sensible to focus on setting out these concepts for the purposes of clarity and focus going forward. From there, subsequent chapters draw on these concepts – alongside empirical interview evidence – to develop the book's argument.

II. Theoretical Background

Luhmann's general theory of social systems is a variation of systems theory developed in the social sciences in the early-to-mid twentieth century.[1] Systems theory generally may be regarded as an all-encompassing concept for different levels of analysis and different kinds of research efforts.[2] The question 'what is a system?'

[1] See J Mingers, *Self-Producing Systems: Implications and Applications of Autopoiesis* (London, Plenum, 1994) 2.
[2] ibid 16.

has attracted different answers; in general, systems are biological, they are groups of people, they are countries and they are societies. Systems theory constitutes a general theoretical description of a model used to analyse 'systems' (eg, a brain, a business organisation), identify their boundaries and examine their relationship with their environment (eg, other systems). Systems theory, however, is an elusive term:

> To be precise, there is no such general systems theory. It is indeed the case that in sociological scholarship there have been, time and again, references to systems theory, as if this concerned something that exists in the singular. But, as soon as one examines the matter more closely and looks beyond sociological scholarship, it becomes difficult to find an object – that is, a theory – that would correspond to this way of speaking.[3]

Luhmann's systems theory is a response to the perceived failure of intellectual endeavours made since the Enlightenment.[4] These endeavours attribute significance to human beings, their ability to shape society and guide it towards a predefined goal (eg, equality for all, a cleaner planet). These endeavours are attractive, highly ambitious and rarely, if ever, successful. These failures have been amplified, in part, by the emergence of a host of concepts, theories and values that have been introduced over the past 300 years, which challenged the existing order of things. Kant's philosophical approach revolutionised Western philosophy in the eighteenth century. The postmodernist theories of Sartre, Derrida and Foucault further challenged accepted philosophical understandings in the twentieth century. Yet, the intellectual gestures made since the Enlightenment have been increasingly remembered with admonition.[5]

Niklas Luhmann, in particular, illustrates the breakdown of 'Old European' certainties by drawing on the invention of language and printing. He argues that these inventions overcame early obstacles (eg, demands on memory, the distance between recipients) to face-to-face communication.[6] Luhmann points out, however, that these inventions presented new challenges (eg, greater scope for disagreement).[7] They 'revealed how much knowledge already existed simultaneously, so that new selection and classification requirements arose'.[8]

[3] N Luhmann, *Introduction to Systems Theory* (Cambridge, Polity Press, 2013) 25.

[4] See N Luhmann, *Social Systems* (Stanford, Stanford University Press, 1984/1995) 6.

[5] ibid.

[6] Luhmann, *Social Systems* (n 4) 302; N Luhmann, *Risk: A Sociological Theory* (New Brunswick, Aldine Transaction, 1993/2008) 38; N Luhmann, *Essays on Self Reference* (New York, Columbia University Press, 1990) 87–88. Luhmann subscribes to the prevalent view that before the invention of language, signs were used to communicate information. The performance of a sign in primitive times, under Luhmann's analysis, could only be successful within close physical proximity. The subsequent evolution of language, coupled with voice projection and volume, could afford greater distance between ego and alter and improve the chances of successful communication with a wider audience.

[7] Luhmann, *Social Systems* (n 4) 150, 162.

[8] Luhmann, *Risk* (n 6) 38.

The potential for different points of view, misinterpretation and dispute to emerge about the world increased:

> [T]he more we know, the better we know what we do not know, and the more elaborate our risk awareness becomes. The more rationality we calculate and the more complex the calculations become, the more aspects come into view involving uncertainty about the future and thus risk.[9]

Luhmann devises a version of systems theory that identifies the limitations of conventional understandings about the individual and society.[10] It avoids the well-trodden path of classical sociology that persons, groups of people, organisations or the state are receptive to direct input from external sources for the purposes of reaching predefined goals (eg, using psychoanalysis to change someone's behaviour or using politics to eliminate poverty). Luhmann rejects the viability of designating individuals and the reductionist concepts (eg, 'the state') they use to realise their utopian ambitions as units of analysis for understanding society and solving its problems.

Luhmann advocates a completely new starting point from which to study society. Rather than beginning with a concept of the world (eg, economic materialism in Marxism), he advocates that society should be framed around the concept of difference:

> [A] system *is* difference – the difference between system and environment ... Theory, insofar as it is intended to be systems theory, begins with a difference, the difference between system and environment; if the theory is intended to be something else, it must be based on a different difference. Therefore, such a theory does not begin with a unity, a cosmology, a concept of the world or of being, or anything comparable. Instead, it begins with a difference.[11]

Everything that means something must, by definition, emerge as a reality that is different from something else. A system is difference, whether biologically or socially. The concept of system will be elaborated on further later in the present chapter. For now, it is sufficient to flag up the point that Luhmann's definition of system as difference is a vital point of departure in the world of systems theory and social theory more generally.

A. Overcoming Conventional Habits

For Luhmann, conventional approaches to the study of society obscure three separate systems of reality: organic life, thought and communication. The Western

[9] ibid 20.

[10] Luhmann, *Social Systems* (n 4) 1. At p xi, Knodt's foreword to Luhmann's 1984 publication describes his theory as a 'counter-genealogy that includes, among others, a cybernetician (Heinz von Foerster), two evolutionary biologists (Humberto R Maturana and Francisco Varela), an obscure mathematician (George Spencer Brown), not to speak of the Devil Himself'.

[11] ibid 44.

intellectual domain is dominated by references to 'human beings', 'individuals' and concepts which accord primacy to human agency. These references are, however, notable for their failure to acknowledge the three separate systems that make up the human being. For Luhmann, a failure to acknowledge these systems is a problem because doing so oversimplifies our understanding of the individual and society.

Luhmann's tripartite distinction between life, thought and communication is a crucial element in his work. It can be broken down in the following way. Livings beings are *biological* systems (eg, cells, bacteria, respiratory systems, immune systems) but some living beings have minds that think and feel. Thinking, pain and emotion occurs in *psychic* systems, a wholly separate process from biological operations such as cell reproduction. Life forms, such as bacteria, do not think and feel but they do – oddly enough – share something in common with humans in addition to having a biological system: they mean something.

Bacteria may have scientific meaning (eg, as laboratory 'evidence' in a petri dish) and so may humans (eg, as 'research subjects' in a clinical trial). Both bacteria and humans may have meaning in medicine too; bacteria may indicate sickness and humans regarded as 'doctors' and 'patients'. Luhmann argues that these meanings (and many others) are produced by overarching structures of life (eg, science, medicine) that are wholly separate from biological and psychic systems. These are *social systems of communication*.

Luhmann defines communication as the utterance (eg, a gesture, a sign, a written word) of information that is understood.[12] The concept of communication has been paramount in Luhmann's work since 1984 and it provides what he regards as the most suitable unit of analysis for describing how society functions. Moeller provides an apt illustration[13] and it is reproduced here with minor adaptations. A student's assignment is awarded a numerical grade. The grade is entered on a spreadsheet (ie, information) and submitted to the examinations office (ie, an utterance) for processing (eg, understanding). Understanding here is socially relevant to the education system in the form of a final grade. If the grade is the highest in the class, it may also have relevance to the economy in the form of a monetary prize. These meanings are not directly produced by the body parts (ie, biological systems) or thoughts (ie, psychic systems) of those involved in uttering the information and processing it. Rather, the direct 'source' for these meanings is communication. Biological and psychic systems must, of course, operate in the background for these communications to be made. It is imprecise however to maintain that these meanings are directly produced by 'the individuals' involved because to do so would attribute the production of socially significant meaning to biological and psychic systems.

[12] Luhmann, *Social Systems* (n 4) 139–40. See generally C Baraldi, 'Structural Coupling: Simultaneity and Difference Between Communication and Thought' (1993) 3(2) *Communication Theory* 112, 117.

[13] See HG Moeller, *The Radical Luhmann* (New York, Columbia University Press, 2012) 133.

All three systems that make up the individual – biological, psychic and communication systems – are wholly separate and autonomous. To illustrate the point thus: a person cannot make their blood circulate by thinking about blood circulation and the thoughts in a person's head are not accessible to others. Blood and thoughts have social significance, however, when they are *communicated about* in one of society's social systems. Until that point, there is no meaning that can be produced about them. They remain outside of communication – and outside of society – as organic matter (ie, biological systems) and cognition (ie, psychic systems). Communication, for Luhmann, is therefore the crucial link required for a reliable sociology. Communications produce meaning for society because nothing else can.

Western intellectual thought, according to Luhmann, has conflated these three system realms for centuries. It is frequently accepted that one system may exercise control over and directly access all others. The 'individual' has been placed at the apex of society by intellectuals and society's elite decision makers because the individual's 'soul' or capacity to reason is often regarded as the ultimate guiding hand over everything else. As a well-established intellectual tradition, the Enlightenment concept of the individual assumes that the individual exercises mastery over organic matter (eg, through medical science), psychological processes (eg, through psychoanalysis) and society (eg, Marxism). For Luhmann, these are fundamental errors because they overlook the systemic complexity of the individual and society. They are tantamount to describing how a cell in the human body works by referring to human emotions. Any attempt to procure desired social change, despite systemic complexity, is thus naïve; the fundamental differences between the three systemic realms preclude the possibility that one system can dominate others.[14] Rather, all three systemic realms are equally important. They are non-hierarchical.

An original, yet reliable, account of how society works, in all its variance and complexity, is achievable according to Luhmann. The problem, however, ceases to be about identifying suitable agents of predefined change and wholly about explaining how meaning in the world is generated in the first place.[15]

i. Social Systems

Luhmann makes a second tripartite distinction within the systemic realm of the *social*. Social systems *are* communication, but only those communications that are relevant to *society* have significance for society and hence significance for a reliable sociology. We can conceive of communications of meaning as personal interactions between two colleagues about out-of-touch politicians. These interactions,

[14] For example, the practice of Communism after its implementation produced a range of unpredictable and deleterious effects on the biological and psychic systems of those subjected to it.

[15] See generally Moeller, *Radical Luhmann* (n 13) 59.

however, have no resonance beyond the interaction itself and the psychic systems of the parties involved. Other types of communication, however, may resonate beyond the interaction and beyond the minds of those involved in it. For example, voting in an election communicates a clear meaning to everyone else that you are a voter who votes for a political party seeking power. As a political communication, it is carried out without having to have a personal interaction with anyone. The communication is, rather, of wider social significance. It is a social communication because it has relevance for one or more of society's social systems (ie, the political system). What is more, if a person votes for the main political opposition party in an election by referring to my colleague's convincing argument about how out-of-touch our politicians appear to be, our personal interaction has become socially relevant to the political system and therefore relevant to society.

Luhmann distinguishes between *society*, *interaction* and *organisations*. He holds that communications constitute society and they are the one viable unit of analysis for a reliable sociology. Luhmann's argument that society has functionally differentiated into separate and distinct function systems that produce unique meanings is crucial. For example, scientific, legal and medical meanings are distinct, differentiated and produce meanings that are fixed, immoveable and impervious to influence from external sources of meaning. Socially relevant meanings produced in one of society's systems are not directly transferable to other systems of meaning. For example, it would be inaccurate to refer to the principles of supply and demand (ie, economic communications) when explaining how a physical disease develops in the human body (ie, medical communications).

Intimate conversations or exchanges between sentient organisms have no innate significance for society. Thousands, perhaps millions, of personal interactions occur every hour of every day. Only a few will have significance for society. Personal conversations about the climate (eg, that it is too dry and warm for the month of January) have no significance for society, but they may do if they are used to justify a decision to relocate an umbrella business to a wetter climate to boost profits (ie, relevant to the social system of economics) or as part of a research effort to prove the truth of global warming (ie, relevant to the social system of science). These conversations, by themselves, amount to interactions between co-present actors that have no societal resonance. They involve communication, in the sense that information is uttered and understood, but that is it. They are not part of society.

Organisations are similarly conceived in Luhmann's theory. Like interactions, they are a type of social system, but they are outside of society. Organisations are visible. They have members, buildings and mission statements. Unlike interactions, their members may be thousands of miles apart and may never contact each other. Social systems are systems of meaning. They are not perceived in the same way as, say, aspects of reality that we commonly associate with organisations, such as courtrooms (ie, law), hospitals (ie, medicine) and the House of

Commons (ie, politics). Courts and hospitals form a separate type of social system (ie, organisations). Their defining and most visible attribute is decision making. Decisions involve a choice between two or more possibilities and it is through a decision that contingency is designated (ie, not knowing what to do because if there were knowledge of what to do, no choice would be necessary). Decisions enable organisations to exist. Decisions are made to admit members and let them go, define goals and abandon others, and settle on a location for activities over other possible locations. Organisations are decision machines.[16] An organisation's decisions designate points of accountability (ie, decision makers).[17] Organisations *are* decisions under Luhmann's theory. It is only when an organisation's decisions have meaning for society that they become part of society. A decision, like a thought in someone's mind, cannot traverse the systemic boundary of the organisation, unchanged, into society. Rather, decisions are communicated about within society and within society's function system on terms constructed by those function systems alone.

ii. A Theoretical Lens

A series of preliminary points will now be made about the patient homicide governance space, based on the theoretical issues examined thus far in the present chapter. Investigators of health services after patient homicides are members of organisations (ie, investigator companies) that regularly interact with members of other organisations (eg, law firms, Clinical Commissioning Groups). These entities are organisations that make decisions about their location, membership and plans. They are all dependent on decisions. Independent investigations are an organisational space of decision making but they also involve the production of meaning about health care services. It is, therefore, insufficient to focus on the organisational reality of investigations to explore the process adequately. Organisations, as decision machines, are best conceptualised as an external environment for social function systems of meaning; organisations are communicated about and constructed as meaningful within society. It may be argued that decisions are content for society. For example, a law firm will make decisions (ie, the social system of organisation) that have meaning in the social system of law (eg, serving papers on the defendant) and economics (eg, billing clients). A bank will make decisions (ie, the social system of organisation) that have economic (eg, loaning money) or legal meaning (eg, recovering defaulted loans in the courts).

The purpose of these illustrations is to begin setting the scene and formulating an original, yet reliable, account of how patient homicide resonates in society, with

[16] A Nassehi, 'Organizations as Decision Machines: Niklas Luhmann's Theory of Organized Social Systems' (2005) 53(1) *The Sociological Review* 178, 178.

[17] ibid.

particular focus on the governance space in which such homicides are investigated. The convenient labels of an 'investigation' and an 'inquiry' merely obscure three distinct types of system (ie, biological, psychic and social systems) and three distinct types of social system (ie, organisations, interaction and society). All of these separate systems are environments for each other and all are operationally closed. All systems rely on the existence of each other to exist. Yet, it is unsatisfactory to conclude that they can directly influence each other's operations. The tripartite distinction set out above is undergirded by the view that different types of system (eg, psychic, biological, social, organisational) are closed off from one another.

iii. A Theory of Communication

Luhmann's systems theory is a theory of communication. It is committed to a serious analysis of society and all serious studies of society must begin at an appropriate starting point. Communication is considered by Luhmann as the most precise unit of analysis to use for these purposes, as opposed to human beings, 'the state' or personal interactions. Academic convention – according to Luhmann – assume all three systemic realities (ie, psychic, biological and social) can merge under the conceptual form of the individual; a questionable argument from a Luhmannian standpoint.

Contrary to some accounts,[18] Luhmann's theory does not destroy the individual or eliminate the individual's significance for society.[19] Rather, Luhmann's theory repositions the individual. His theory goes behind convention, correcting what it sees as a gross oversimplification of society and the human condition. It questions accepted explanations of society that champion human beings as agents of desired social change.[20] Individuals, as biological and psychic systems, remain essential to the existence of society and are necessary for giving coherence to the social world.[21] The crucial point, however, is that meaning in society is impervious to adequate explanation if the systemic plurality of the human being is overlooked. The only way society can be adequately understood is by referring to communication. Communications *are* society. Organic life and thoughts remain outside of it.

[18] A Wolfe, 'Sociological Theory in the Absence of People: The Limits of Luhmann's Systems Theory' (1992) 13(5) *Cardozo Law Review* 1729, 1742.

[19] Luhmann, *Social Systems* (n 4) 256.

[20] M King, 'The "Truth" about Autopoiesis' (1993) 20(2) *Journal of Law and Society* 218. See also G Verschraegen, 'Human Rights and Modern Society: A Sociological Analysis from the Perspective of System Theory' (2002) 29(2) *Journal of Law and Society* 258, 264.

[21] See King, '"Truth" about Autopoiesis' (n 20) 228; G Teubner, *Law as an Autopoietic System* (Oxford, Blackwell Publishers, 1993) 44 and 45. Teubner claims that systems theory reinstates the individual. It 'breaks up the unity of the individual and society, and makes us view human thought and social communication as autonomous processes which reproduce themselves according to a logic of their own'.

In taking these arguments further, Luhmann's theory of social systems proposes that human beings are constructs produced by society's social systems:

> Human beings, concrete individual persons, take part in all social systems. But they do not enter into any of these as determinate parts themselves nor into society itself. Society is not composed of human beings, it is composed of the communication among human beings. It is important to keep this starting point in mind. It distinguishes the systems-theoretical theory of society from the older tradition of political thought and forms an indispensable condition for an analysis of the environmental relations of the system of society and its subsystems.[22]

Human beings, therefore, are indeterminate participants in social systems. They are 'politicians' (the social system of politics), 'doctors' (the social system of medicine), 'lawyers' (the social system of law) and 'loving spouses' (the social system of intimacy). These constructions are possible because previous communications of the same type provide an overarching structure informing their meaning for everyone.[23] Individuals – depending on their necessities, situation, skills and other qualities – are constructed according to roles that mean something for a particular social system of communication.[24] Human beings are semantic artefacts.[25] They are living beings with minds that are communicated about. Communications operate above the heads and behind the backs of those perceived to have most control in society.[26]

Luhmann, however, considers communications to be problematic. He argues that it is wrong to assume communications can be transmitted, unchanged, from a sender to a receiver.[27] The closed systemic qualities of communication systems preclude transmission. To accept otherwise would locate 'what is essential about communication in the act of transmission' and direct 'attention and demands for skilfulness onto the one who makes the utterance' and assume that 'the information transmitted is the same for the sender and the receiver'.[28] The assumption that meaning is transmittable implicitly accepts that two or more meanings can occupy the same side of a coin. It assumes, for example, that a legal communication is

[22] N Luhmann, *Political Theory in the Welfare State* (Berlin and New York, de Gruyter, 1990) 30.

[23] King, '"Truth" about Autopoiesis' (n 20) 267.

[24] See N Luhmann, 'Gesellschaftliche Struktur und semantische Tradition' in *Gessellschaftstruktur und Semantik*, Vol. 1, *Studien zur Wiessensoziologie der modernen Gesellschaft* (Frankfurt, a.M: Suhrkamp) 9–17 and N Luhmann, 'Invididuum, Individualität, Individualismus' in *Gessellschaftstruktur und Semantik*, Vol. 3, *Studien zur Wiessensoziologie der modernen Gesellschaft* (Frankfurt a.M: Suhrkamp) 149–258 cited in EJ Novella, 'Mental Health Care and the Politics of Inclusion: A Social Systems Account of Psychiatric Deinstitutionalization' (2010) 31(6) *Theoretical Medicine and Bioethics* 411, 415, 420.

[25] G Teubner, 'How the Law Thinks: Toward a Constructivist Epistemology of Law' (1989) 23 *Law & Society Review* 727, 737.

[26] KJ Kramar and WD Watson, 'The Insanities of Reproduction: Medico-Legal Knowledge and the Development of Infanticide Law' (2006) 15(2) *Social & Legal Studies* 237, 251.

[27] Luhmann, *Social Systems* (n 4) 139, 140, 148.

[28] ibid 139.

also not a legal communication. Luhmann considers it more reliable to eschew the transmission metaphor; it is easier and sounder to regard social systems of communication as closed off from direct contact (ie, transmission) from other social systems.[29]

Luhmann's argument challenges the common assumption that human beings, groups of people or 'the state' can transmit information, unchanged, to a receiver. Luhmann's challenge, for the present work, enables a deep questioning to commence of the stated ambitions of patient homicide investigators and policy makers to establish truth and learn lessons. These ambitions assume that all parties and interests involved in these arrangements are able to share information universally, for the purpose of ensuring that predefined goals of service improvement and progress are attained. The assumption, however, ignores functional differentiation. Society's functions are diverse, unique and founded on the meaning that communication systems each produce. Society's social systems function by producing unique meanings *about* each other (ie, their environment), in their own image and in accordance with their internal logic. They are unable to acquire or be given a new identity derived from beyond their boundaries. By way of illustration, medicine has a distinctly medical identity (ie, improving and maintaining health). It will, however, lose systemic integrity (ie, the proliferation of illness and sickness) if it is used politically (eg, treatment is denied to persons of a specific political persuasion).[30]

B. Social Autopoiesis

A social system's operations (eg, its processes, rules, principles, concepts) remain within its boundary. These operations are connected to each other through communication and therefore make sense of reality for that system. Social systems are operationally closed under Luhmann's social systems theory; social systems are immune from direct interference by other social systems in their environment. Social function systems are established through closed cycles of communication that link to each other internally. Society and the social systems that constitute society are created from the inside and never from the outside. Communication cannot be considered 'in the same way in which one grabs one thing or another off the rack'.[31] 'Meaning always refers to meaning and never reaches out of itself for something else'.[32] For example, *scientific* truth is considered true because the

[29] ibid 140.
[30] On systemic integrity, see generally HG Moeller, *Luhmann Explained: From Souls to Systems* (Chicago, IL, Open Court, 2006) 15.
[31] Luhmann, *Social Systems* (n 4) 140. Cf L von Bertalanffy, *General Systems Theory* (New York, G Braziller, 1988) 4. Von Bertalanffy advocated the 'open' systems theory model, which provided support to the argument that social systems engage 'in exchange of matter with its environment, presenting import and export, building up and breaking down of its material components'.
[32] Luhmann, *Social Systems* (n 4) 62.

means used to establish it – *scientific* methods – are considered true according to *science. Scientific* methods meet *scientific* standards produced by *scientifically* accredited experts.[33] Similarly, a declaration of *legality* by a *legally* constituted court relies on previous *law* to deliver *legal* decisions – these decisions are *legal* acts exercising *legal* authority to declare something as *legal* or *illegal.*[34] Social systems are socially autopoietic. They create their own reality through their own operations.

Luhmann rejected the idea that social systems go through stages of partial autopoiesis to full autopoiesis (ie, a 'hypercycle').[35] Social systems arguably acquire their own self-producing life and refer to their own values for their continued existence.[36] Law is said to have evolved to the extent that it is completely free of other social values.[37] It consists of elements that refer to each other for meaning and validity. For example, law relies on the concept of justice for self-validity, yet the law itself defines what justice requires. Partial autopoiesis may occur when a function system 'has not crystallised its elements self-referentially, but relies to a great extent on seemingly external contributions, such as scientific findings, ethical impedimenta and political issues of participation and democracy'.[38] Luhmann's weakness here concerns his lack of explanation for how social systems emerge. For him, social systems are 'all or nothing'.[39] Nevertheless, it is accepted by others that social systems have different capacities. For example, politics is more prominent in society than other social systems. Indeed, the cognitive capacity of a system arguably determines whether it is fully autopoietic or not.[40] For example, to ascertain the degree to which the cognitive domain of a system is open to external references in other systems will enable a determination of whether a system is fully autopoietic or not.[41]

For Luhmann, society emerges when its function systems become differentiated from each other and a strong case may be made that society is, indeed, functionally differentiated. Society's subsystems are environments for each other. They communicate about each other, but in their own image. For example, a person may step into the social system of psychiatry as a psychiatrist to

[33] See Y Fujigaki, 'Filling the Gap Between Discussions on Science and Scientists' Everyday Activities: Applying the Autopoiesis System Theory to Scientific Knowledge' (1998) 37(1) *Social Science Information* 5.

[34] Teubner, *Law* (n 21) 2: 'Legal validity cannot be brought in from the outside; it can only be produced within the law'.

[35] ibid 26.

[36] ibid.

[37] ibid 35.

[38] A Philippopoulos-Mihalopoulos, *Absent Environments* (London, Routledge-Cavendish, 2007) 191.

[39] The debate over whether social systems emerge gradually is a credible one, although it is not relevant to the present work. The latter is concerned with playing to the conceptual strength of Luhmann's account of modern society.

[40] Philippopoulos-Mihalopoulos, *Absent Environments* (n 38) 190.

[41] ibid. See also King, '"Truth" about Autopoiesis' (n 20) 224.

construct a patient's utterance that they hear voices as evidence of a psychiatric illness, whereas the same person may step into the social system of religion as a religious fundamentalist who constructs the hearing of voices as evidence of demonic possession. Furthermore, society's social systems are environments for biological and psychic systems (and vice versa). For example, a polluted river is a biological system that can acquire legal significance as evidence of a crime. The same polluted river, however, may be communicated about in the social subsystem of medicine as a hazard to human health. In each instance, the social systems of law and medicine are their own authority for the meaning they produce. A fatal stabbing is a criminal offence in law but may be regarded as the breaking of a loving bond in the social system of intimacy. In the social system of economics, the act of killing will signify economic scarcity for the victim's family if the victim is the sole breadwinner. The law, however, may construct economic scarcity as legally relevant and filter the family's economic hardship through its operations; the family may comply with legal rules for lodging a claim for compensation or seek advice about their legal entitlements under the victim's contract for life insurance. A biological process, such as death, will, however, be constructed as an event of spiritual significance in the social system of religion.

These illustrations show that social systems, according to Luhmann, construct unique significance around 'events'. In the process, they produce their own boundary and construct their own social environment. It is impossible for other function systems to be directly accessed by others and their operations transferred to another function system. Society's social systems differentiate themselves from others by communicating about themselves (ie, their function). They construct each of their environments by referring to their function.

i. Observation, Not Explanation

Luhmann's argument that a system is a difference between system and environment is strongly informed by George Spencer-Brown's *Laws of Form*.[42] Luhmann draws on Spencer-Brown's work to argue that experiences of the world, descriptions of it, the acquisition of knowledge and understanding must begin with the drawing of a distinction. Spencer-Brown, a mathematician, argues that a distinction designates a marked area of interest for the person drawing it. An unmarked area of interest not indicated by the drawing is brought into existence at the same time: the world 'must cut itself up into at least one state which sees, and at least one other state which is seen'.[43] The drawing of a distinction between what something is and what it is not may then lead to the drawing of further distinctions inside the marked area of interest. Drawing distinctions is inescapable. Experiences draw

[42] GS Brown, *Laws of Form* (London, George Allen and Unwin Ltd, 1969).
[43] ibid 105.

a distinction between what that experience is and what it is not. Understanding something involves drawing a distinction between that understanding and what that understanding is not (eg, other understandings).

Luhmann makes the novel argument that social communications operate in the same way.[44] Communications produce meaning by drawing distinctions. Communication designates meaning from its opposite (ie, meaninglessness). The distinction designates an identifiable state for a social system from a second, unmarked state: 'All identity is constituted by way of negation'.[45]

In *Law as a Social System*, Luhmann shows that law – its theories, concepts, doctrines, rules and principles – designate law as a sense-making system that distinguishes law from what it is not (ie, non-law).[46] Law distinguishes between legality and illegality. Law's distinction, however, presupposes the existence of an original, essential, distinction that began law's evolution between law and non-law. Law designates legality from illegality but only after an original distinction is made designating law from non-law. The marked state of the distinction (ie, law) therefore occupies a space for further distinctions to be made inside it (ie, legal and illegal). These distinctions, however, always reproduce the original distinction. The original distinction is the crux of law's identity. According to Luhmann, the identities of all social systems hinge on an original distinction between what that subsystem is and what it is not.

For Luhmann, social systems *observe* by drawing a distinction between what something is and what it is not. For systems theory, observation occurs biologically, psychically and communicatively. A cell, a thought or a communication observes by distinguishing itself from its environment. A cell in the body draws a distinction through its membrane and continues to distinguish between what it is and what it is not, inside the membrane. A psychic system draws a distinction through cognition. Social systems draw a distinction through communication. All systems observe. Social systems observe by continually drawing distinctions in the marked side of the original distinction drawn.

Observing involves drawing a distinction between what is observed and unobserved and it also involves distinguishing the observed from the observer.[47] The distinction that is drawn by a social subsystem between itself and its environment is reintroduced to make sense of what the system actually does (ie, distinguishing itself from its environment). For instance, a thought inside someone's head observes its environment and hence distinguishes itself from its environment. The production of further thoughts involves distinguishing one thought from another

[44] Luhmann, *Social Systems* (n 4) 6.

[45] Luhmann, *Essays* (n 6) 36 and 43. See generally: M Schiltz, 'Space is the Place: The Laws of Form and Social Systems' (2007) 88(8) *Thesis Eleven* 8; J Arnoldi, 'Niklas Luhmann: An Introduction' (2001) 18(1) *Theory, Culture & Society* 1; T Hernes and T Bakken, 'Implications of Self-Reference: Niklas Luhmann's Autopoiesis and Organization Theory' (2003) 24 *Organization Studies* 1511.

[46] Luhmann, *Law as a Social System* (Oxford, Oxford University Press, 1993/2008) 67 and 385.

[47] See Moeller, *Luhmann Explained* (n 30) 69.

(ie, making sense of sense-making). Communication systems, for Luhmann, operate in the same way. The social systems of law and medicine observe their respective environments and hence distinguish themselves from them. Medicine distinguishes itself from what is not medicine and law distinguishes itself from what is not law. In performing these distinctions, however, the designated side of the distinguished form (ie, medicine, law) is reintroduced into itself. Medical communication must be distinguished from other medical communications and legal communications must be distinguished from other legal communications to make sense. Over time, these systems communicate about their environment by referring to their own operations (ie, their previous communications). The result is that social autopoiesis builds up.

Luhmann refers to the observations of social systems as first-order observations. First-order observation means that an observer who observes is invisible in the observation; the act of observation and the observer making it cannot be observed *at the same time*. Observations, as distinctions, must designate a marked area of interest from an unmarked area of interest; law cannot at the same time be non-law and legality cannot at the same time be illegality. First-order observations observe their object of focus and that is the end of it. For a reliable understanding of society to emerge, however, Luhmann insists that the observer and the act of observation must be brought into view together through second-order observation.[48]

Second-order observation involves observing observers drawing distinctions between objects of focus on the one hand and unmarked states of interest on the other. Meaning in society may, then, be produced in different ways. King and Thornhill point out that Luhmann asks his readers 'to become observers of observations – observers of all those theories, concepts and beliefs which people use to understand events, attribute causes, make predictions and so on'.[49] The distinction between first- and second-order observation is therefore crucial for enabling Luhmann's argument that society generates meaning for itself, as opposed to deriving meaning at the first-order level by objectively researching facts 'out there', devising inviolable moral systems and building unquestionable political ideologies.

It is important to note that Luhmann applies the reasoning underpinning his theory to his own theory; he advances his theory as one of observation, not explanation. As a theory of second-order observation, it is advanced as a more reliable way of studying society, but it too is an observation that may be subjected to third-order observation (ie, observing a second-order observer and their object of focus). Third-order observation may then be subjected to fourth-level observation and so on. Observation, not explanation, is all there is; there is no final destination

[48] Luhmann, *Introduction* (n 3) 111.

[49] M King and C Thornhill, *Niklas Luhmann's Theory of Politics and Law* (Basingstoke, Palgrave Macmillan, 2003) 2.

at which an observation of society – including the one provided by Luhmann – can arrive and declare the final word.[50] Yet, the 'Old European' tradition has done so for centuries and continues to do so.

Luhmann's theory is therefore unexceptional. It too is positioned inside society as meaning in the social system of science (ie, sociology). Luhmann's theory avoids assuming a privileged and final observation of society that can guide all others. It exudes ambitious modesty by illuminating the limitations of conventional intellectual projects, while refusing to self-allocate observational supremacy.[51]

These theoretical angles inform a new look at independent investigations after homicide. These investigations frequently buy into standard conventions: truth seeking, accountability, learning lessons and bringing about improvements. The chapters that follow question these ambitions through the theoretical prism of Luhmann's work.

The present chapter continues exploring Luhmann's unique conceptual apparatus by examining how it depicts social systemic identity. Social systems of communication produce meaning about their environment and that specific meaning founds their identity. Two concepts that support Luhmann's theory of social autopoiesis are relevant here: *coding* and *programming*. These concepts will now be explained.

ii. Identity and Paradox

The labels 'independent inquiry' and 'investigation' are convenient shorthand for something more complex on closer inspection. Patient homicide investigations resonate as moments of observation. These moments involve the drawing of distinctions by observers between what has meaning for society and what does not. These observations are made by social systems of communication that produce meaning, forming society. These systems have an immoveable identity. According to Luhmann, their identity is formed through a binary *code*. Social systems produce meaning by coding their external environment (eg, other social systems, psychic systems).[52] They establish certain expectations by selecting information from their external environment on their own terms, through the code. People, events, values, concepts, bodies and norms are all cognitively available to all social systems but they are all uniquely coded by each social subsystem as part of their sense-making capabilities. Social systems, accordingly, self-create their identity. They remain normatively closed and yet are able to learn (albeit on their own terms).[53]

[50] See Teubner, 'How the Law Thinks' (n 25).

[51] See M King and A Schütz, 'The Ambitious Modesty of Niklas Luhmann' (1994) 21(3) *Journal of Law and Society* 261, 262.

[52] Luhmann, *Social Systems* (n 4) 142.

[53] N Luhmann, *A Sociological Theory of Law* (London, Routledge & Kegan Paul, 1985) 25. 'Coded events operate as information in the communication process, uncoded ones as disturbance (noise)'.

The distinction that the legal system draws between legality and illegality is a familiar example of a binary code. Law designates what is legal and illegal conduct by applying the *legal/illegal* code to its external environment. The social system of politics generates meaning about power by applying the *government/governed* code. The economy produces meaning about scarcity and abundance by applying the *payment/non-payment* code to its external environment. Each system utilises an immoveable code to reconstruct its external environment on its own terms. Codes cannot be replaced by other codes or transferred to other social systems because they have an identity that is distinguishable from other function system identities.

The code of a social subsystem is irreplaceable and impervious to transmission among other social systems. A code gives meaning to a social system's identity and enables it to make sense of its self-created environment.[54] To further illustrate: a deliberate and fatal stabbing of a person is an event that involves a host of communications made within different social systems of communication about their uniquely coded environments. A fatal stabbing is a meaningful event in law's environment as a homicide. It constitutes illegal conduct and involves distinguishing what is legal from what is illegal. The same event is constructed as an expiry of biological life in the social system of medicine, pursuant to the code *health/illness*; a fatal stabbing is filtered through the code of the medical system as endangerment to health. No other social subsystem is able to make such a determination. For law, medicine and all other social systems that communicate about such events, they rely on their internal code – rather than a higher, superior, code – from which meaning about an event is derived.[55] Each code is fixed and unchanging.

Behind independent inquiries into patient homicides are moments of observation in which events are coded legally (eg, by considering whether the Mental Health Act 1983 was fully complied with), medically (eg, whether the administration of medication to the perpetrator on a particular occasion benefited his mental and physical health) and economically (eg, how much an investigation is going to cost) in society. These examples indicate just a few of the numerous moments of observation that occur where the codes of function systems are applied. Law, medicine and economics are environments for each other, insofar as each function system filters the operations of the other through its unique code. An investigation that considers the legality of a decision to discharge from hospital (ie, a legal communication) is an instance of law applying its code to its external environment, whereas a clinician on an inquiry panel might construct a past decision to discharge as medically necessary (eg, the patient ceased to display symptoms of *illness*) or economically expedient (eg, the resources needed to care for the patient became too *scarce*).

[54] Luhmann, *Law* (n 46) 93.
[55] Luhmann, *Social Systems* (n 4) 178.

It is clear, however, from court judgments, scientific theories and economic practices that the codes of social systems are inconspicuous. Rarely is the world crudely divided in reductionist fashion for all of us to see. The binary code that founds the identity of social systems is concealed by a complex raft of content; procedures, concepts and routines. Codes self-validate a social system's identity but they are mediated by content that refers to a range of values associated with other social systems of communication.[56]

On the one hand, law may refer to values generated by psychiatry (eg, a defendant's mental state) or economics (eg, the profit earned by a company prosecuted for fraud). An investigator company commissioned to conduct a patient homicide investigation may have their findings challenged in a judicial review action on the basis that these findings are unfair – a value usually associated with morality rather than law. These values may be amended, revised, discarded, replaced or overruled over time in judicial review cases, but the legal meaning given to an administrative issue by the legal code remains the same.[57] These values are solely relevant to an application of the legal code. Medicine's content may refer to legal (eg, obtaining lawful consent to administer treatment) and scientific (eg, the extent to which a drug has undergone testing) values for the purposes of making decisions to diagnose and treat patients (ie, applying the *health/illness* code). These values may be replaced with others or they may be modified on occasion by a social system's operations, but the medical code remains intact. Communicating about the improvement of human health and the curing of sickness remains unchanged. Science is still science, even if scientific theories are rejected and replaced. Law is still law, even though laws are occasionally repealed.

The values used in social systemic communication form patterns that organise information in ways that enable the binary codes to be applied to a multitude of events. Luhmann refers to these patterns as *programmes*. Programmes ensure that codes are applied to different areas of social life. They lay down the particular circumstances in which codes are correctly applied.[58] They may be conditional (ie, refer to previous communications) or they may relate to future conditions in which a code should apply.[59]

Codes and programmes establish the autopoiesis of social systems; events in a social system's environment (eg, the communications of other social systems) that

[56] See Luhmann, *Law* (n 46) 203; Teubner, *Law* (n 21) 105.

[57] See King and Thornhill, *Niklas Luhmann's Theory* (n 49) 24.

[58] See Luhmann, *Law* (n 46) 144; Arnoldi, 'Niklas Luhmann' (n 45) 6; M King, 'Future Uncertainty as a Challenge to Law's Programmes: The Dilemma of Parental Disputes' (2000) 63(4) *Modern Law Review* 523, 534; R Nobles and D Schiff, *Observing Law Through Systems Theory* (London, Hart Publishing, 2012) 10; Teubner, *Law* (n 21) 105; E Sevanen, 'Art as an Autopoietic Sub-System of Modern Society: A Critical Analysis of the Concepts of Art and Autopoietic Systems in Luhmann's Late Production' (2001) 18(1) *Theory, Culture & Society* 75 at 82.

[59] Luhmann, *Law* (n 46) 199. An example of a purpose-oriented programme would be risk management in economics; hedging capital is an economic programme designed to avoid the loss of profit through continual calibration (see also King (n 58) 534).

meet the criteria laid down by a programme are pre-formulated as meaningful for a social system through its code.

The meanings that social systems produce about themselves and their environment create the illusion of a seamless transmission of information and control in society.[60] Luhmann, however, argues that these illusions conceal a crucial paradox: the absurdity of social systems applying their code to their own operations. It would be paradoxical from the law's point of view for a court to subject a finding of illegality to an assessment of the finding's legality.[61] To accept that a legal finding could be subjected to such an examination would be to conclude that illegality is legal because the law designates illegality under its code.[62] Law's programmes conceal the paradox. Programmes refer to relevant values and events in law's environment but they are filtered into meaning by the social system's binary code. Programmes validate a rational application of the function binary code. Without programmes, social systems expose themselves to their own paradox and frustrate their function (ie, their meaning).[63] Programmes, however, create a 'semblance of certainty'.[64] They provide an evidence base for a code's application. Law, for instance, relies on legality to validate and reproduce the operations it uses to make law. Science relies on truthfulness to validate the operations involved in producing scientific truth. A social system's code 'is a tautology and is, if applied to itself, a paradox', while programmes deflect the system away from its own paradox and give its communications the appearance of rationality.[65] Social systems therefore ensure the continuation of society (ie, communication) by producing meanings that avoid paradox.

iii. System Contact

Biological, psychic and social systems are all equally important under Luhmann's theory. The operations of each are confined within their boundary but they have a relationship. To put it crudely, a thought in one's head cannot be produced without the presence of one's physical body. Each system relies on their mutual existence in order to operate, but reliance is non-causal. Organic processes and

[60] See King and Schütz, 'Ambitious Modesty' (n 51) 269.

[61] Luhmann, *Law* (n 46) 175. At p 197, Luhmann comments that 'the distinction between legal and illegal is obviously legal, because otherwise there could be no orderly administration of justice'. Similarly, it would be inconceivable for the psychiatric profession to decide whether the distinction between sanity and insanity was sane or not. Luhmann describes the paradox as a 'blind-spot' of social systems.

[62] ibid. See also Teubner, 'How the Law Thinks' (n 25) 736. Instead of eschewing paradoxes, systems theory is predicated on paradox. To use Teubner's phrasing, systems theory 'makes productive use of them!' But see R Münch, 'Autopoiesis by Definition' (1991–1992) 13 *Cardozo Law Review* 1463, 1465.

[63] Luhmann, *Law* (n 46) 54. See also Luhmann, *A Sociological Theory* (n 53) 19; D Cornell, 'The Relevance of Time to the Relationship between the Philosophy of Limit and Systems Theory' (1992) 13(5) *Cardozo Law Review* 1579, 1580.

[64] Luhmann, *Risk* (n 6) 189.

[65] Luhmann, *Law* (n 46) 19, 191.

consciousness, as we have seen, are not directly connected to each other; thoughts cannot make my lungs inflate because thoughts and respiration are operationally closed systems. Yet, consciousness needs a set of lungs to exist in order to operate. As explained earlier in the present chapter, psychic and social systems are similarly coupled.[66] For example, the extent to which people cope with everyday life at the level of individual consciousness involves operations (ie, thoughts) that are wholly distinct from the meanings produced in law (ie, communication). Yet, law's function (ie, stabilising expectations over time) is essential for psychological coping processes.[67] It would be impossible to psychologically cope in the world without knowing what conduct is legal and illegal.

The present chapter explains that causal relationships of dominance or influence in society are unable to occur under Luhmann's theory because social systems are not made of the same type of communication. Social systemic identity and meaning is generated within social systems, through their immoveable codes, as opposed to outside social systems from an objective source of authority. Social systems 'create everything that they use as an element and thereby use recursively the elements that are already constituted in the system'.[68] A social system's communications are closed and refer back to themselves with a view to validating their identity.[69] Communications are made *about* a system's environment however (eg, other social systems, psychic systems) and not with it.[70]

Reality is meaningful to a social system *because* of its closure as a system, not despite it: Luhmann's theory is a theory of difference as opposed to a theory of unity. Social systems exist because they differentiate themselves from their environment. Social systems are nevertheless responsive to information in their environment at a *cognitive* level. They are cognitively open. The picture that emerges of society here is a contingent one. Social systems create the meaning that they apply to the communications of other social systems by referring to their past communications on terms unique to their identity (ie, their code). A neat exchange of information between social systems is precluded. Rather than there being cause and effect, there is irritation, resonance and perturbation.[71] Communication happens because other communications happen.

[66] ibid 384. See also D Lee, 'Niklas Luhmann's The Society of Society' (2000) 18(2) *Sociological Theory* 320, 326. See generally Moeller, *Radical Luhmann* (n 13) 131.

[67] Luhmann, *Law* (n 46) 84.

[68] ibid 444.

[69] Luhmann, *Social Systems* (n 4) 144; King and Thornhill, *Niklas Luhmann's Theory* (n 49) 26.

[70] Luhmann, *Social Systems* (n 4) 37. See also Luhmann, *Law* (n 46) 80; N Luhmann, 'The Unity of the Legal System' in G Teubner (ed) *Autopoietic Law: A New Approach to Law and Society* (New York, de Gruyter, 1987) 12–15 cited in King, '"Truth" about Autopoiesis' (n 20) 225. See also Teubner, *Law* (n 21) 89. Teubner posits that there is no real contact with the outside world beyond the system. Social systems, rather, *irritate* one another, stimulating reactions that happen because other things in other social systems happen.

[71] N Luhmann, 'Operational Closure and Structural Coupling: The Differentiation of the Legal System' (1991–1992) 13 *Cardozo Law Review* 1419, 1436.

Social systems may resonate with the communications of other social systems on an ongoing basis, but on terms meaningful within their operational closure. Taxes are political communications but they resonate economically; taxes have political meaning (ie, it is fairer to tax the rich more than the poor) but they irritate the economic system at the same time when capitalists *pay* their taxes. When capitalists pay their taxes, the political system is at the same time irritated; these payments are politically meaningful because they secure vital political premises (eg, social equality). One communication is solely concerned with power and the other is solely concerned with payments. A contract for goods has economic meaning (ie, the transfer of payment) and a legal meaning (ie, the point at which ownership begins). Legislation is 'the will of the people' in politics, but at the same time embodies rights and obligations in law.[72] Even expensive portraits have meaning economically (eg, capital investments) and aesthetically (eg, beautiful works of art).[73] Taxes, contracts, legislation and art are 'events' around which moments of coupling are created between two or more social systems. These systems preserve their systemic integrity and remain distinct as operationally closed systems of meaning and each produce expectations in each other about how events will be communicated about.[74]

The concept of structural coupling (referred to by Luhmann as interpenetration in his early work on systems theory) is Luhmann's answer to an important question: how can systems be open and closed at the same time? Luhmann defines structural coupling as 'the specific form in which the system presupposes specific states or changes in its environment and relies on them'.[75] Social systems are created through formulae that enable them to produce self-created meaning about their environment on an ongoing basis.[76] Social systems produce communications separately around certain concepts or ideas.[77] These concepts and ideas permit a functional description of how a relationship between social systems can be conceived of without relying on notions of causality.[78] Simply put, *structural couplings* involve social systems of meaning producing their own communications about the recurring communications of other social systems in their respective environments.[79] It is a relationship of 'mutual existential dependency'.[80] Law and science are well known to be incongruent,[81] but the concept of structural coupling allows for a relationship to exist between them. There is contact.

[72] ibid at 1436. Luhmann, *Law* (n 46) 417.
[73] Sevanen, 'Art as an Autopoietic Sub-System' (n 58) 95.
[74] G Teubner, 'The Two Faces of Janus: Rethinking Legal Pluralism' (1992) 13 *Cardozo Law Review* 1443, 1447.
[75] Luhmann, 'Operational Closure' (n 71) 1432.
[76] Luhmann, *Law* (n 46) 391.
[77] Luhmann, 'Operational Closure' (n 71) 1432. But see Münch, 'Autopoiesis' (n 62) 1468.
[78] Luhmann, *Law* (n 46) 381; Luhmann, *Social Systems* (n 4) 9, 444.
[79] Luhmann, *Social Systems* (n 4) 328.
[80] Moeller, *Radical Luhmann* (n 13) 131. See also Luhmann, 'Operational Closure' (n 71) 1437.
[81] N Eastman, 'Ethical and Legal Applications' (2006) 11(1) *Criminal Behaviour and Mental Health* 124, 124.

Luhmann's concept of structural coupling may be able to explain why complex services, such as health care, are deliverable despite the involvement of different disciplines (eg, law, psychiatry) seemingly at odds with each other.[82] Structural coupling may also be used to explain how social systems of communication operate after patient homicide by coupling around certain concepts and ideas. Homicide has meaning for the law as an illegal act whereas for the social system of medicine it has medical significance (eg, injury, blood loss, cardiac arrest). The concept of structural coupling implies coordination between these social systems, but not synchronicity.[83] There is contingency, adaptation and adjustment, but not a causal relationship of influence or interaction between one system and another.[84]

Critics argue, however, that the concept of structural coupling lacks integrity, is overly metaphorical and resistant to empirical verification.[85] In addition, the comparison Luhmann makes between biological autopoiesis and social autopoiesis has also been questioned.[86] In response, it may be argued that these criticisms are made within the humanist paradigm of social and legal theory. They assume that (scientific) verification is the touchstone for understanding how society works. Yet, to assume that any one viewpoint can be a guiding touchstone for society is explicitly critiqued and rejected by Luhmann in his work. They imply that there is an end goal to reach – a final understanding of society – provided that the criticisms they make are overcome with theoretical adjustments. Luhmann would regard these criticisms as embedded in an 'Old European' style of thought that is unreliable as a point of reference for a robust study of society. Others comment that Luhmann's theory fails to achieve anything.[87] An example is a lawyer who refers to policy documents or Parliamentary debates when constructing a legal argument. An open systems-theoretical account would refer to the lawyer's effort as law communicating with the political system, whereas autopoietic theory would claim that it is a matter of law constructing the political system in its own image in order to reach a legal finding.[88] Accordingly, the charge is that Luhmann's work does not make for a novel conclusion.[89] Yet, the centrality of Luhmann's work and the growing impact it has on wider regulatory and organisational research

[82] See J Peay, 'Decision Making in Mental Health Law: Can Past Experience Predict Future Practice' (2005) *Journal of Mental Health Law* 41, 52, 56.

[83] Luhmann, *Law* (n 46) 42.

[84] See generally Mingers, *Self-Producing Systems* (n 1) 35.

[85] See S Diamond, 'Autopoiesis in America' (1992) 13(5) *Cardozo Law Review* 1763; MBW Sinclair, 'Autopoiesis: Who Needs It?' (1992) 16(1) *Legal Studies Forum* 81; Wolfe, 'Sociological Theory' (n 18) 1729.

[86] KD Bailey, 'Towards Unifying Science: Applying Concepts Across Disciplinary Boundaries (2001) 18(1) *Systems Research and Behavioural Science* 52, 52. Bailey complains that social autopoiesis and cellular autopoiesis are not the same thing. Any comparison between them is, accordingly, impoverished.

[87] Münch, 'Autopoiesis' (n 62) 1465.

[88] Sinclair, 'Autopoiesis' (n 85) 89–90.

[89] ibid 83 and 87. See also Münch, 'Autopoiesis' (n 62) 1464; Bailey, 'Towards Unifying Science' (n 86) 52.

would suggest otherwise. The criticisms of Luhmann also appear to understate the significance of his crucial tripartite distinction between biological, psychic and social systems. Indeed, the tripartite distinction gives his theoretical effort its paradigm-shifting quality and mounts a formidable challenge to conventional policy-making orthodoxies. It is inevitable that traditional intellectual approaches struggle to engage with Luhmann's work. It is only by rejecting the 'Old European' way of theorising society that Luhmann's concepts start to make sense.

III. Conclusions

Luhmann's theoretical position has an unusual ability to reframe conflicts and relationships in society without getting drawn into messy ideological debates. It empties a study of society of humanist content and replaces it with the intangible: communication, meaning and difference. All meaning is difference and all communication is meaningful because of the difference social systems draw between themselves and their environment. The concepts of cause-and-effect and input-output are abandoned in favour of a theory that provides an account of reality as self-created observation inside systems of meaning that carry out social functions. For Luhmann, these theoretical positions meet a need for greater reliability in social theory building and academic research.

For the author, Luhmann's position provides a way to conduct an assessment of the patient homicide governance space. The space involves a series of taken-for-granted assumptions (eg, truth seeking, universal learning) that the theoretical lens constructed by the present chapter will help break down and analyse in subsequent chapters. The price of taking up the book's theoretical position, however, is the abandonment of convention and engagement with high theoretical abstraction. The concepts explained in the present chapter will be counterintuitive and controversial to Anglo-American readers unfamiliar with an anti-humanist theory of society. Health care adequacy and public safety are issues where intentions are widely considered to matter and control over the behaviour of professionals is possible. For the professionals and families involved with independent investigations after patient homicide, it is vital that something must be done to alleviate misunderstanding and error in health care services. The stakes are high for the parties involved. Luhmann's theory of social systems is therefore an unfamiliar fit because it calls these ambitions into question.

Furthermore, the criticism that Luhmann demotes the status of individuals in society has long been in circulation. A solid reading of Luhmann's work, however, leads to the conclusion that the individual is simply repositioned. Luhmann simply draws attention to the individual's systemic plurality. He is picking up on detail missed by the Western intellectual tradition and using it to identify a problem long obscured: the problem of securing progress through human agency.

Generally, Luhmann insists that an understanding of society through analyses of the relationship between individuals and society is mythical because it assumes individuals have special primacy in the world (ie, that they are outside of society and have a special relationship *with* society). It was explained earlier, however, that human beings are systemically fragmented and the systems that constitute them lack a direct and special relationship with each other. These systems acquire significance for society by being constructed within society. Human bodies and minds are outside of society but they acquire a communicative existence; they are constructed as meaningful for society, within society and by it. References to biological and psychic systems, in the form of 'the individual', are a communication about these systems. These systems remain outside of society. As communicative constructs, individuals enter society but never as whole persons. Luhmann, rather, replaces the individual–society relation with the distinction between system and environment.[90]

Luhmann's systems theory refrains from taking up normative positions. It is neither a manifesto for acting or not acting in the world and nor is it a critique or defence of social structures.[91] Again, the parties involved in independent investigations may view systems theory with suspicion because it avoids taking sides. Patient homicides are traumatic for those involved and inquiries are engulfed in demands for services to work better. These parties may regard it as inappropriate to use an anti-humanist theoretical framework to examine how these incidents are investigated. A closer appreciation of Luhmann's work may, however, convince sceptical readers that Luhmann's ideas are not as forbidding as they seem. They may help reframe conflicts between different roles in society.[92] Their use helps place homicide and health care into a social context that other theories are unable to do. It helps illuminate the different social systems involved (eg, the mass media, politics, law) and helps analyse the relationships between them. Ultimately, it may enable policy makers to reappraise their conventional normative commitments.

The current chapter has sought to initiate contact with Luhmann's concepts and how they interact with each other. The next chapter uses Luhmann's theoretical arguments to examine the patient homicide governance space more closely and to use the theoretical lens constructed hitherto as a reference point for the examination.

[90] Luhmann, *Social Systems* (n 4) 176.
[91] See Moeller, *Radical Luhmann* (n 13) 29.
[92] J Peay, 'Themes and Questions' in J Peay (ed), *Inquiries after Homicide* (London, Duckworth & Co, 1996) 20.

4

The Patient Homicide Governance Space

I. Introduction

The present chapter builds on the conceptual framework presented in the previous chapter. It helps contribute to a novel and highly rigorous understanding of the patient homicide governance space as a field of observation in which homicide and health care are communicated about in society's communication systems. The terms 'inquiry' and 'independent investigation' are useful shorthand but they potentially obscure the dynamics of the patient homicide governance space and inhibit a reliable description of what it is and what it is capable of. In particular, the present chapter refers to Luhmann's argument that there are three distinct spheres of social reality: *interactions* occur between entities with minds and bodies and *organisations* are comprised of decisions. Interactions and decisions, furthermore, may have meaning in one or more *social systems* of communication. Organisations (eg, decisions made by investigator companies, NHS England), interactions (ie, conversations inside organisations) and communications (eg, law, medicine) are essential elements of the patient homicide governance space. A novel and detailed analysis of the latter and, crucially, its social significance, emerges in the present chapter.

By way of illustration, when conducting the investigations and speaking to witnesses, an independent investigator's interview with a psychiatrist about the perpetrator's treatment record will begin with a decision to conduct the interview. The decision constitutes one of many decisions that make up the organisation responsible for conducting the investigation (ie, the investigator's company). The interview itself may involve small-scale interactions (eg, a private interaction between the parties about their availability) that do not acquire meaning in society. For instance, many interactions will not have legal or medical significance. Some interactions will, however, acquire significance in society because they resonate in one or more society's social function systems. The perpetrator's medical history may be raised in an interaction and hence become relevant to the social subsystem of medicine; an understanding here is likely to emerge about past medical decisions made about the perpetrator, their effect on his or her health and how subsequent change is conceived by policy makers. Other decisions of an organisation (eg, a decision made by an investigation manager to submit a contract tender to health care commissioners) have meaning in the social system of economics (ie, the payment of money) and law eventually (ie, the creation of contractual obligations). Interactions and the decisions of organisations acquire social significance when they have meaning for one or more of society's social systems of communication.

The aims of an inquiry (eg, 'learning lessons') may become formulated through social systems of interaction within a relevant organisation (ie, an investigation company, a Clinical Commissioning Group (CCG), a law firm), but they may then become relevant to social systems of communication in different ways. An NHS Trust, for instance, is governed by a Board of Directors. Each member of the Board interacts personally and they often make decisions to implement inquiry recommendations. There is a stated need to identify learning on a clinical (eg, producing medical communications in relation to how to treat patients differently) or economic level (ie, producing economic communications in relation to increasing resource levels at a particular psychiatric unit).

The tasks of a CCG, alternatively, are focused on how resources are distributed (ie, economic communications) and the impact of resource distribution on the treatment of certain medical conditions in the community (ie, medical communications). CCGs may also decide to seek safety assurances from independent investigators and generate social communications about risk (ie, the possibility of future loss) in the social system of medicine (eg, fears about the impact of service safety level on health). From investigators to other relevant parties, their interactions and decisions acquire social significance for certain social systems of communication.

The present chapter will go on to show that the patient homicide governance space is constituted by different realities of meaning produced within autopoietic communication systems. The remainder of the present chapter explores these realities, their dynamics and how they interact. It examines the legal realities, political realities, scientific realities, medical realities, economic realities, moral realities and mass media realities of the patient homicide governance space. It develops the argument that each reality is produced by an autonomous, functional sphere of communication. Each sphere is unable to determine the operations of others, although they are mutually reliant. These spheres of communication observe their self-created environment (eg, other social communication systems). Furthermore, their operational closure provides a crucial entry point into a discussion regarding whether independent investigations into health care services after patient homicide are capable of fulfilling their ambitions to learn lessons, enhance public safety and improve the adequacy of health care services.

The present chapter is not intended to be an exhaustive account of all systemic operations that occur within the patient homicide governance space. Rather, it identifies a series of notable communicative operations for the purposes of developing a new understanding of independent inquiries, their aims, their challenges and the governance space they occupy. For example, it is common for investigators to express the belief that an objective vantage point of observation may be reached through their investigation, which can expose the reality of patient homicides to the gaze of interested parties. Luhmann's theory helps place these concerns into a different, albeit radical, perspective that raises questions about these beliefs. In particular, it helps call the conventional normative commitments of policy makers into question.

II. Legal Realities

The previous chapter explained a series of important concepts in Luhmann's writings. These concepts underpin the argument that normatively closed observation is all there is in society and that a reliable study of any governance space must take them into account.

Observations are made by observers (eg, psychic systems, social systems). In society, these observations are coded in a certain way. One particular code of relevance here is the legal code: *legal/illegal*. The legal code provides an entry point at which the present chapter can begin depicting an original picture of how the legal realities within the patient homicide governance space are constructed. These realities operate as moments of legal observation, produced by legal communications and endowed with an immoveable identity pursuant to a legal code.

On the one hand, the interpretation of Article 2 of the ECHR is a legal communication. A government's failure to hold a full and fair investigation pursuant to the ECHR may be challenged in the courts as illegal; the courts may be called upon to establish a series of relevant facts and consider relevant case law in order to reach a legal judgment. For law, a full and fair investigation is a lawful act that is distinguishable from an unlawful act (ie, a failure to conduct the investigation fairly, a failure to conduct it at all). Moreover, an independent inquiry may acquire legal significance in the context of an action for judicial review. Judicial review is carried out by a judge after an application to a court by a party who complains to be adversely affected by a decision made by a public body. The judge will review the decision made in accordance with a specific set of legal principles. The judge must review the procedural propriety of the decision, its reasonableness and consider whether it is 'fair', 'rational' and consistent with 'natural justice'. These principles may be used by qualified legal officials in their assessment of an independent inquiry's findings and whether or not they are 'legal' from a judicial review standpoint. Lawyers draw on legal communications previously established by the courts. Investigations, then, become socially meaningful for law. Legal communications are, then, socially available communications that produce legal meanings about investigations. These communications frame a series of questions about the legality of investigation findings. These investigations acquire legal significance when a complaint is lodged by lawyers with legally constituted courts.

Under the theoretical framework established hitherto, the legal system codes the patient investigatory domain using the binary distinction *legal/illegal*.

Article 2 requirements and the principles of judicial review are expressed in complex ways. They refer to a range of values (eg, fairness, rights, justice, mental health, safety, due process) rather than the crude distinction between legality and illegality. These communications are, however, legal communications. Law codes investigations as lawful and unlawful. At the same time, law determines the relevance of investigations to its operations (ie, the distinction between law and non-law). In other words, law operates on the marked side of the distinction *law/non-law* when distinguishing legality from illegality in relation to independent investigations. The different ways in which these legal communications are applied, however, (eg, by drawing on concepts like fairness, mental health, rationality) are value patterns. These patterns are reintroduced into the marked side of the *law/non-law* distinction. These value patterns are *programmes*. They enable law to reduce social complexity through its binary code. The complexity of health care services and independent investigations (ie, the functionally differentiated communications that constitute these processes) is such that it is impossible to reduce these things down to crude distinctions between what is lawful and what is unlawful. Law would not get very far if it insisted on making such crude distinctions each time an investigation was charged with making improper findings. For instance, the recruitment of different values in legislation and case law does not mean that law ceases to be law in these instances. Law is unable to determine what 'mental health' is, for example, but 'mental health' is used in law all the time.[1] Rather, law applies its code to events through these values. These values are filtered through the legal code.

Law is a relevant moment within the governance space in other ways too. Legal expertise has taken a back seat in inquiries since the Guidance was amended in 2005 but law remains important for providing answers in investigations. Investigators sometimes explore the extent to which professionals could have taken advantage of certain legal mechanisms (ie, detention) when providing care to the perpetrator:

> Trying to draw that direct correlation between the omission and the eventual catastrophic event is very difficult and I think we've only ever done that on two or three cases: the one involving the Metropolitan Police, the judicial review. That was why they didn't like it. We basically said there was a root cause there: the failure of the police to exercise their authority and use section 136 of the Mental Health Act to detain the person. There was a direct link between not doing that and what eventually unfolded. They didn't want that direct link. We worked it through from that. It's very rare and unusual to come across that. You can see it more in acute care, where a wrong limb is taken or something like that. It's a more simplistic understanding of what went on, but in psychiatric terms it's difficult. **Investigator 10**

[1] M King and C Thornhill, *Niklas Luhmann's Theory of Politics and Law* (Basingstoke, Palgrave Macmillan, 2005) 24.

The investigator's comment shows that law may become a crucial link in the chain when ascertaining root causes in investigations. For the investigator, the police's failure to communicate legally was an answer to the vexed question of whether the homicide could have been prevented. Legal measures are, therefore, a touchstone for investigators, in some instances. Law may be used as a way of reducing causal complexity or it may be used to reach the conclusion that the care provided was inadequate.[2] Legal knowledge is, therefore, an essential element in investigations:

> [Law] is absolutely essential … What your legal member was doing was hopefully an understanding of fairness and procedure to both sides. They were mental health lawyers. They also brought expertise on the Mental Health Act. … Michael Stone – you know that name well – the Stone Inquiry was chaired by a friend of mine … who's a barrister. … very much about process and a really good understanding of the law. **Investigator 6**

The investigator added that inquiries today do not have adequate legal knowledge to properly investigate. For him, communicating legally is a crucial element of a reliable investigation:

> Whether the outcome could have been different, I haven't got a crystal ball. I don't know. It could have been a very different outcome, a person killing themselves because they came so close to killing someone else. Anything is possible. So, all we can do is say 'look – particularly in my expertise on the Mental Health Act – was the criteria met?' Someone's got to understand the Act. [A recent investigation], which I'm very cross with … accepted the person wasn't sectionable at face value, because they haven't got the expertise. **Investigator 6**

It is understandable that, for some investigators at least, law stabilises expectations and helps to produce certainty. Luhmann argued that law's function in society is to stabilise normative expectations in the face of disappointment.[3] It is assumed generally that law is able to reduce risks (eg, future conflicts, future loss) in society through its generally applicable rules. Law's responsibility lies in immunising society from disadvantages in ways that do not involve a point-for-point correlation between itself and the conflicts that occupy its focus. Law is society's way of coming 'up with ways of preventing, solving, and compensating for disadvantages which affect individuals differently'.[4] For Luhmann, the legal norm is 'presupposed as a risk-free structure' and 'there is no risk in being guided by it'.[5] Law overrides defeated cognitive expectations. Homicides are occasions where cognitive expectations are crushed. These incidents incite doubt in the ability of health care services to make us better when we are ill, but law appears to provide 'support

[2] For example, see H Waldock et al, *Independent Investigation into the Care and Treatment provided to Mr Y by the Cornwall Partnership NHS Foundation Trust* (Health and Social Care Advisory Service, undated) 15.

[3] N Luhmann, *Law as a Social System* (Oxford, Oxford University Press, 1993/2008) 148.

[4] ibid 470.

[5] N Luhmann, *Risk: A Sociological Theory* (New Brunswick, Aldine Transaction, 1993/2008) 55.

against resistance and disappointments'.[6] It stabilises the expectation that certain events will be described as legal and illegal in the future, despite the experience of disappointment.

Law, then, is a 'risk-free' structure which investigators may rely on from time to time to address disappointments. Luhmann, however, advances the argument that law is put under increasing strain by society's growing preoccupation with risk and safety. There are no absolute guarantees in a functionally differentiated society but more is expected from law to address a range of different conditions and problems.[7] Unexpected developments occur more often that prove legal decisions to be wrong.[8]

Inquiries after homicide appear, on occasion, to refer to legal norms as a supreme guide for judging health services but Luhmann's systems theory demonstrates that law is one observation in society out of many that builds its own distinct reality and has its own 'blind spot'. Law itself becomes a risk if relied on as an authoritative guide for understanding an increasingly uncertain world.[9] Health care services are constituted in a range of different communication systems, especially medicine. Law is only able to represent itself. It is unable to represent other communication systems because it is operationally closed. Its operations are fundamentally different from those used to produce meanings relating to health and sickness, for instance.

These questions about law are echoed in the dissatisfaction expressed during an interview with Julian Hendy, a family representative and high-profile campaigner. He commented that legal processes consistently fail to meet the expectations of family members and provide clear answers. Perpetrators are put on trial in the criminal courts before independent investigations into health services begin and he described the process as wasteful for families:

> I think typically what happens is they'll go in, the defendant will plead guilty to manslaughter by diminished responsibility and what that means is typically you've wasted nine months to a year to come through all that where you think 'I'll get the answers to all my questions'. Usually, you get a manslaughter by diminished responsibility plea accepted by the Crown Prosecution Service, so there's failure of discussion at that point. Everything's been decided before we get to the court case. And I have been to cases … where the prosecution said 'we've found all the psychiatry reports, you've read them, I've read them, so we don't need to go into them in this case'. And the family are saying 'we'd like to know what happened'. What happens in cases of manslaughter by diminished responsibility, often, the court cases are very short. Typically, what will happen is the prosecutor will get up and give a very brief outline of what happened on that day, the psychiatrist will get up and say 'yes, the defendant has got a recognisable mental disorder which explains his act and we've got a place for him at a secure unit' and the judge will say 'right, detention hospital order, section 37, 41'. Those cases can be

[6] Luhmann, *Law* (n 3) 471.
[7] Luhmann, *Risk* (n 5) 59 and 60.
[8] Luhmann, *Law* (n 3) 469.
[9] ibid 471.

> over within an hour and you've waited for, like, nine months to a year, thinking you'll possibly get answers to your questions and then you don't get answers.

Law appears to inhibit families' search for answers. Some investigators, however, consider law to be capable of providing answers. Families are sometimes frustrated. Legal processes are considered to be too brief, ignorant of wider questions regarding the adequacy of health services and impervious to the needs of families to find out more. It may be argued that the frustration felt by families exemplifies law's operational closure. Law is committed to establishing its 'truth' and families are committed to establishing their 'truth'. Lawyers agree a set of defined charges and ensure that the elements of a manslaughter offence are present. In doing so, however, law excludes those who do not directly deal in its currency (ie, legal communications). A family's desire to know more about the services provided to the perpetrator is not a meaningful event for the legal system. Those events that are meaningful for the legal system's operations are relevant, such as the past reports of the perpetrator's state of mind and the accounts of eyewitnesses to the homicide. They are relevant because they enable law to piece together the *legal* elements of the criminal offence.

Law and families, then, read from different scripts. Julian Hendy explained that the governance space is typified by different narratives:

> We essentially may get a family or a legal narrative about what went on and we'll get a narrative of what went on in the medical notes. If the inquiry is just looking at the medical notes, it would be incomplete and partial. So we say, they should talk to the family. 70 percent of homicides happen between friends and families and neighbours, about 30 percent happen to strangers. So, often, the families have personal patient information about when they were deteriorating, when they tried to get them help and they've been refused – which would be important in examining the gaps in the services. You know, unless you talk to the family, the investigation is not going to know that. It is important, we always say, the investigation and the Trust should always talk to the families because you don't know what you're missing otherwise.

Julian Hendy also identified the use of technical jargon in legal narratives as a problem:

> Sometimes when people are bureaucratic, talking jargon, treats the families and the victims as a 'tick-box' exercise and not being emotionally engaged with it, that can get people's backs up and they can say 'well, I'm not interested really'.

It is arguable, therefore, that investigators – when stepping into legal communications for answers – may generate conflict with a family's construction of the killing and the wider circumstances. The exclusion of family interests from legal processes appears therefore to be an issue. Legal constructions of homicide incidents are known for their reductionism. Causation in law is a well-known example also. Law focuses on the intentions and actions of individuals present at the scene when the incident took place. It is, therefore, unsurprising that court proceedings will focus on these elements and exclude considerations that do not fit into the legal agenda.

The issue of family alienation emerges in other aspects of investigations, particularly those aspects relating to the law on confidentiality. The family representative and campaigner interviewed by the author commented that strict application of the law on confidentiality made investigations inhumane and irrational. Final investigation reports are anonymised for medical confidentiality reasons. The victim and the perpetrator will often be referred to using single letters. Julian Hendy questioned the use of such techniques:

> [N]o one's ever made a credible argument to me why the perpetrator and the victim are not named in these reports. Often, people are named when the incident first happens, they'll be named at the time of the court case, everybody will be named … An inquest will be made, but with the NHS everybody is covered up. It doesn't take a lot to find all the names anyway, so in whose interest is it to actually not to name the people? … It's distancing, it's distancing and it's inhumane … I've questioned people and they say 'well we've always done it like that' and I say 'well that's actually not good enough'. You know, you have to have a good reason for not doing it rather than 'this is how we've always done it'.

For the families of victims, therefore, legal communications are reconstructed as dehumanising and out of touch.

Moreover, an investigator interviewed expressed the clear difference between how law enforcers think about patient homicides and how he, as an investigator, thinks about them:

> I'm kind of almost not interested in laying blame at the door of individuals except in extreme cases. And that's just my mentality, I suppose. We used to grate with that approach when I was in the Health and Safety Executive, with the police, because the police are concerned with the individual. **Investigator 5**

It is clear, therefore, that not all investigators will subscribe to reductionist understandings of patient homicides in ways that law enforcers and the courts do. However, some investigators step into legal communications on certain issues and these communications appear to irritate other social systems of communication. For instance, the law's operations appear to be wholly ignorant of issues relating to the need for families to contribute, honour the victim's memory and pursue investigation leads as a way of doing justice in the case. Conflict and disagreement may then follow between families and the law. Irritation is, therefore generated in both.

The experience of legal alienation in the context of independent investigations is quite varied. It is felt by families, of course, but it is also felt by investigators. An investigator reported his feelings about a judicial review action launched against his practice by the police:

> It was very worrying for us. We, as a company, felt quite isolated with this. We were seen as a party to the judicial review, separate to the others, so we got no coverage from NHS England with regards to this. Although they commissioned us, we were seen as … we should have our own legal advice and the rest of it. And it could have gone a number

> of ways. It could have been financially ruinous for us, because of the costs involved. It's an expensive process. Even if in the end, we won the argument, the criticism was just unfair. **Investigator 10**

Investigators may step into the social system of law in order to produce answers during the course of their investigation but it is clear that they find law alienating and intimidating in instances where they are targeted with legal argumentation and threats of judicial review:

> [W]e as a company were dragged through the courts for 18 months and what I witnessed was what I would call institutional bullying … for us to change the report: 'if you say that and drop criticism against us, everything will be okay. If that continues, then we go to court' … They commissioned … one of the highest profile QCs [Queen's Counsel] in the country … Fairly heavy duty on the judicial review. **Investigator 10**

Investigators are not lawyers. They are clinically trained specialists. They are able to step into legal communications, but communicating legally is something that they rarely do. If they do step into legal communications in the context of a legal dispute, they are more likely to find the experience confusing, hostile and uncertain. Investigators rely on medical and psychiatric communications to construct reality, predominantly, and legal actions are bound to produce irritation in the form of confusion and uncertainty relating to their medically informed findings. They may question their own judgements. They may revisit themes and verify their conclusions. The police are, however, well used to navigating law as a way of addressing conflict. It is understandable, then, that when asked to engage in detailed legal complaints against them, investigators are likely to regard the complaints as threatening. Investigators and law enforcers appear to clash because both 'step into' different operationally closed social systems of communication at distinct moments after the publication of the final investigation report.

Some investigators interviewed by the author commented that law fixates on reaching firm answers to certain questions that are not firmly answerable in non-legal moments of meaning construction. One investigator commented that the bygone practice of appointing legally qualified chairs to inquiry panels cannot lead to 'a great learning product':

> You've got a barrister leading a review and there's going to be an awful lot of money knocking around and not necessarily for a great learning product. They investigate from a different construct. It's not about having all the answers and I don't know many people who have got all the answers. It's about the premise from which you're doing the investigation from. **Investigator 2**

The investigator went on to comment that an approach involving the use of legal communications to inform the inquiry process would create investigatory bloat and cease to be meaningful:

> If I'm doing an investigation from a legal framework point of view, you're looking for causality, you're looking for duty of care, you might be looking for negligence, but also

> in the legal field you may be giving too much attention to detail. That is the nature of their work. If you're going to defend or prosecute a case, every line matters … You'd have reports that were hundreds of pages long that were dense and not particularly readable or engaging. **Investigator 2**

These extracts show conflicting views among investigators regarding how panels should be constituted and how investigations into health services should be set up. Law may be regarded as rendering the task of investigation meaningless because it conflicts with aims to produce learning about health care; making services better and safer requires modifications of medical and clinical practices in a manner that is user friendly to the medical and psychiatric profession. Legal approaches to independent investigation are bound to make sense from a legal point of view (eg, procedurally sound, rational), but the scope to learn medically and psychiatrically, for example, is limited. Law's potential resonance in the social systems of medicine and psychiatry is one of sluggish learning, confusion and a frustration of clinical practice. The same can be said of law's strained relationship with families. Legal communications are unable to directly speak to many of the needs, concerns and ambitions of families.

III. Political Realities

Chapter 3 alluded to the argument that there is a social subsystem of politics that reproduces communications about its environment through a political code. The political code distinguishes between those who govern (ie, exercise power) and those who are governed (ie, those who lack power). The present chapter provides an opportunity to elaborate on the relevance of the political system to patient homicide, health care and society. The present section, in particular, establishes the argument that the patient homicide governance space is a construction of political reality within society's political system.

Politics functions by generating collectively binding decisions.[10] Enforcing these decisions through *power* is a critical aspect of the subsystem of politics; in the same way that money is the necessary medium of economic communication (ie, payments), power is the necessary medium of political communication (ie, distinguishing government from the governed). As an autopoietic social subsystem of society, politics constructs its environment politically through its binary code. As a communication system of socially relevant meaning, politics observes its environment by distinguishing between events that are relevant to the exercise of power and those that are not. The social subsystem of politics, like all other social systems that make up society, is a polycentric, self-referential system of communications that legitimates itself.[11]

[10] N Luhmann, *Political Theory in the Welfare State* (Berlin and New York, de Gruyter, 1990) 73.
[11] ibid 18 and 19.

These arguments question the traditional view of politics as society's superintendent. They also have implications for the study of the patient homicide governance space and its resonance in society more generally. Politics is considered to be a central point of reference for problem solving in society. From health to welfare to big business, politics is regarded as an authoritative guide for action. Luhmann challenges the primacy of politics in modern society. Attributing primacy to politics assumes society, in its complexity and fragmentation, is directly receptive to political prescriptions.[12] It is clear that a theory of social autopoiesis does not attribute such qualities to any social subsystem of society.

A systems-theoretical perspective of politics holds that politics manages itself and, over time, has built up enough internal complexity to a degree where it has created new communicative possibilities in response to a functionally differentiated society. Politics, at some point in history, became meaningful through the drawing of an original distinction between what constituted politics and what did not constitute politics (ie, an unmarked, formless state). A series of further observations (eg, *government/governed*, *government/opposition*) have since been made on the marked side of the political form (ie, politics) as society has become more differentiated into specific functions, resulting in today's modern political system.[13] The political system has differentiated itself gradually from other function systems, building up internal complexity to the extent that it has differentiated itself into three political subsystems: politics, administration and the public.[14]

The three subsystems of politics communicate about power cyclically, albeit in different forms, thus reducing the complexity of society generally. *Politics* constitutes a set of decision premises (eg, boundaries and priorities) for the *administration* (eg, Parliament, agencies) to package into decisions (eg, legislation) and addressed to the *public* (eg, voters). The public react to the decisions of the administration through expressing 'public opinion'. Public opinion and its role in Luhmann's theory are discussed at various points in the present work. In brief, public opinion for Luhmann has nothing to do with what the public actually think. It is impossible to reach and identify public consensus out of the millions of psychic systems in existence. These systems are invisible and extremely diffuse. They are observable only to the minds that produce the necessary material (ie, thoughts) for these systems to operate.[15] Rather, public opinion – in the context of the political system – is a political construction. It is a symbolic medium of power derived from political communications in the form of elections, opinion polls and mass media topics.[16] The present chapter later explores the significance

[12] ibid 19.

[13] See Luhmann, *Political Theory* (n 10) 46 and 169–70. See generally King and Thornhill, *Niklas Luhmann's Theory* (n 1) 13.

[14] Luhmann, *Political Theory* (n 10) 47 and 48.

[15] ibid 205.

[16] ibid 48, 60 and 215. See also N Luhmann, *The Reality of the Mass Media* (Cambridge, Polity Press, 1995).

of the mass media because it too is a social system of communication that the political system couples with through the concept of public opinion. For now, it is apposite to point out that public opinion may assume the form of news reports and bulletins for the political system to recognise as politically significant (eg, as relevant to re-election, for instance). Mass media topics may have a distinct and unique relevance to the social subsystem of the mass media, but they may also have obvious relevance for politics for the purposes of formulating decision premises, making decisions and addressing those decisions to the public.[17] Public opinion, then, is a semantic construction of the political system that founds the political system's legitimacy (ie, that it is democratic).[18]

The Guidance mandating inquiries in response to a mental health homicide is a political communication that reproduces the distinction between those that govern and those who are governed. It is a political communication (ie, a premise for requiring investigations to be conducted). It is a collectively binding decision about patient homicide governance made by those who exercise power on the matter in question (ie, the Secretary of State for Health and Social Care, the Department of Health and Social Care) and addressed to those that do not exercise it (eg, NHS England, independent investigators, the public). The Guidance also designates the issue of patient homicide investigations as something for the government to deal with through the currency of power (ie, requiring that investigations must be launched in the event of a patient homicide). The Guidance, then, is a political communication because it organises, allocates and enforces the governmental decision to investigate patient homicides over those who do not wield power.

The Guidance itself refers to a host of values that are not typically associated with the political system. It refers to terms like 'homicide' and 'mental health'. They are values that are more at home in other social systems, such as law and psychiatry. Politics applies its code through these terms. Politics is unable to distinguish a homicide from a non-homicide because doing so would require dealing in legal communicational currency (ie, distinguishing legality from illegality). Terms like 'homicide' are values for the political subsystem and constitute its programmes. Political programmes enable the fixed code of politics to be applied to a multitude of complex situations that require a decision (ie, the exercise of power) to do something.

Within an investigation itself, political meanings may be generated about homicides and health care services in different ways. It is not just government departments that step into political communications when communicating about investigations. Investigators themselves, as decision makers in the broader political bureaucratic landscape, may step into political communication if it transpires that a homicide occurred in close physical proximity to the corridors of political power:

> I think there's a distinct difference that people get much more excited about those cases that were in London. There's something about proximity to Parliament and all the rest

[17] Luhmann, *Political Theory* (n 10) 215.
[18] ibid 204 and 210.

> of it and the fact that it's on the front of the Evening Standard. And the second one is stranger homicides. People get very anxious about those. The majority we look at would be where the victim is known to the perpetrator or is within the family. But the few cases where it's a stranger homicide – out of the blue – then you can see that anxiety from the general public. You know, 'that could have been me'. And that raises the profile and hence the amount of press coverage you get … We've dealt with very high profile cases; first item on the 9pm news, even though they're [the cases] five years old. And that's because they meet those two criteria. So, if you kill a member of your family in Scotland you probably won't even get a line in the press. If you kill a stranger outside Parliament, then you're going to be the main item on the 9pm news. **Investigator 10**

Investigators will construct homicide incidents carried out close to Parliament politically. The tenor of the investigator's comment is that patient homicides committed close to Parliament potentially pose a threat to political power. The incident and subsequent investigation of health services are, consequently, exposed to greater media scrutiny. Media exposure may provide relevant topics for the political system to select for the purpose of continuing political communication about the issue. For instance, these topics will indicate that public opinion requires politics to formulate decision premises (eg, enhanced public safety) for the administration to implement through, say, the passing of legislation or a policy renewal. These decisions will be directed to the public as a way of improving electoral prospects and 'feeding' the cycle of public opinion.

Independent investigations are communicated about politically in other ways also. NHS Trust management may step into political communications when communicating about homicide and health care. These organisations may resist the findings of these investigations because they are concerned about their reputation and position:

> [An NHS] Trust is sometimes, is not very happy. **Investigator 7**

An NHS Trust may, furthermore, engage investigators defensively:

> [NHS Trusts] send strongly worded letters telling us that the investigators have got it wrong … that their version of the truth is the real truth. **Investigator 8**

The investigator added that NHS Trusts do not provide evidence in support of such views. It is arguable that there is a political dynamic to the responses of NHS Trusts on these occasions, particularly when investigators are commissioned to review clusters of homicide cases under one health authority (otherwise known as thematic reviews):

> There's another political dynamic you get from the thematic inquiries, that sometimes mental health Trusts are looking to protect their own back so that they can say 'we've had a run of these problems, but we've taken care of it and had it reviewed. We know where the problems are' … It won't work out quite like that. It rumbled on and they got all of the opprobrium of the press and all the rest of it and the report came out some time later. That was commissioned partly by the Trust and partly by NHS England. That went up to Ministers in the end. **Investigator 11**

The investigator continued by describing NHS Trusts as lobbyists. They sometimes go behind the backs of investigators and attempt to persuade those with oversight in the power network (ie, NHS England) to force a change in an inquiry's findings:

> [T]he lobbying from the Trusts, I'm sure that goes on. In the thematic review we did … they were obviously talking to [NHS England] behind our backs and trying to put pressure on us to change it. **Investigator 11**

Another investigator interviewed drew attention to a health care provider's concern with its reputation before the media and avoiding negative coverage:

> It's all about the press release. What the organisation is solely preoccupied on is the possibility that this is going to come back and bite [it] further. **Investigator 6**

The investigator's view was echoed by another investigator who commented that a rigorous analysis of causation by investigators is undesirable from the NHS Trust's point of view. NHS Trusts prefer to insulate their organisation from public criticism and avoid close scrutiny:

> I think those internal reports [by the NHS Trust] are poor because they don't correctly identify root causation and, therefore, the lessons that the organisation really needs to take on to improve. I think part of that is defensiveness about exposing the organisation to criticism. **Investigator 5**

Further empirical research into how NHS Trusts think politically about inquiries could unfold more important observations. The points above, however, raise questions about why NHS Trusts are defensive. One possible explanation is that the defensiveness of NHS Trusts is politically driven. These organisations are situated in a politically constructed hierarchy. They are delegated the governmental responsibility of providing publicly funded health care services and it is arguable that they resist unfavourable investigation findings on the basis that they will attract opprobrium from those who govern. NHS Trusts are extensions of governmental authority. They provide health care on behalf of the government. They communicate medically and psychiatrically but they also communicate politically. They appear keen to avoid perceived threats to their power within the political hierarchy.

In developing the theme that the patient homicide governance space is constituted with political realities, one investigator described how NHS Trusts attempt to minimise their culpability after the occurrence of a patient homicide incident:

> [T]here is a lot of challenge and pressure applied to the independent investigators by the Trust and whilst the Trust don't commission the work, they can throw a lot of mud back at the independent investigators to try and throw them off-course basically. It sounds a bit paranoid but I think what happens is that the Trust are very defensive understandably and I think that's because of this ambiguity about causation potentially, they are quite … they are not as open as they would be and that kind of culture pervades the rest of the team … They challenge you, which is fine in and of itself, but we basically

> produce a draft report for our customer, which is the commissioner and they wanted us to consult with the Trust on the publication of this prior and we provided the Trust with a copy. The Trust then tried to throw uncertainty at our work such that it would paint them in a better light. **Investigator 5**

The same theme was echoed in the comments of another investigator, a former NHS Trust non-executive director:

> I think at times you're getting less experienced people doing them [investigations], less confident people doing them. They may know the mechanics of how to investigate but they don't come with background and experience. So this very experienced Director of Nursing went into a meeting with the investigators and she said to me afterwards 'we got away with a load of it'. In the draft report, they were mindful to criticise the Trust. She had pushed back at the investigators who didn't feel confident in their position and so omitted that or changed it in relation to the report. And that, sort of, set some alarm bells ringing. **Investigator 10**

The possibility that 'heads will roll' in the event that an investigation concludes inadequate care was provided is a real one. One investigator interviewed commented that serious cases involve mass firings, defensive posturing and attempts by NHS Trusts to influence the situation:

> [T]he consequences for [the Trust] was that most of the Board went … NHS Trusts are very sensitive to criticism. … [they] will make attempts to minimise, try and influence things. **Investigator 10**

It is arguable, therefore, that independent patient homicide investigations involve the construction of unique political realities. In particular, NHS Trust management express resistance to those findings of an investigation that appear to threaten their political power as providers accountable to the government. They attempt to deflect responsibility, question findings without cogent evidence in support and use 'pushback' at key moments when incidents produce 'heat'. Investigators are, on the whole, focused on generating medical and psychiatric communications in their investigations. It is understandable, then, that when their findings show inadequacies in care, the political system is irritated in the form of defensiveness and resistance throughout society's power networks.

IV. Scientific Realities

The patient homicide governance space is constituted by moments of observation. These moments include the construction of scientific realities. Like the social system of law and politics, the social system of science is an operationally closed system of communication. Its identity is immoveable and located in its code: *true/false*.[19] The currency of science is truth; something is scientific when it can

[19] N Luhmann, *Ecological Communication* (Cambridge, Polity Press, 1989) 76.

demonstrate truth as opposed to falsehood. Money, legality and power may irritate science by making it easier or more difficult to conduct scientific research, for example, but only science alone can produce truth. Money and power struggle to produce objective truths about the world. For example, we are more likely to question the truth produced by scientific research that downplays the harms of smoking tobacco if that research is funded by a tobacco firm. Of course, others may not question the research and step into the social system of science when asserting the truth produced by it. Observers may point to the reliable research methods used, for example. Others, however, may step into the social system of the economy and conclude that truth is absent due to bias; economic communication is concerned with payments, wealth and scarcity rather than truth.

The social subsystem of science produces truth through its communications that other communication systems are incapable of producing. It performs a unique and irreplaceable function. As mentioned above, however, science may become irritated by the communications of other social systems; in the example above, scientific communications may become irritated by the economy when those communications are criticised for economic bias. These irritations are likely to take the form of scientific defences of the research and further research substantiating the questioned claims. Alternatively, a shortage of funding (ie, an economic communication) may irritate the function system of science in the form of stifling scientific research processes.[20] Regardless of the manner in which irritations emerge, these function systems retain their distinct integrity as meaning systems (unless function systems become de-differentiated as a result of one system commandeering another).

Like law and politics, the scientific code is rarely applied in crude form. It relies on scientific programmes because society is too complex to be divided up into what is true and what is not true. Rather, science relies on theories, concepts, equations and taxonomies when constructing its environment. These are programmes that enable the scientific code to be applied to a host of issues and situations.[21] Natural phenomena (ie, organic systems) irritate the social system of science often, as seen in scientific observations and theories about quantum mechanics, the human body and the planets. Scientific communications are also produced about society, in the form of the social sciences. Disciplines like sociology may be regarded as communications produced by the social system of science because they use scientifically accredited techniques of observation. These techniques are the structures science creates and relies on to observe its environment (ie, other social systems, the ecological environment).[22]

Investigators of patient homicide often use root cause analysis (RCA) in their investigations and it is relevant here for demonstrating the argument that their

[20] See ibid 83.
[21] ibid.
[22] ibid.

investigations are constituted with moments of scientific observation. RCA is an exploratory technique. Its main purpose is to identify the 'root' of a problem and extract it for the purpose of ensuring that the problem does not grow back. It is a technique carried out using human factor taxonomies. These taxonomies incorporate a range of headings that are used to attribute root or contributory causes to an adverse event.[23] Patient homicide investigations often identify many contributory causes. There may be staff shortages (ie, workforce issues), technological issues (ie, equipment) or regulatory concerns (ie, external stakeholder issues). One investigator described RCA as important for obtaining 'a better perspective':

> A lot of the nub of the training that I do is about people having a better perspective of where they should be, having a human factors approach or a systems analysis approach. What we call in the NHS root causes analysis. So, that if there are significant lapses in care, be it health or social care management, it's about deconstructing those but also being confident about whether things are okay because I don't think I've ever looked at a case where the whole pack of cards come down. **Investigator 2**

Another investigator regarded RCA as useful for structuring information:

> [I]t helps you get your thoughts into ... I think what happens is that you have a lot of information and it helps if you start by putting it into sections. **Investigator 7**

The origins of RCA lie in the area of business management[24] and it has been adapted to draw logical relationships between events when investigating mental health homicides.[25] Investigators expressed the view that these tools give the investigations objectivity or at least a veneer of objectivity. It has, however, been criticised for ignoring the feelings (eg, fear, anxiety and hostility) that accompany difficult decisions on health care matters.[26] Nevertheless, one investigator agreed that RCA introduces objectivity into investigations:

> I think the objectivity and independence bit do. I think they do for NHS England, the perpetrator, relatives and the media. **Investigator 3**

Another investigator explained that RCA creates an illusion of objectivity but conceded that it provides a way of structuring certain aspects of an investigation:

> [RCA] help[s] a lot in structuring thoughts and structuring findings and looking at things in an ordered way. **Investigator 7**

[23] These headings include patient, individual practitioner/staff member, workforce and team issues, environmental and equipment issues, task and process, organisational issues and external stakeholder/legislative issues.

[24] See LA Neal et al, 'Root Cause Analysis Applied to the Investigation of Serious Untoward Incidents in Mental Health Services' (2004) 28 *Psychiatric Bulletin* 75, 75. See also RAM Iedema et al, 'Turning the Medical Gaze In Upon Itself: Root Cause Analysis and the Investigation of Error' (2006) 62(7) *Social Science & Medicine* 1605, 1613.

[25] JHM Crichton, 'A Review of Published Independent Inquiries in England into Psychiatric Patient Homicide, 1995–2010' (2011) 22(6) *The Journal of Forensic Psychiatry & Psychology* 761, 780.

[26] G Adshead, 'Root Cause Analysis' (2005) 29(2) *The Psychiatrist* 71, 71.

In equal measure, other investigators refrained from using terms like 'objectivity':

> [RCA] provides a background framework for what we find out and we use it to weigh up the evidence ... we'll come out with a very good picture of what services were like at the time and what they offered. Then it becomes 'how does that compare against what should be offered, NICE [National Institute for Health and Care Excellence] guidance or whatever, the commissioning contract or whatever.' So, we use that framework to guide the 'finding out' of things. **Investigator 9**

The pursuit of certainty, also, appeared to be significant to investigations:

> I think they [commissioners] ... want certainty. I think the reality is it's very difficult to be certain. There might be the odd one which is certain, but in many cases – in mental health – everybody can do everything right but someone can still go and kill somebody. So it's not the same as someone amputating the wrong leg. **Investigator 3**

These comments indicate that independent investigations strive to reach findings that are reliable and certain. An investigator went as far as to describe her role as 'a bit like a research project', where the data collected from the documentary analysis and interviews of witnesses is 're-worked' to an extent that the investigator judges that the investigation is sufficiently robust:

> [Y]ou re-work the data and if they've done a reasonable job you've got all of their data, you should come out pretty close. But also, you can see where they've asked the right questions, where they haven't explored things sufficiently enough, then you also find out whether they have a nice looking report with no data to support it. **Investigator 2**

There is a strong emphasis on methodology, peer review and reliable data collection that is familiar to that found in the sciences:

> [W]hen it went through legal checks, the legal team said 'are you absolutely sure? Can you really prove that that homicide could have been prevented?' I sat back and I read the report again and I read my evidence again and I had a very long conversation with a peer reviewer and I realised that actually my personal opinion about the inaction of an organisation had clouded my objective judgement. And for me that's one of the key benefits of peer review because, you know, when we talked it through at length and we talked about actions that were taken and talked through potential outcomes of actions that might have been taken, none of those that I could have said with 100 percent certainty that that would have guaranteed the safety of the individual who died. **Investigator 4**

Investigators also regarded the development of specialist analytical skills as crucial to a reliable investigation. These skills relate to activities that would usually appear in a scientific inquiry:

> If the team are competent both technically and behaviourally, then all the other things fit into place. So, the difficult interaction with the family, managing families' expectations and getting to good root causation and all of that is a function of the team and how good they are in terms of their clinical knowledge and experience but also their ability to be a good investigator. **Investigator 5**

One investigator remarked that the possession of specialist analytical skills differentiated professionals from 'amateurs':

> I would disagree … that these 'amateurs' aren't able to investigate – I think they are – but they do need some core skill development first. **Investigator 2**

The investigator continued, describing her use of psychology-based models when interviewing witnesses and mining data:

> I like the psychology-model, which is cognitive-based. Strong tell-all instructions; 'tell me about', 'describe', 'walk me through'. Those strong, openly directed questions; 'tell me everything you can remember about', 'leave nothing out', 'no details are too small' … What I also pull out of my data mining is added value learning and rubbish. You know, you collect stuff during an investigation that you are not going to include in your report. For me, I sift the data. **Investigator 4**

The investigator went on to describe how small investigations involving four or five people would present limited 'opportunities for validated and triangulated data' and that a choice would be made in these instances to 'bring a peer group together' or 'issue a semi-structured survey'. The investigator praised these techniques: they 'really help you substantiate what it is you want to say'. She described her role as one of 'watching', 'observing' and picking up 'unconscious incompetence'. She concluded:

> You don't get that stuff when using only a traditional model because you never ever get to see it. **Investigator 2**

In using these techniques, the investigator described the independent inquiry as an exercise that establishes whether the 'right' questions were asked by professionals prior to the homicide occurring and that NHS Trusts need to demonstrate evidence using data when it came to reporting on their implementation of inquiry recommendations:

> I have yet to go to a Trust that is able to show me quantifiable evidence of improvement. And that's not because it hasn't improved, it's because they have not collected the data. **Investigator 2**

The adaptation of RCA and the emphasis on mining health care service data for systematic analysis in independent investigations is quintessentially unscientific if juxtaposed with how the natural sciences are regarded as scientific. The natural sciences are known for validating their hypotheses through laboratory testing. Like the natural sciences, however, RCA and other analytical tools are used by investigators for purposes related to data validation. Child welfare knowledge is an example. Child welfare knowledge is considered to be more questionable than knowledge produced by the natural sciences but it is nonetheless knowledge that is scientific.[27] The production of knowledge about a child's development – when

[27] See M King, 'Child Welfare Within Law: The Emergence of a Hybrid Discourse' (1991) 18(3) *Journal of Law and Society* 303, 309. See also M King and C Piper, *How the Law Thinks About Children*, 2nd edn (Aldershot, Arena/Ashgate Publishing, 1995) 45.

analysed through observational techniques such as interviewing – appears less reliable than knowledge produced about the human body. Child welfare knowledge is, however, generated scientifically. It is produced by scientific programmes and strives to produce 'objective facts' about children.[28] Health care services are equally open to scientific analysis. These techniques – data mining, surveying and verifying information – are scientific programmes that produce objective facts about health care services after a patient homicide. These are moments of scientific observation produced within the social subsystem of science. They are moments of crucial importance because they illustrate how the patient homicide governance space resonates scientifically.

It is telling that Julian Hendy, the founder of Hundred Families, commented during interview that families 'view it [RCA] as a load of nonsense generally' and that 'it doesn't mean very much to them'. He continued by expressing doubt about a recent investigation he was involved in:

> [T]hey've [the investigators] chosen very bizarre root causes … it's got this veneer of pseudo-scientific analysis, but it's all rather subjective it seems to me. If you gave three lots of investigators the same circumstances and said 'what's the root cause analysis, what's your fishbone analysis' … it will come up with different things. It's not, like, scientifically tested or testable, like we think 'it's this', we think 'it's this' or we think 'it's this'. I'm not sure it's the best way forward.

Again, the family representative's comment indicates a site of resistance. In addition to law, scientific communications are equally alienating to families. Families seek justice and vindication for their loved one. As Chapter 5 argues, families step into morally charged communications that harness protest and conflict with social systems such as law, politics and science.

Scientific knowledge may be combined with legal communications in situations of conflict.[29] It is arguable that similar combinations are formed in the context of independent investigations after patient homicide. One investigator described her recruitment of solicitors to help evaluate the standard of care provided by health care services at the time of the incident:

> We worked with solicitors and we came up with a 'predictable and preventable' test, which I can't remember now but we were the first company to do it. I think other companies have used the same words or similar words and we work with Capsticks [law firm] and asked them to come up with a 'predictable and preventable' test … So the predictability test is 'did the person say that they were going to harm somebody? Did they, through their words or actions, show that they were going to harm somebody?'
> **Investigator 3**

Independent inquiries therefore strive to obtain objective truths through law and science as a way of bolstering the credibility of their investigations. The two social systems of communication known for their ability to be objective and reliable are

[28] See King and Piper, *How the Law Thinks* (n 27) 45.
[29] See generally ibid 49.

science and law. Yet, the 'truths' produced by science and law do not directly speak to the truths produced by other social systems of communication. The resistance of families demonstrates the point and it is a point that reoccurs throughout the present work.

The systems-theoretical concept of 'enslavement' provides further possibilities of theoretical development. Enslavement refers to the reconstruction of knowledge created in one social system within another; controversial meanings produced by one social system are reconstructed anew, with wholly different meanings, in another.[30] A court's reliance on, say, evidence given by a psychiatrist in a homicide trial is an attempt to establish the defendant's guilt rather than the status of his health. The court enslaves psychiatry for the purpose of answering the question of whether a certain act was legal or illegal. The law is unconcerned with the niceties of controversial research on psychiatric illnesses and the reliability of the scientific methods used to formulate the research that informs the witness's opinion.[31] Law demands firm answers to questions of legality, which medicine and psychiatry often cannot give.[32] Many of the questions that usually occupy the focus of an inquiry relate to the adequacy of the care and treatment received by the perpetrator (ie, the social system of medicine or psychiatry). It was explained above that investigators step into the social subsystem of science to answer some of the questions raised by their investigations. Another possibility, however, is that, in some instances, scientific communications may be enslaved by the social systems of medicine and psychiatry in order to produce 'facts' about the adequacy of health care received by the perpetrator. These facts will point to the implications services have – and have had – for the *health* of the patients. The use of RCA is crucial to the task of answering questions, posed by investigators, about the adequacy of health care services. However, the use of these methods may be described as instances where scientific communications are put to the service of medicine and the application of medicine's binary code (ie, *health/illness*). There are, then, fine observations to be made using Luhmann's system's theory about how scientific communications are produced within independent investigations after patient homicide.

[30] M King, 'An Autopoietic Approach to "Parental Alienation Syndrome"' (2002) 13(3) *The Journal of Forensic Psychiatry* 609, 620. Experts are recruited and their statements about a child's future welfare, for example, are assessed for their ability to support judgements about what kind of behaviour is legal and illegal. See also K Keywood, 'Rethinking the Anorexic Body: How English Law and Psychiatry "Think"' (2003) 26 *International Journal of Law and Psychiatry* 599, 603: 'if the English legal system were to acknowledge the lack of certainty as to what anorexia nervosa 'is', the law's credibility would be severely compromised for the law would lose its authority to determine the appropriateness of treatment and detention of patients diagnosed with anorexia nervosa'. See also M King, 'Psychology and the Legal Process: Is Science and Law an Impossible Marriage?' (1995) 7 *Current Issues in Criminal Justice* 20.

[31] King, 'Child Welfare' (n 27) 312; M King and D King, 'How the Law Defines the Special Educational Needs of Autistic Children' (2006) 18(1) *Child and Family Law Quarterly* 23; M King, 'Children and the Legal Process: Views From a Mental Health Clinic' (2008) 13(4) *Journal of Social Welfare and Family Law* 269.

[32] King, 'Child Welfare' (n 27) 313; King, 'An Autopoietic Approach' (n 30) 620.

V. Medical Realities

Medical and psychiatric communications are important aspects of the patient homicide governance space. It is easy to see why. Investigators must investigate past medical decisions. They must be able to identify those roles that are relevant to medicine and psychiatry (eg, doctors, psychiatrists), understand the medical reasoning behind their decisions, judge these decisions and produce a report explaining them. These abilities are hard to come by:

> It's a small world. There's not a huge number of people who've got the expertise really to comment on others when there's been such a tragedy. **Investigator 6**

Medical and psychiatric communications operate in a similar way to all other social systems of communication. They both construct their own unique social environment through a unique binary code. Generally, both acquire their form and identity through the code *health/illness*, albeit psychiatry is concerned with the distinction *mental health/mental illness*. The operations that make up these systems (eg, diagnostic tests, taxonomies) are all meaningful as communications about health and illness. Identifying illness is an occasion for further communications to be made within these systems for the purposes of bringing about health improvements. Of course, if non-medical or non-psychiatric communications are used to navigate a medical procedure, the outcome is medical dysfunction. For example, medicine ceases to have meaning if a doctor receives financial kickbacks (ie, economic communications) from pharmaceutical companies in return for over-prescribing a company's products.

From a system-theoretical perspective, investigators step into the social systems of medicine and psychiatry, at all stages of an investigation:

> I always read it [the NHS Trust's internal investigation report] and I will come to a judgement about how good it is, whether I've pulled out the right issues … Is it about forensic psychiatry? Is it about general adult psychiatry? So, that will be my heads up number one. Who I'm going to need and the context of care will inform that as well and whether they had hospital-based care, mainly community based care, substantive-based care. So it may be a case where they've been assessed in A & E [Accident & Emergency] by the Crisis and Home Treatment team for example. They may have had minimal contact. So what I read will inform what I do … I may bring in a drug and alcohol nurse to help out … So, is this someone [the perpetrator], for example, who has had lots of safeguarding issues? In which case, we would want someone who understands adult safeguarding. We nearly always need a psychiatrist. It depends on how the patient presented and what services they received. And then we look to see if we've got the expertise in-house and, if not, we bring somebody in … What you want to be assessing is the care and treatment against a peer group, a relevant peer group. **Investigator 2**

Another investigator commented that an initial judgement will be made regarding whether an investigation requires certain tranches of medical expertise:

> [T]hey [the investigation lead] will sometimes say to me, because of the circumstances, 'do you think we need a social worker?' 'Do you think we need a nurse?' I might provide

> input into whether we need further professional expertise, depending on the incident. So, for example … draft in some nursing advice. You need to have expertise in the area to comment on it … You bring your expertise as a psychiatrist and then you have a clearer understanding as to how things should happen. If you understand how things should happen then you have a better understanding of what should have happened. Unless you have that expertise, how would the inquiry know? **Investigator 7**

In developing a picture of how investigations are organised, one investigator made it clear that it was important for investigations to constitute their panels with clinical expertise. The key demand of an investigation is to make sense of the specialist tasks and professional conduct of those involved in delivering health care services and those who possess the expertise to understand these tasks are best placed to produce findings that 'make sense'.

The investigator quoted above further commented that it was 'fairer' to judge the conduct of clinical staff against the standards set by their profession, as opposed to requiring external parties to make those judgements:

> Those completely outside of the system – the patient's solicitors, the CCG or something – they might have a different view. I think probably the best balance is that you have to have some people on the outside to scrutinise because you don't want it to be an old boys' cover up but I think it is important to have grounded advice as well. I think it has to be independent. I don't think I'm soft on people, but I am aware you have to be realistic on what's achievable … I suspect different people have different aims within the same inquiry. I suppose the Trust may be to identify any particular learning about it really. For the CCG, the external commissioners, it might be to get assurances about whether commissioning is safe, it might be to provide answers to the family. So I think people come at them with a variety of different aims. You probably want different things from the inquiry. **Investigator 7**

The investigator regarded certain groups known for communicating legally and economically (ie, solicitors and the CCG) as 'outside of the system' – a theoretically significant point. It indicates that the social systems of law and economics are irrelevant and potentially harmful to the task of judging medical and psychiatric decisions. Lawyers trade in legal communications. CCGs possess medical knowledge of course, but they are somewhat distant from service provision. Service provision is 'at the coalface'. Medical and psychiatric communications are produced there in abundance. It is understandable therefore that lawyers and CCGs are regarded as outsiders by investigators.

A curious point that emerged during the interviews conducted for the present research is that investigators communicate psychiatrically in order to make judgements about the mental health of the witnesses they interview. An investigator considered that one of the inquiry's responsibilities is to judge the psychiatric well-being of these witnesses:

> We've seen staff years after the event so traumatised that we feel that they shouldn't be at work and we have alerted people to that. Those staff themselves have elements of post-traumatic stress in some form and live the consequences of the fatal day every day in their work. Sometimes that makes them even better practitioners. Sometimes I think

> 'how do they get through the day?'. They get really angry – the very thing happened which they could foresee happening and they tried to tell people and they weren't listened to. **Investigator 8**

Medical and psychiatric communications are, therefore, produced within the independent investigation in different ways and are often used by investigators to demarcate fault lines between medical and psychiatric communications on the one hand and non-medical and non-psychiatric communications on the other. Either side of these fault lines are roles that are relevant to the investigation's aims (ie, front-line health professionals) and those that are not so relevant (eg, lawyers, CCGs). Medical and psychiatric communications are produced about the past decisions of clinical staff responsible for the perpetrator's care and treatment and they are produced about witnesses, in the form of provisional diagnoses of mental illness. These communications constitute moments of observation within the social systems of medicine and psychiatry. They reproduce the social realities of medicine and psychiatry within the patient homicide governance space.

VI. Economic Realities

Chapters 1 and 2 referred, at various points, to the economic dimensions of the patient homicide governance space. These dimensions primarily relate to the costs of investigations, the payments made to fund them and the competition involved in securing contracts with commissioners for investigators to carry out their investigations. These elements underpin a series of practices. Investigators must be skilled at managing their resources and mindful about the need to secure future work as a way of maintaining economic stability. These dimensions of an investigation are theoretically relevant to the present chapter because they may be theorised as moments of economic observation observed by the social function system of economics. These observations produce an economic reality for the patient homicide governance space more generally.

It was explained in Chapter 3 that the economic subsystem is an operationally closed system of communications. It communicates about its environment through its code: *payment/no payment*. Economic communications are validated by the economic code. It is impossible for economic communications to be anything other than economic, inviting the conclusion that they are internally validated and self-made. The purpose of the present section is to draw on systems theory and explore some of the main economic dynamics behind independent investigations.

It is telling that many of the investigators interviewed referred to economic constraints. One investigator pointed to the issue of capacity (ie, resources) as crucial to an investigation start-up:

> [W]e've all got different backgrounds, different skill-sets, different areas of expertise … the substantive team will say 'Ok, which of our associates best fit, what can we already

> see are the key issues in this investigation?' And then there is the conversation about capacity. But, you know, that is always the first question. **Investigator 4**

Another investigator – a psychiatrist regularly drafted in by investigation managers to work on inquiries – reported that psychiatrists tend not to lead investigations because of the cost implications involved:

> You don't tend to lead the investigations. It's more that you provide the medical input. Which is partly I suspect is for reasons of cost. **Investigator 7**

For some investigators, issues of cost are dominant in investigations. Only a small community of investigators is available to conduct investigations and navigate the governance space. They compete with each other for contracts and, combined with minimal vetting, issues like cost become significant:

> [I]t could be that cost is one element they look at, but I think there's a distinct possibility that cost is pretty fundamental. It might also be about delivery type. It might be who's been less critical in previous inquiries of the organisation and will give us a soft touch. **Investigator 6**

The investigator continued by commenting that the significance of cost is sometimes accompanied by a lack of reassurance from commissioners that those involved in conducting the investigation possess the requisite expertise to judge the conduct and decisions of others:

> I think now, it [the investigation] seems to be put out to competitive tender and who's willing to do it for the cheapest, without any reassurance by those commissioning it that the people who are going to do the job have actually got the expertise to pronounce on others. **Investigator 6**

Similarly, another investigator made the following statement:

> [T]here's been a dumbing down of the investigations and I think part of that is driven by finance. **Investigator 10**

The investigator went on to explain the economic implications of entering into legal conflict:

> In one sense you can see why people are prepared to change it [the investigation] because, in the end, it's easy. You get paid at the end of the day. What does it matter? … On the other side we've had the extremes of pressure on us to change reports because of what they are prepared to throw at us in terms of resources and you're in danger as a company of being drawn into something where you're paying tens of thousands to defend yourself going to judicial review. **Investigator 10**

Economic communications are prominent. What is more, it may be argued that they produce uncertainty (ie, perturbations) about non-economic aspects of investigations. In other words, economic communications resonate in other social systems of communication (ie, medical and psychiatric communications). Investigating health services for their resourcefulness (ie, their economic efficiency) provides only a partial picture of health services in the context of patient homicide. Economic communications are unable to produce meanings about health services beyond resource issues because the social subsystem of economics cannot directly communicate with medicine or psychiatry. Economics can only communicate about other social systems by filtering the communications of other systems through the economic code. Irritation may emerge in the form of uncertainty and doubt about the clinically reliability of an investigation's findings.

The investigator quoted above doubted that commissioners were unable to provide reassurance that investigators could do a good job of judging those involved because commissioning arrangements emphasised issues of cost at the expense of other issues. These doubts may be regarded as evidence of irritation; economic considerations irritate medical and psychiatric communications in the form of more questioning and greater uncertainty about an investigation's ability to produce findings informed by medical and psychiatric communications. Economic communications are concerned with payments and resources as opposed to health and illness. They are unable to directly speak to health concerns, but they may irritate communications about health in the form of calls for greater emphases on medical and psychiatric expertise in investigations. In turn, economic communications may be irritated; the expression of doubt about the reliable use of expertise to judge clinical staff and calls for greater emphasis on medical and psychiatric expertise (ie, medical and psychiatric communications) may irritate in the form of greater resource demands. The social systems of the economy and medicine (along with psychiatry) are, in such instances, *structurally coupled*. Both communicate about each other through the issue of investigative competence, but neither have direct influence over the operations of each other. Rather, both systems are irritated by each other's operations but their communications remain operationally closed.

The drive to reduce costs and limit scarcity as much as possible perturbed other aspects of an investigation too:

> [W]e were basically being driven commercially to reduce panel sizes and to try and do these investigations. So, for example, I can't remember off the top of my head, but I think this investigation cost £160k and we were under pressure to deliver all future investigations for £40k. So, they basically tried to divide the effort by 3 effectively. We just didn't feel we could do justice to … I mean it's not like these are slip-and-trip accidents, a homicide has occurred and these are deeply complex. **Investigator 5**

Medical and psychiatric communications, in particular, involve identifying relevant decisions of concern in a dense network of decisions and processes. Ample expertise and time is dedicated, both of which are communicated about economically. Payments must be made for experts to take the time and apply their skills in an investigation. The pressures exerted by commissioners to reduce costs as much as possible irritate other social systems of communication (eg, medicine). Economic communications communicate about health care by referring to costs, resources and payments rather than the adequacy of certain medical practices and their implications for people's health. It follows that scope for health care-related learning may be reduced.

The present chapter earlier discussed the construction of legal realities within the patient homicide governance space and that judicial review may become relevant where an investigator's findings are challenged by parties contending that the investigation is flawed. Legal actions, like judicial review, perturb the social subsystem of economics because legally defending an investigation finding costs money:

> It [judicial review] could have been financially ruinous for us, because of the costs involved. It's an expensive process. **Investigator 10**

An investigation, in its systemic plurality (eg, its economic realities, its medical realities), is an environment for law and law constructs the environment through applying the legal code; investigations in law will be challenged on the basis of their legality or illegality. A host of arguments will be made that, while not applying these distinctions in crude fashion, will nonetheless produce legal programmes (eg, legal arguments, legal principles) that apply the legal code. Economic considerations are irrelevant although both law and economics will perturb each other's operations. Without an abundance of resources to mount a legal defence with, law will be perturbed in the form of a quick settlement, a concession that the investigation is legally dubious or a stubborn court battle if both parties possess the resources to fund the process. Law itself will perturb economic communications in the form of payments to lawyers. In extremis, investigators may be financially ruined and go out of business. Resources become scarce. Law and the economy are therefore *structurally coupled*; both systems are cognitively open to each other's communications and rely on each other's existence to function but they are operationally closed and are immoveable as sense-making function systems.

VII. Moral Realities

Chapter 1 briefly referred to the moral dimensions of the patient homicide governance space. It is apposite now to explore these moral dimensions in more detail. Luhmann expresses dissatisfaction with attempts to frame morality as rooted in human nature and prefers a conceptualisation of morality as a function system of communication. In other words, moral communications reduce social complexity using the binary scheme *esteem/disdain* or *respect/disrespect*.[33]

Luhmann singles out morality as a function system that used to perform a socially integrative function that it no longer performs.[34] Universal morality used

[33] N Luhmann, *Social Systems* (Stanford, Stanford University Press, 1984/1995) 235 and 236; N Luhmann, *Theory of Society, Volume 1* (Stanford, Stanford University Press, 1997/2013) 239.

[34] Luhmann, *Social Systems* (n 33) 235.

to be designated by religiously derived rules and it promoted certain behaviours that were connected to a person's social position. The aristocrat would be esteemed by others if he conformed to the rules of behaviour (eg, manners) demanded by his position. In equal measure, the peasant would be esteemed for conducting him or herself in ways that were consistent with his or her position in society. The advent of functional differentiation, however, has meant that society is no longer organised according to supreme religious conventions and fixed social positions.[35] Morality has lost its magical underpinning.[36] Morality has changed. 'Morality indicates the conditions under which persons can praise or blame one another and themselves' but morality becomes increasingly inadequate as a universal formula in complex societies. Its 'zones of tolerance must be overextended' and it becomes pluralised.[37]

Belonging to a royal bloodline, for example, means little in the social systems of politics, economics and law. Like everyone else, royal family members are relevant to these system's operations in the same way they are relevant to everyone else. Everyone, regardless of bloodline, may become politically relevant as a citizen, legally relevant as a litigant and client, and economically relevant as a consumer of products. The breakdown of religious protocol and fixed social status through social upheaval (eg, scientific revolution, political reform) has meant that morality is now unanchored from its long-standing social throne.[38] Morality no longer integrates society because social function systems obey their own codes.[39] The 'crisis of morality' resulted, according to Luhmann, in lofty ambitions to relocate morality's seat in itself, in the form of moral philosophy:

> Ethical theories seek to compensate theoretically for this structural problematic to prevent morality from being devalued semantically. For a long time this occurred by smuggling morality into nature and finally, in reaction, by the rigorous, transcendental-theoretical grounding of the moral law.[40]

The pioneers of moral philosophy, Kant and Bentham, sought to uncover universal truths about morality through their moral principles. They were ambitious men who set out to establish a philosophical ethics that could, once and for all, anchor morality to a firm ground of irrefutable justification.[41] Luhmann concludes that the efforts of these philosophical heavyweights were doomed to fail because society is too complex to be represented by single universal truths. Society is functionally differentiated and morality's function cannot be wholly reflected in all of society's function systems. A different portrayal of morality is required, one that

[35] ibid 234–35.
[36] Luhmann, *Theory of Society* (n 33) 240.
[37] Luhmann, *Social Systems* (n 33) 82.
[38] See generally HG Moeller, *Luhmann Explained: From Souls to Systems* (Chicago, Open Court, 2006) 110.
[39] Luhmann, *Theory of Society* (n 33) 243.
[40] Luhmann, *Social Systems* (n 33) 238 (footnote omitted).
[41] Luhmann, *Theory of Society* (n 33) 240.

regards it as relocated in itself. Luhmann presents morality as a function system that produces meaning about what is moral and immoral or good and bad (eg, through moral ethics). It reflects on itself but constructs the reflection as a serious pursuit of universal truths by which society should live.[42]

Luhmann sets himself the task of establishing a shift from philosophical ethics to theoretical ethics.[43] Theoretical ethics is an ironic pursuit of moral deconstruction and acknowledges that morality has no foundation outside itself; morality makes sense to itself but it is, at the same time, nonsense.[44] To assume that morality does have a foundation outside of itself (eg, in objective reason or God) is to pursue a fruitless endeavour. Furthermore, to regard morality as a supreme reference point for society generally is likely to lead to deleterious outcomes.[45]

Luhmann, however, added that morality is a type of communication that communicates esteem and disesteem in a plurality of contexts ranging from the political to the economic. Morality, according to Luhmann, attaches quite easily to the communications of other social systems (politics especially), while remaining separate as a function system. The moral code *esteem/disdain* is, then, unlike the codes of law or science because it is able to freely appear in different social systems without compromising the meanings produced in these systems. It refers to the general recognition and evaluation of people and their conformity with our expectations of what we consider to be necessary for social relations to continue.[46] Morality is a type of communication that processes information about 'persons' (as opposed to particular skills or achievements of specialists) on the basis of their 'moral agency' and the extent to which they are worthy of esteem or disdain.[47] Luhmann adds that moral communications are ubiquitous and diffuse for these reasons.[48] Morality, then, may operate in contexts alongside other function systems.

Moral communications may easily attach to political (eg, 'all capitalists are evil') or religious (eg, 'all non-believers are evil') communications, leaving these political and religious meanings untouched. A 'moralization of themes', rather, occurs.[49] For example, a person may disagree with someone politically and still sustain their disagreement by adding that the person with whom they disagree is a bad person for believing in the political ideology that they believe in. Moral communications do not replace the meanings generated by society's function systems but the difference they make is crucial; when attached to social communications, moral communications generate greater conflict.

[42] See Moeller, *Luhmann Explained* (n 38) 110.
[43] ibid.
[44] ibid. See also Luhmann, *Social Systems* (n 33) 236.
[45] See HG Moeller, *The Radical Luhmann* (New York, Columbia University Press, 2011) 114.
[46] Luhmann, *Social Systems* (n 33) 235.
[47] Luhmann, *Theory of Society* (n 33) 239.
[48] Luhmann, *Ecological Communication* (n 19); Luhmann, *Theory of Society* (n 33) 239.
[49] Luhmann, *Theory of Society* 238.

Moral communications also emerge in situations where a social subsystem's code is 'threatened'. For instance, political parties strive to increase power to the point where politics becomes morally charged through appeals to 'fair play' if governmental or oppositional power is difficult to realise.[50] The result is that it is impossible to avoid esteeming oneself while disdaining others who do not conform to one's point of view. The polarising tension of moral communications materialises with greater intensity in those instances where problems persist and solutions are absent:

> There is much to suggest that morality now assumes a sort of alarm function. It emerges where urgent societal problems come to notice that cannot obviously be solved by means of symbolically generalized communication media and in corresponding function systems. Society clearly recruits moral communication for serious problems caused by its own structures and above all by its differentiation form.[51]

Moral communications are relevant to the patient homicide governance space because they attach to a whole range of communications about health services. Moreover, notions of what is 'right' and 'respectful' in relation to investigations and learning outcomes are visible from the interviews conducted with investigators. Moral communications combine with medical communications, for instance, whereby competent medical care is grounded in the expectation that those involved act with honesty and respect:

> I tend to work on the premise that most professionals in health and social care are honest, that they want to support the review process, they want the right learning to come out, they want their case management to be respected. **Investigator 2**

The investigator, quoted above but alluded to here again, commented that it was 'fairer' to judge the conduct of clinical staff against the standards set by their profession, as opposed to requiring external parties to make those judgements:

> Those completely outside of the system – the patient's solicitors, the CCG or something – they might have a different view. I think probably the best balance is that you have to have some people on the outside to scrutinise because you don't want it to be an old boys' cover up. **Investigator 2**

The investigator continued by commenting that clinically trained investigators produce fairer outcomes for the people in the service, although he expressed doubts over whether external interests (ie, non-clinically trained investigators and observers) could achieve the same result. Clinical skills are esteemed because they can be used to 'fairly' judge the behaviour of clinical staff targeted for investigation. Communicating medically or psychiatrically is, then, supplemented with moral weighting. At the same time, other ways of investigating and

[50] ibid 243.
[51] ibid 244.

judging professionals (eg, through the use of legal judgments) are considered to be ineligible for the same degree of esteem. Of course, there are exceptions:

> What your legal member was doing was hopefully an understanding of fairness and procedure to both sides. **Investigator 6**

Investigations are sometimes embroiled in conflict and moral communications are recruited at various times that polarise the parties involved. These conflicts may arise from misunderstandings between one social system of communication and another (eg, between economic and medical communications), but they may also be related to the assumption of moral positions by the parties involved. An investigator considered his resistance to the police's disagreement with his criticism of the force as an occupation of 'moral high-ground' and an occasion to afford his work greater esteem vis-à-vis the perceptions of others (ie, the police) that countered his position:

> I sense that we were perceived as not easy to work with. 'Intractable', 'not prepared to', whatever. I took a different view that our moral high-ground was a principle and we were prepared to argue a principle. **Investigator 10**

A different investigator described 'being straight, honest and objective and sticking to the rules of the game was vital' because doing so would result in 'a fair outcome':

> [T]he meeting in the media, that was even more interesting because they weren't prepared for the type of reception they would not normally get from the media and others. They were very complimentary. The fact that this had happened because of being straight, honest and objective and sticking to the rules of the game. And it resulted in a fair outcome. **Investigator 13**

The role of families is especially relevant here. Their role prompts a range of moral issues to surface. Chapter 1 referred to an investigator's view that families give investigations moral authority. For the investigator, families are a morally respected aspect of an investigation. They are, at times, afforded a higher level of esteem than those paying for the investigator's services (ie, commissioners):

> I use phrases like the mandate coming from the family. That's my authority, as much as if not more so than the people actually paying me. I'm not sure that's common. **Investigator 6**

Julian Hendy, a high-profile representative of bereaved families, expressed respect and esteem for families because they – as victims in need of support – articulate important questions that strike at the heart of any investigation (eg, what happened to their loved one). These questions complement the questions investigators seek to answer as part of their terms of reference but, owing to the different ways in which these questions may be approached, a divergence of opinion may occur. Divergence seeds a fertile ground of morally charged conflict. On the one hand,

Julian Hendy depicted the disdain families commonly express for certain aspects of the investigation process, particularly investigators' use of RCA:

> I don't think they [families] understand, it doesn't mean very much to them … I don't think there's any evidence for it working very well … I think it's partly a way of escaping responsibility and accountability because it's trying to distance itself, it's not like this is a systems problem.

Julian Hendy furthermore expressed scepticism about tranches of expertise involved in investigations. For him, techniques like RCA leave the family's questions unanswered and are disdainful attempts to help health services evade responsibility. The investigators are singled out for disdain too because they often answer questions in ways that families do not understand. Julian Hendy comments further that investigators should 'have the courage of [their] convictions to write the report how [they] saw it'.

In conclusion, the esteemed role of families is maintained by combining attempts to elicit satisfactory responses from investigators with a moral discourse that frames some investigators as unworthy of esteem, obstructive and difficult to deal with. Moral communications are, then, an important element of independent investigations after patient homicide. They attach to non-moral communications in the form of additional judgements from those involved about the level of esteem that investigators and others involved deserve. For example, a family's desire to vindicate their deceased love one – a communication produced in the social subsystem of intimacy – remains intact, as does the non-moral communication it attaches to. The non-moral communication becomes morally charged however, especially where there is an impasse within the investigation. Conflict may, therefore, proliferate.

VIII. Mass Media Realities

The present chapter surveys a series of different realities that resonate throughout the patient homicide governance space. The reality of the mass media is yet another social self-construction that is relevant. The mass media is a 'rising star' of social systemic communication because it is relatively new on the scene as a mode of communication and it constructs a very distinct reality for society.[52] Luhmann's *The Reality of the Mass Media* reminds us that 'whatever we know about our society, or indeed about the world in which we live, we know through the mass media'.[53] Books, magazines, newspapers, documentaries and the internet

[52] See Moeller, *Luhmann Explained* (n 38) 121.
[53] Luhmann, *Mass Media* (n 16) 2.

are salient examples of the copying technologies institutions use and which Luhmann claims define the mass media.[54]

Luhmann's sociology depicts the mass media as a social subsystem of society that self-creates its own reality by communicating about its environment (eg, other social systems) through its own unique code: *information/non-information*.[55] The mass media generates a *general* reality about the world in which we live through its binary code, rather than a specific reality informed by rigorous scientific examination or legal enquiry.

The mass media may draw on scientific and legal 'events' as *topics*. Ultimately, however, topics have informational value for the mass media as opposed to legal value or scientific value. The mass media generates accessible realities for everyone by selecting topics. Society relies on the mass media to know what is to be known and nothing more. Information, furthermore, is what is selected by the mass media for dissemination. Once information is selected, it becomes non-information;[56] the mass media is always forcing itself to provide new information because, otherwise, it makes itself obsolete and ceases to communicate (ie, have meaning).[57]

Luhmann's concept of communication, as explained in Chapter 3, is flexible. Communication may emerge in different ways. It may involve spoken word, gestures or a technological separation between those that disseminate mass media and those that constitute its audience:

> [I]t is the mechanical manufacture of a product as the bearer of communication – but not writing itself – which has led to the differentiation of a particular system of the mass media. Thus, the technology of dissemination plays the same kind of role as that played by the medium of money in the differentiation of the economy: it merely constitutes a medium which makes formations of forms possible. These formations in turn, unlike the medium itself, constitute the communicative operations which enable the differentiation and operational closure of the system.[58]

Mass media communication is non-interactional. There is no face-to-face interaction between the disseminator of the information and the audience. Anyone in society, however, anywhere and anytime, may access the information provided by the mass media. The technology involved in mass media communications (eg, televisions, websites, print) gives mass media communications their non-interactional qualities.

[54] ibid.

[55] ibid 1. See also R Nobles and D Schiff, 'A Story of Miscarriage: Law in the Media' (2004) 31(2) *Journal of Law and Society* 221.

[56] Luhmann, *Mass Media* (n 16) 20.

[57] ibid. Advertising appears to be an exception but Luhmann argues that advertising relies on repetition for the purposes of generating information: 'the reflexive figure of the information value of non-information must be used, as an indicator of significance and meriting remembrance. The same advertisement is repeated several times in order to inform the reader, who notices the repetition of the value of the product'.

[58] ibid 2.

Mass media technologies are external to the mass media's operations. They are to the mass media what human bodies are to human thoughts; there is no direct relationship of causality between them. The operations of both, however, are a precondition for their mutual existence. Technology and mass media communications are, then, environments for each other. When we disseminate information through a website or online blog, electronic impulses and heat are produced within our computer. These effects, however, are incidental to the information on our website or blog. The electronic impulses and heat generated inside our computer are irritations; the information has resonated with our computer's hardware and software, making it work harder. It is, however, inaccurate to conclude that the information causes the electronic impulses and heat to occur. Yet, if the information is not produced, our computer does not have to work as hard; there is less perturbation in the form of electronic impulses and heat.

On the other hand, mass media communications may be irritated by technology (eg, clearer images, better audio, blackouts). The informational value of mass media content is, however, generated independently, in the social subsystem of the mass media. To argue otherwise would be to do away with the tripartite distinction of biological, psychic and communication systems that is essential to Luhmannian sociology. Technology and the mass media are environments for each other. They register each other indirectly (ie, cognitively) but they are both operationally closed systems. The computer technology involved and the information on the website in the above example are structurally coupled. Yet, their closure enables their operation.[59]

The mass media's code, like all other function systems, rarely (if ever) applies in crude form; society is too complex to be divided up into information and non-information. Like other social systems, the mass media uses programmes to apply its code. News and entertainment are programmes that the mass media uses to apply the code. News uses selectors (eg, surprise, conflict, quantities, scandals, disasters)[60] that help determine information from non-information, and entertainment sequences information from certain fields of selection (eg, politics, law) in ways that create topical narratives for the viewer. News stories must change from day to day to be news. Of course, the narratives produced by documentaries may be rerun on television but the narrative may still retain informational value; a documentary may be broadcast several times on television but its repetition may be interpreted as a way of getting the audience to think more deeply (ie, acquire informational value) about the issues covered and to ask themselves (and others) new questions.

All social systems have a 'currency' that they 'trade' in. In the economy, it is money. In politics, it is power. In law, it is legality. The currency of mass media communications is 'public opinion', defined by Luhmann as a medium of

[59] ibid 3. See generally Moeller, *Luhmann Explained* (n 38) 124.
[60] Luhmann, *Mass Media* (n 16) 28–35.

self-description produced within the mass media system of communication.[61] We all have an opinion on the news, the weather and yesterday's wrangle in the House of Commons. As explained earlier in relation to the political system, public opinion does not translate to real consensus. Luhmann is clearly not interested in public opinion as a form of psychological consensus. Public opinion in Luhmann's theoretical apparatus is a symbolic medium of exchange that enables mass media communications to be produced. Indeed, there is always an opinion to be made about information selected by the mass media, regardless of whether we all share that opinion. What is more, the opinions we form today about information selected by the mass media inform our opinions tomorrow. Otherwise, we know much less about what there is to be known, which, according to Luhmann, is crucial for socialisation and the avoidance of embarrassment.[62]

The mass media's drive to avoid obsolescence through the production of new information provides other function systems with a memory that provides opportunities for structural couplings to emerge. The mass media, in the form of news reports and documentaries, refers to medicine and politics. Medicine, law and politics refer to the mass media, perhaps in the form of defensive statements by doctors to senior managers and journalists, legal statements about confidentiality and political responses to allegations in the media. The mass media, law, medicine and politics are operationally closed function systems but they observe each other and resonate mutually. For example, irritation may take the form of ongoing news reports in the mass media, clinical defensiveness in medicine, legal explanation in law, political disagreement in politics.

Mental health homicides, for instance, may be reported about in the news and irritate the political system in ways that involve the revision of a policy or new political appointments. At the same time, health services may assess the extent to which services are beneficial for the local population. A government minister with an eye on the press (ie, public opinion) and re-election may make a statement about the need to investigate health care services after an unusually high number of mental health homicides. As a communication made within the political system, the mass media is likely to select the minister's statement as information to be reported in the news. After all, it is a statement that has surprise-value. Both systems of communication – politics and the mass media – are distinct arenas of communication that structurally couple around the topic of patient homicide. From a systems-theoretical perspective, neither system controls the other. Both systems, however, rely on each other to carry out their internal operations and continue their communications; without a news story about a mental health homicide there would be no political and medical communication made to address the topic and vice versa.

[61] See ibid 105.
[62] See generally Moeller, *Luhmann Explained* (n 38) 138.

Homicides committed by mentally disordered persons clearly have informational value for the mass media:

> I think that people are less likely to be comfortable in managing risk than in the past because everything now is media-fuelled. So, I think years ago people would say 'it's rare, but occasionally, someone's going to go out and do something awful and there's probably not a lot we can do about it'. I don't think anyone would dare utter those words now. Everything is seen as predictable and preventable. We see it all the time, on the news. **Investigator 3**

An investigator commented that NHS Trusts often utilise their press offices for the purposes of protecting the reputation of the organisation. Mass media and politics, arguably, become structurally coupled; the NHS Trust – as a government-affiliated health care provider – engages the mass media about a matter that it wishes to address politically. The two systems of politics and the mass media remain separate systems but both are coupled by the NHS Trust's press release:

> [T]hey had the press office involved and they were very paranoid about the wrong messages that were painting the Trust in a bad light. I think that's part of the problem. **Investigator 5**

Politics and the mass media are function systems that irritate each other. One is irritated into further communications about the NHS Trust's 'response to the allegations' (ie, mass media news stories) and the other is irritated into communications about political accountability and disciplinary action taken against NHS management (ie, political communications).

A mental health homicide may become a topic for the mass media if the homicide becomes socially relevant to the system of politics:

> I think there's a distinct difference that people get much more excited about those cases that were in London. There's something about proximity to Parliament and all the rest of it and that it's on the front of the Evening Standard. And the second one is stranger homicides. People get very anxious about those. The majority we look at would be where the victim is known to the perpetrator or is within the family. But the few cases where it's a stranger homicide – out of the blue – then you can see that anxiety from the general public, you know: 'that could have been me'. And that raises the profile and hence the amount of press coverage you get. On the cases we've dealt with, we've dealt with very high profile cases. The first item on the 9pm news, even though they're five years old. And that's because they meet those two criteria. So, if you kill a member of your family in Scotland you probably won't even get a line in the press. If you kill a stranger outside Parliament, then you're going to be the main item on the 9pm news. **Investigator 10**

Mental health homicides acquire informational value for the mass media if homicides resonate politically; the act of killing in close proximity to the corridors of power perturbs the social system of politics and the mass media in turn will select the event as having informational value. It is selected as a topic because of its ability to shock and surprise (eg, a potential threat to political power). Some mental health homicides committed by strangers therefore have more informational value for the mass media than others for these reasons.

Mental health homicides have received unique levels of mass media attention in recent years. Julian Hendy is a trustee of a charity that supports and represents the families of mental health homicide victims and he is an experienced television producer and documentary filmmaker. He produced a moving documentary about his father's murder at the hands of a mentally disordered person who, at the time, was known to health authorities. The documentary was broadcast by the British Broadcasting Corporation (BBC). An investigator interviewed for the present research commented that the documentary had a major impact on how investigations are carried out.

The investigator commented further that Julian Hendy's documentary made the NHS 'very nervous'. NHS Trust managers, in particular, became concerned about the media involvement because of fears around negative coverage and reputational damage. It is not surprising that these fears were reported, as mass media communications tend to select information that is novel, surprising, unsettling and scandalous. The investigator accepted that the NHS 'at all levels is very nervous about the press'.

The mass media, in the form of Julian Hendy's documentary, appeared to irritate the social system of politics in the form of NHS managerial anxiety about provider performance and reputation. It may also be argued that the documentary – as a mass media communication – irritated the social system of medicine, in the form of fresh clinical reviews of practice. Medicine and politics, in turn, may irritate the social system of the mass media in the form of fresh news topics about the most recent developments on these issues. For instance, the defensive statements of NHS managers and Department of Health and Social Care politicians are likely to be reported in the media as responses with informational value to the ongoing story. Modifications to health care services in response to a homicide incident are likely to resonate in the mass media as an 'overhaul of services', 'failure' or 'sackings'. These events are topics with informational value that keep a newsworthy item going and maintain the functional integrity of the mass media system.

Structural couplings between the mass media and politics are evident in the responses of investigators interviewed for the author's research. The reported anxiety expressed by NHS institutions in response to mass media coverage of mental health homicides forms part of a wider set of observations about how NHS institutions cope with crisis. An investigator interviewed by the author described Hendy as being influenced by NHS England; the investigator was of the view that NHS England brought Julian into its domain, to the extent that he is now involved in judging investigation reports on behalf of NHS England South and being actively involved in cases. The investigator criticised NHS England South for being unwilling to take the position that families are supported by other processes, such as victim impact statements in court and police liaison.

The investigator's views paint a picture of rich complexion. They show a suspicion of NHS England's appointment of a family campaigner and experienced television producer to one of its committees. The investigator's concern is that, in appointing Julian Hendy, NHS England is seeking to directly influence him for political advantage. It is a depiction of NHS England looking to control what is reported about the organisation by a vociferous campaigner and filmmaker. The investigator also commented that the appointment of Julian Hendy has led to the imposition of unhelpful requirements on investigators to appoint additional members to their panels tasked with oversight of family-related issues. The investigator's suspicion clearly demonstrates a concern that investigations are being hindered by certain appointments made within NHS England. The assumption here is that investigations would work better without NHS England making such appointments. The investigator comes close to implying manipulation on the part of NHS England, describing the arrangement as inviting Julian 'into its tent'.

The root of the investigator's concern above arguably oversimplifies a complex social process. Systems theory claims that individuals are not capable of direct manipulation and control; it is no more possible for individuals to manipulate the mass media than it is for the thoughts inside someone's head to manipulate their blood flow. Both individuals (ie, as psychic and biological systems) and the mass media are autopoietic systems of social communication that are unable to determine each other's operations. In a similar manner, the political system is unable to manipulate the mass media and vice versa. The idea that a public organisation can directly manipulate the mass media for political advantage (eg, minimising the possibility of ministerial sanction) is impossible, according to systems theory, because cause-and-effect relationships between the two systems would imply that hierarchies may form between them. Systems theory invites the suggestion that the suspicions expressed by the investigator are erroneously imbued with human agency. What is perceived as manipulation is, rather, a structural coupling of politics and the mass media. There is mutual resonance but politics and the mass media represent society in their own image. They are unable to directly manipulate each other or dissolve their operations into each other. A mass media communication, in the form of a website post or a documentary, remains a mass media communication irrespective of whether the individual considered to be responsible for it is perceived as politically controlled. The topics referred to by these communications (eg, mental health homicide, homicide statistics) do not cease to have informational value for the mass media. The social systems of politics and the mass media continue to communicate as closed systems in these situations, albeit mutually reliant on the existence of each other to operate around a particular issue. To illustrate, a political communication about a news broadcast on the inadequacy of health services is impossible to produce without the production of the news broadcast itself. Nonetheless, both politics and the mass media remain operationally closed function systems of communication.

IX. The Implications of Social Autopoiesis

To summarise the argument of the book thus far, the patient homicide governance space is a communicational space of observation. The space requires the operation of biological and psychic systems but, crucially, it acquires a meaningful existence in social communication. Communications operate at the level of personal interactions and the decisions of organisations but the present work lays most emphasis on how the patient homicide governance space resonates in society's social communication systems. The governance space is a self-construction of meaning within these systems. Law, politics, science, the economy and the mass media (to name a few) communicate about their environment (eg, about each other). They make sense of homicide events, structure problems relating to patient homicide through their unique binary codes and sometimes attempt to influence a target area of scrutiny.[63]

The present chapter illustrates how different communications, produced through a social subsystem's binary code, create distinct, non-replicable realities for the patient homicide governance space. Their non-replicable qualities, in particular, render them impervious to direct exogenous influence. Function systems have immoveable identities. They are unable to control or commandeer others. If social autopoietic theory is anything to go by, the attempts of independent investigators and health care providers to resolve or alleviate perceived health care inadequacies after a patient homicide are likely to be unsuccessful or yield undesired consequences.[64] No one systemic perspective is able to wholly represent the social complexity involved, thus leading to the conclusion that the conventional normative commitments of policy makers (eg, 'learning lessons', 'improving safety') calls for a re-evaluation.

Demonstrable efforts have been made to introduce economic forces into areas previously untouched by such forces. The NHS in general has experienced grave problems as a result of economic communications becoming too dominant on hospital wards. A fixation on cost cutting has adversely impacted health care quality and has led to a slew of deaths.[65] Independent investigations into patient homicide occupy a different seat of health care governance however. They investigate. Investigators do not administer medication and care but there are similarities

[63] See generally G Teubner, 'Introduction to Autopoietic Law' in G Teubner (ed), *Autopoietic Law: A New Approach to Law and Society* (New York: de Gruyter, 1987) 19; J Paterson, *Behind the Mask: Regulating Health and Safety in Britain's Offshore Oil and Gas Industry* (Aldershot, Ashgate, 2000) 57–59.

[64] In relation to law, see Teubner, 'Introduction' (n 63) 19. Generally speaking, the 'regulatory trilemma' refers to attempts by law to reach beyond its autopoietic boundaries and interfere with its target area at the risk of damage to the regulated area.

[65] R Francis, *Report of the Mid Staffordshire NHS Foundation Trust Public Inquiry: Executive Summary* (London, The Stationery Office, 2013).

between front-line hospital governance mechanisms and independent investigations after patient homicide. Both involve observation. Both involve medical and economic ways of communicating. Both involve a process of making sense of health services. It is therefore unsurprising that making sense of health services from different perspectives, particularly from a medical and economic perspective, will lead to unintended consequences, misunderstanding and disagreement if those perspectives underpin decisions to do or not do something (eg, decisions to reform services).

The present chapter earlier explained that economic communications may limit the ability of an inquiry to generate clinically informed understandings about health care. These understandings require time, expertise and the expenditure of resources. If investigatory resources are tight, the scope to recruit expertise (eg, medical, psychiatric) is constrained and the ability of investigations to produce understandings about the degree to which services benefit the health of patients becomes compromised:

> [T]here was pressure from the Trust to try and pare-down the team size and to try and make it more of a generalist investigation ... I think they're trying to reduce the cost and also the complexity and understandably the timescales involved in these investigations. **Investigator 5**

The investigator's comment links up with the concerns of other investigators. These concerns point to a tension between communicating economically about the investigation itself, the non-economic aims of gauging a comprehensive understanding of services across different agencies and conducting a satisfactory investigation. Inquiry resources (eg, panel sizes) were being reduced in some instances. These resource reductions were being carried out in response to commercial imperatives, resulting in a constriction of investigatory breadth and experience:

> They [investigations] would just focus on his [the perpetrator's] last episode of care and there certainly wouldn't be involvement from any of the different agencies. There would just be a focus on mental health services and perhaps how they communicated with other agencies, but now you wouldn't be interviewing the police, the ambulance services like you were 10 or 12 years ago ... the commissioners commissioning investigations now are not as experienced. For example, in the old days, those commissioning investigations had a good knowledge of mental health services and I don't think – and I'm speaking very generally – I don't think they've had that over the years. The second thing is money. In the old days, investigations came to about £90,000. Investigations now tend to come in at 15 to 30. So, they don't commission the breadth of it. You're just looking at mental health services. The outcome of that is that you get a very narrow-focused investigation that actually doesn't tell the whole story. **Investigator 3**

The abundance and scarcity of resources is, therefore, communicated about frequently by investigators and commissioners after a patient homicide. Economic considerations may, however, jar with the central tenets of learning lessons about the connection between services, health and welfare. If these investigations are supposed to excavate findings that inform better health care for the future, an attempt by certain parties (eg, NHS Trusts and commissioners) to limit investigative reach on financial and economic grounds may stymie these aims. Furthermore, if economic communications dominate an investigation, there are sound reasons to argue that the overall level of investigative quality will diminish:

> If the team are competent, both technically and behaviourally, then all the other things fit into place. So, the difficult interaction with the family, managing families' expectations and getting to good root causation and all of that is a function of the team and how good they are in terms of their clinical knowledge and experience but also their ability to be a good investigator … I think part of the problem is the move to try and pare these down and the push to do these things quick and dirty. I think that will affect the quality basically. **Investigator 5**

If economic communications become too dominant in an investigation, medical and psychiatric communications may undergo a diminution in their functional integrity. The significance of the investigation's findings for the medical profession will be reduced because of an inability to inform health care practice with a sufficient level of detail and precision commensurate with having enough resources (eg, expertise, time) at the disposal of the investigation. At worst, it could lead to a loss of functional integrity in medicine and psychiatry; a lack of resources to conduct the investigation may lead to a 'quick and dirty' investigation that is thin on explanation and learning capacity for clinicians.

There are also visible conflicts between the inquiry's scientific approach and the expectations of family members. An investigator described one case in particular that depicted conflict in clear terms:

> [T]he family were quite keen that the care was so poor that it resulted in the death of their loved one because they very much saw this as a criminal act and that her mental health was not causative of the event. So, that is another dimension in there and, yes, there are challenges in the objective search for the truth and the expectation of the family and other people in there because we also spoke to the offender's family and they had quite a strong view that her poor quality of care has led to her offending. And so, there's that issue. Quite a complex mix in these sort of cases. **Investigator 5**

The overarching point is that independent investigations involve the operation of functionally differentiated observations that describe society in fundamentally different ways. An attempt to manipulate, change or steer a complex sphere of industrial life – such as health care services – will resonate unpredictably and create misunderstandings, ignorance or objection. One investigator expressed awareness of these tensions:

> Lots of recommendations have unintended consequences. A lot of the stuff we've learned has come from aviation, a lot of the human factors things. So, you have to be careful and hand it over to the Trust to make it happen because we don't know all the 'ins and outs'. They know the culture and they have to make it work. Nothing is infallible. The public think it is. **Investigator 3**

The same investigator commented that making recommendations may manufacture new problems:

> I remember as Director of Nursing at a large Trust, we had a problem observing service users on the ward, making sure that they were observed properly. I spent ages doing it. And then I kept going on the ward and seeing somebody sitting on the ward all the time. Inadvertently, by introducing this new policy, people had misunderstood it and thought they had to sit by the door and go in and out all the time. A totally unintended consequence. This took out a lot of resources and we had to change it. **Investigator 3**

Combined with the book's empirical data, systems theory helps capture an image of the patient homicide governance space as a non-hierarchical sphere of sense making and observation. A privileged vantage point from which to observe events and relationships and generate a superior meaning about them is impossible. The difficulty of managing the economic dynamics in investigations vis-à-vis clinical learning underlines the point. Something may make sense from a psychiatric point of view (ie, increased patient monitoring) and indeed justify an inquiry recommendation, but the same measure may demand action in the future. The action could take the form of reappraising clinical practice from an economic perspective (ie, modifying staff observational practices in a way that reduces resource expenditure).

Social systems of communication continually confront one another.[66] The recommendations made by an inquiry are, if implemented, bound to irritate social function systems in a way that is unpredictable. The implementation of clinical training regimes, the production of economic communications about costs and the pursuit of objectivity through selected investigatory techniques are occasions on which irritation will occur. Independent investigations are, nevertheless, primarily focused on producing medical and psychiatric communications about the health and physical safety of the perpetrator and the public.

The implication, therefore, is that the notion of learning lessons is not as accurate as policy makers portray it to be. The idea of learning lessons has gained much currency in recent years however. It is gaining ground in statutory provisions on adult safeguarding in social care[67] but the phrase is elusive, open to interpretation and assumes that learning is a uniform experience for all those involved in health and social care practices. It also assumes that decisions can be made and assumed to have precise consequences within complex public services. The author questions those assumptions. For one investigator, the concept of learning lessons was something that only certain parties were capable of understanding:

> Families aren't interested in learning lessons. They're interested in someone losing their job. **Investigator 12**

[66] See generally M King, 'The "Truth" about Autopoiesis' (1993) 20(2) *Journal of Law and Society* 218, 222.

[67] DP Horton, 'Tackling Elder Abuse and Neglect: Adult Safeguarding under the Care Act 2014' (2016) 4 *Elder Law Journal* 333.

Another investigator was similarly candid:

> What is interesting in this case is that the family were quite keen that the care was so poor that it resulted in the death of their loved one because they very much saw this as a criminal act and that her mental health was not causative of the event. **Investigator 5**

Julian Hendy, however, depicted a more complex picture about what learning lessons means:

> They have a thing in the reports called 'lessons learned'. To any normal person, 'lessons learned' are things they've done to make improvements. In the NHS, it means 'things we've identified we still need to do to make improvements'. So not 'lessons learned', past tense. These are lessons to be learned. And the usage in the NHS is that they always use 'lessons learned', as if it's already happened. It hasn't always happened so I'm always thinking, have I missed something? So it's interesting to ask what they mean by 'lessons learned'.

For the family representative, 'learning lessons' is used in different ways by parties connected to an inquiry. The above statement shows that NHS institutions regard it temporally: as a plan for the future as opposed to something having already been done. As the next chapter will explain, time is a crucial dimension of meaning in society, in addition to the other meanings society produces about itself and its environment. It is also crucial to the patient homicide governance space.

X. Conclusions

The present chapter develops the systems-theoretical lens established in Chapter 3. It elaborates on the theoretical issues raised in Chapter 3 by focusing sharply on the different communicational realities that make up the patient homicide governance space. What is commonly referred to as 'the inquiry' or the 'independent investigation' conceals the operation of organic systems (ie, the bodies of humans), consciousness (ie, psychic systems) and, critically, different types of social systems (ie, interaction, organisations, societies). Of particular interest are the social systems at the level of society. The act of killing, the roles and decisions of those responsible for the perpetrator's care and treatment, the illness the perpetrator was suffering from (ie, psychiatric communications), the cost of investigations (ie, economic communications) and whether or not the perpetrator has been previously convicted of a crime (ie, legal communications) are all socially relevant to society's function systems of meaning. These systems are functionally differentiated from each other but their communications are cognitively available to other systems and are reconstructed anew by each one. A fatal stabbing committed by a mentally disordered perpetrator will have significance for, say, the social system of law in the form of homicide and the social system of psychiatry in the form of a health service investigation. Both law and psychiatry are environments for each other. The fatal stabbing is an event that perturbs both systems; each system couples around the event and self-generates its meanings through its own operations.

In other instances, there may be enslavement. Inquiry panels are typically comprised of psychiatrists. Psychiatric expertise is brought to bear significantly on questions over whether the care and treatment provided to the perpetrator benefited the latter's health and whether it influenced his decision to end the life of another. Answering these questions may involve recruiting scientific approaches (eg, using data analysis, reaching objective conclusions and examining causality between events), perhaps in order to answer questions framed by medical and psychiatric practice.

More generally, the patient homicide governance space is made up of different communications about health services and the ability of these services to improve patient health (ie, the application of the binary code *health/illness*). Inquiry recommendations indicate the application of the medical code by proposing ways of improving the health of local populations (eg, new staff training programmes, better communication about psychiatric conditions). Yet, other forms of communication are relevant. Economic and legal communications appear, making the governance space more complex. The conclusions, findings and recommendations of independent investigations may originate in one specific functional perspective (eg, improving health, improving resource efficiency), but the complexity of the health care governance space and the operational closure of the communication systems that constitute it means that not any one perspective can wholly represent the complexity of the space or commandeer it for the purposes of normative change.

These theoretical arguments enable an original and searching critique of central policy ambitions (eg, the learning of lessons). They also help recognise the limitations (eg, unintended consequences) associated with patient homicide investigatory governance. These arguments are, admittedly, eccentric and unusual in design because they are derived from Luhmann's social systems theory. Readers may question the utilisation of a theory that, according to some scholars, empties society of all its content and eradicates the individual. The questioning is understandable. Independent investigations engage with highly contentious and emotive issues that are traumatic for families and staff. Some readers may wonder whether recruiting Luhmann's theory for the purpose of examining these concerns diminishes the experiences and significance of these groups. The author's response to these concerns is categorical; individuals matter more than ever but not in a way that we are used to. Luhmann does not eradicate the individual. He repositions the individual. The essential qualities that we associate with individuals (eg, consciousness) are recognised by his theory. Luhmann's work constitutes a more precise assessment of these qualities and their relevance to society. From a person's thoughts to how they are communicated about, Luhmann's work helps realise the significance of those involved in patient homicide inquiries. The notion that inquiries are formal procedures that uncover truth and secure accountability are not incorrect portrayals. However, they oversimplify a complex health care governance space. The present chapter represents an effort to recapture the complexity involved. It reliably depicts the communicational complexity by referring to society's complexity and differentiation.[68] After all, independent investigations are expected to engage with some of the most important and complex aspects of society (eg, health care services, public confidence, safety, the mass media). A theory (ie, systems theory) that acknowledges complexity as communicational is, therefore, the most suitable one for framing questions and concerns around these aspects.

The following chapter focuses on a major challenge that investigators commonly face: time. Inquiries communicate about individuals and events, as we have seen, but they also communicate about time. Health services are well known for their regular and sizeable administrative changes. Inquiries may take up to four years to commence. Changes in services occur. It is challenging for investigators to look back into the past and investigate health services because services become unrecognisable in a short space of time. For Luhmann, time is of significance too. Social systems of communication are oriented to their past communications. They communicate about the past and the future. Time is a crucial concept that is worthy of further examination. The following chapter also explores the concept of accountability, which is another familiar element associated with patient homicides. The development of the accountability concept was outlined in Chapter 2 but it is theoretically repositioned in the following chapter. Accountability – traditionally understood – is humanist in design (eg, a touchstone of democracy in politics). It is sometimes referred to as eliciting information and establishing facts. The following chapter, however, repositions it around the concept of communication explained in Chapter 3. In brief, the following chapter considers the argument that accountability is a relationship constructed within social systems of communication as opposed to being a formulaic process of information transmission between account renderers and account elicitors. In the later stages of the next chapter, the concepts of accountability and time are considered together and understood as communicational self-constructions within the patient homicide governance space; both involve society's social systems communicating about the past, in the present, for the purpose of making judgements and decisions that have future implications. These arguments link up with the book's broader thesis that the patient homicide governance space is a communicational space of observation that involves the self-construction of meaning within functionally differentiated autopoietic social communication systems in society. The argument precludes the possibility of directed steering and change, post-homicide, inviting the conclusion that policy makers re-evaluate their normative commitments to improving services and minimising risks.

[68] See also M Brans and S Rossbach, 'The Autopoiesis of Administrative Systems: Niklas Luhmann on Public Administration and Public Policy' (1997) 75(3) *Public Administration* 417, 436.

5

Accountability and Time

I. Introduction

The present chapter focuses on two challenging elements associated with the patient homicide governance space: time and accountability. Chapter 2 explained that a main lever of the governance space – independent investigations – is regarded as occasionally engaging in hindsight bias and counterfactual reasoning. Bias and counterfactual reasoning link up with issues of time and accountability because they involve eliciting utterances from relevant individuals and organisations about past events with a view to forming a socially relevant understanding of them. The relevance of time and accountability to the patient homicide governance space is therefore deserving of closer examination.

The present chapter situates the concepts of accountability and time within the domain of Luhmann's systems theory and continues the task commenced in Chapter 4. Society's communications constitute the fabric of social meaning in situations where investigators elicit accounts (ie, conventional accountability) from health professionals during an interview. The present chapter reframes accountability as a communicative event. Accountability is a communication made within social function systems and it is also a communication about time; it involves the construction of a unique version of time at various moments by function systems that structure relevant events in sequence within the patient homicide governance space. The chapter proceeds by first examining accountability, followed by its relevance to the concept of time.

The issue of time is a problem for independent investigations after patient homicide because they take an average of four years to be completed. An investigator interviewed for the present research commented that it is not uncommon for investigations to begin six or seven years after the incident. These are long periods of time. Significant service changes are bound to occur during the intervening years. One report vividly commented that 'the passage of time may hinder the recollection of clinical witnesses and yield a poor standard of available information within the clinical record'.[1] Clinical documentation may be incomplete. Key witnesses may be untraceable.

[1] A Johnstone, *Independent Investigation into the Care and Treatment of Mr X by the Lincolnshire Partnership NHS Foundation Trust and the Avon and Wiltshire Mental Health Partnership NHS Trust* (NHS South West SHA and East Midlands SHA, Health and Social Care Advisory Service (undated)) 15.

The problem of time is amplified by institutional change. The NHS is known for its regular shake-ups at local and national level. The NHS underwent the largest reorganisation in its history in 2012. Market conditions were strengthened. Health care commissioning was placed further into General Practitioner (GP) hands. Regulatory oversight was revamped. Investigators have had to adapt to these conditions. At a local level, NHS Trusts regularly reorganise their departments. Teams, agencies and organisations are disbanded, reconfigured and created. Staff members move on. New staff members are recruited. Services today will not resemble what they were when the homicide was committed. A period of a few years may bring untold change. Investigators are expected to examine the health care services provided to the perpetrator around the time of incident but it is difficult to investigate services that no longer resemble what they once were. Establishing accountability, producing understandings and advancing recommendations for change to services that have changed beyond recognition creates a contradictory dynamic.

The present chapter explores Luhmann's concept of time in order to inform its analysis. For Luhmann, time is self-constructed by social systems of communication.[2] For example, law produces a version of time that is meaningful for its own operations. The relevant legal past in a court case will consist of previous legal decisions and legally relevant 'facts', rather than moral or political arguments. Law may also take months or years to produce a communication (eg, a legal principle) about an event (eg, a fatal stabbing) because litigation proceedings are protracted. The social system of medicine, however, constructs the past medically. The past is relevant according to what is medically significant (ie, previous communications about treatment methods). A stabbing will have significance for the law because the act is filtered through the legal code (ie, *legal/illegal*) and medicine will construct the act through its medical code (ie, *health/illness*). The act's biological consequences for the human body, the treatment required and past communications about how best to stabilise the health of the victim are relevant to medicine. Medicine will produce communications about these events much more quickly than law will produce communications about legality. The temporal rhythms of law and medicine are different. Each social subsystem constructs time uniquely. The concept of time may therefore be used to explain how accountability is constructed within the patient homicide governance space in a dynamic and changing institutional environment.

These problems of time raise implications for what it means to hold services to account for lapses in care. Accountability is often associated with probing individuals for information; a simple equation of asking questions and eliciting answers for example. The problem of time complicates the issue however. The purpose of the present chapter, therefore, is to reconceptualise what it means to

[2] N Luhmann, *Social Systems* (Stanford, Stanford University Press, 1984/1995) 42.

establish accountability in the patient homicide governance space. It theorises the governance space as an observational space of meaning about time produced by society's function systems of communication. Again, following from the previous chapter, the implications of the present chapter's reconceptualisation of time and accountability are assessed. In particular, the thesis that time and accountability are observational self-constructions produced within communication systems opens up an entry point to question and moderate the ambitions (eg, 'learning lessons', 'improving services') that support policy responses to patient homicide.

II. Accountability as Communication

Communication systems, according to Luhmann, are outside the bodies and minds that make up 'the individual'. Communications are accessible by communications only. Individuals, in their systemic plurality, perturb communications but they do not create communications or have a direct relationship with them. Psychic systems couple with communication systems through language, for example. Psychic systems, however, produce thoughts only and they are unable to exercise direct influence over communication systems. Society's communication systems are frameworks of life that operate independently from psychic systems. Psychic systems are fundamentally different from the operations of communication systems (ie, communication). Yet, human beings have been routinely placed at the apex of society. They are assumed to steer society towards improvement, instigate change according to predefined goals and share information harmoniously. Luhmann's theory, replete with unfamiliar terminology, usurps conventional routine. It holds that human beings are unable to occupy a primary vantage point of observation or control over society. Society is too complex for human beings (or anything else) to exercise mastery over. The human being has no transcendental authority or existence. The idea that governance mechanisms, such as independent patient homicide investigations, are procedures that enable individuals to access truth and produce objective facts about homicide is misleading.

The traditional concept of the individual developed in the Western philosophical and political tradition masks the individual's systemic plurality. Similarly, terms like 'inquiry' and 'investigation' mask operatively closed biological, psychic and social systems operating to form the patient homicide governance space.

The general development of the accountability concept was set out in Chapter 1. It explained that accountability is understood in different ways. Traditional understandings reflect its hierarchical portrayal as a legal and political phenomenon. More recent understandings of accountability emphasise its fragmentation. Accountability relationships may be non-hierarchical, formed horizontally between non-state actors and formed for different reasons (eg, financial, performance). Many formulations of the accountability concept emphasise the significance of individuals, the answering of questions and the transmission of information about past conduct between persons or organisations.[3] These different understandings are united by their expressed or implied humanism; they accept that accountability is a vehicle through which individuals steer society towards specific, predefined, goals (eg, truth, legitimacy). Chapter 3, however, explained Luhmann's rejection of humanist explanations on the basis that they are imprecise and unreliable. His work, nevertheless, exhibits diffidence in that it refrains from dismissing these understandings of accountability as wrong. Although Luhmann's work does not, explicitly, study the concept of accountability, his work nevertheless facilitates new understandings of it from a new starting point. The reductionism of conventional accountability concepts sits awkwardly alongside society's complexity. These concepts encourage oversimplification. The present chapter is an opportunity to reconceptualise the concept of accountability within the patient homicide governance space and rehabilitate the concept as a communicative moment in which socially available meaning is produced. Rather than accountability being considered as a procedural relation between an investigation panel and an account-rendering subject (ie, a mental health professional), it is more accurate to frame it as a relation that acquires a distinct, self-constructed meaning within social systems of communication.

The following illustration demonstrates the present chapter's argument. Before an inquiry is commenced, an initial review is undertaken by the investigating company. The initial review will determine what particular issues are relevant and what are less relevant or irrelevant. The reviewer's determination will influence the recognition of relevant account renderers (ie, 'roles' pertinent to the case). These roles are primarily, but not solely, drawn from the medical and psychiatric profession (eg, doctors, psychiatrists, nurses). These roles, clearly, have significance for the social systems of medicine and psychiatry because they are constructions of these systems. The investigator's initial review will also determine the manner in which those occupying these relevant roles are to be questioned. Again, these questions will predominantly hinge on topics relating to the expertise of those in certain roles (eg, doctors, nurses) identified for their relevance (eg, the past administration of treatment to the perpetrator, the health of the perpetrator). Furthermore, the panel is constituted in a way that enables it to address and understand the specific issues raised by these cases. Its members will be selected for the 'roles' they play, the knowledge they have and the experience they hold. These attributes will, primarily, be meaningful from a medical and psychiatric perspective although investigation panels may identify other relevant roles (eg, probation officers, lawyers) that – in one way or another – are relevant to

[3] R Mulgan, '"Accountability": An Ever-expanding Concept?' (2000) 78(3) *Public Administration* 555, 555.

the case but are constructions of other social function systems. If a perpetrator experienced considerable social worker contact preceding the crime, then an investigation will be carried out with social worker expertise on its panel (ie, an expert in communicating through the binary code *help/no help*).[4] If the perpetrator had considerable contact with nursing staff or a probation officer, the panel will be constituted with experts in these fields:

> You focus on the profession. If we're interviewing a consultant psychiatrist, I would take the lead. If we're interviewing a nurse, then a nurse on the panel might take the lead. You might try and line up the interviewee with professional backgrounds sometimes. **Investigator 7**

Furthermore, companies will look to specialist advisers to help them draw out meaningful events:

> Generally, there'll be the key players involved in the patient's care and treatment. I will look at the case management. I will identify with my specialist advisors what I feel we need to understand. **Investigator 2**

Once set up, independent patient homicide investigations will identify relevant account renderers (eg, 'doctors', 'nurses') and formulate leads of interest.

Tables 5.1, 5.2 and 5.3 present a conceptual overview of accountability theorised as a communicative moment. The content of the tables is non-exhaustive. They do not capture all the communicative dynamics that constitute accountability in the patient homicide governance space. Rather, they showcase a series of typical communicative dynamics relating to the constitution of investigation panels (Table 5.1), their investigative approach (Table 5.2) and the identification and significance of the roles they identify for account-rendering purposes (Table 5.3). These dynamics are broken down into relevant organisational systems (ie, the forum), communication systems (eg, medicine, law, the specific roles constructed by communication systems) and the social function (eg, maintaining expectations) they carry out. Furthermore, the tables provide a series of possibilities relating to how a panel might be put together, how an account-rendering witness would be identified and what would normally be expected from both panel members and witnesses. Some roles (eg, psychiatrists), in particular, sit regularly on panels and act as witnesses and some feature less frequently (eg, lay members and probation officers sitting on panels). Nevertheless, panels are always tailored to the facts of a case and investigation managers are prepared to enlist relevant expertise of any description to participate in conducting the investigation.

[4] See JV Wirth, 'The Function of Social Work' (2009) 9(4) *Journal of Social Work*, 405; A Kihlström, 'Luhmann's System Theory in Social Work: Criticism and Reflections' (2012) 12(3) *Journal of Social Work* 287.

Table 5.1 Accountability as communication in the patient homicide governance space: roles

Organisational forum	Accountee	Accountee roles	Function of accountee's role	Significance of account-render's role	Particular expectation met	Relevant function systems
Independent investigation	Independent panel and panel members (eg, psychiatrist, nurse, social worker, etc)	Investigation manager	Distinguishing between abundance and scarcity; distinguishing between payment and non-payment	Providing functional authority; meeting expectations	Providing meaningful accounts of abundance, scarcity, payments and non-payments	The economy
		Psychiatrist	Distinguishing between health and illness; distinguishing mental health and mental illness	Providing functional authority; meeting expectations	Providing meaningful accounts of diagnosis and treatment	Medicine; psychiatry
		Nurse	Distinguishing between care and neglect; distinguishing between health and ill-health	Providing functional authority; meeting expectations	Providing a meaningful accounts of caring practices	Medicine; psychiatry; care

Organisational forum	Accountee	Accountee roles	Function of accountee's role	Significance of account-render's role	Particular expectation met	Relevant function systems
		Social worker	Distinguishing between help and no help; distinguishing between helping and not helping	Providing functional authority; meeting expectations	Providing meaningful accounts of help	Help/social work
		Probation officer	Distinguishing between rehabilitation and no rehabilitation; distinguishing between legality and illegality	Providing functional authority; meeting expectations	Providing a meaningful account of rehabilitation practices	Law; morality
		Lay Person (NHS England (South))	Distinguishing between intimacy and hate, distinguishing between respect and disrespect; distinguishing between esteem and disesteem	Providing functional authority; meeting expectations	Providing meaningful accounts of intimacy and esteem	Intimacy; morality

Table 5.2 Accountability as communication in the patient homicide governance space: methods

Organisational forum	Accountee	Account-eliciting method	Relevant communication subsystem	Significance of accountee's role	Particular expectation met	Relevant communication subsystem
Independent investigation	Independent panel and panel members (eg, psychiatrist, nurse, social worker, etc)	Question and answer	Distinguishing between mental health and mental illness; distinguishing between help and no help; distinguishing between helping and not helping	Providing functional authority; meeting expectations	Reaching truthful findings; verifying adequacy of service provision	Medicine; psychiatry; help social work
		Peer group review	Distinguishing between truth and falsehood; distinguishing between health and ill-health	Providing functional authority; meeting expectations	Providing meaningful accounts of caring practices	Medicine; psychiatry; science
		Psychology-based models	Distinguishing between truth and falsehood	Providing functional authority; meeting expectations	Providing a meaningful account of help	Science
		Conflict	Distinguishing between respect and disrespect	Providing functional authority; meeting expectations	Providing a meaningful account of rehabilitation practices	Morality

Table 5.3 Accountability as communication in the patient homicide governance space: account rendering

Organisational forum	Accountor	Accountor's role	Accountor's function	Significance of account renderer's role	Particular expectation met	Relevant communication systems
Independent investigation	Roles deemed relevant to the investigation	Doctor; psychiatrist	Distinguishing between health and sickness and mental health and mental illness	Providing functional authority; meeting expectations	Providing meaningful accounts of diagnosis and treatment	Medicine; psychiatry
		Nurse	Distinguishing between care and neglect, health and sickness	Providing functional authority; meeting expectations	Providing a meaningful account of caring practices	Medicine; psychiatry; care
		Social worker	Distinguishing between having social problems and absence of social problems; helping and not helping	Providing functional authority; meeting expectations	Providing a meaningful account of the helping practices	Care
		Probation officer	Distinguishing between rehabilitation and no rehabilitation; legality and illegality	Providing functional authority for the investigation; meeting expectations	Providing a meaningful account of rehabilitation practices	Law; morality
		Families	Distinguishing between love and hate; esteem and disesteem	Providing functional authority; meeting expectations	Providing meaningful accounts of love and esteem	Intimacy; morality
		NHS Trust directors	Distinguishing between health and sickness and mental health and mental illness; distinguishing between truth and falsehood; distinguishing between power and no power	Providing functional authority; meeting expectations	Providing meaningful accounts of recommendations, health service adequacy and reliable investigation findings	Medicine; psychiatry; science
Courts; law firms	Roles deemed relevant to law	Lawyers; judges; law enforcers; defendants	Distinguishing between legality and illegality	Providing functional authority; maintaining expectations	Providing meaningful accounts of legality and illegality	Law

Table 5.1 demonstrates that calling, say, a psychiatrist to account for his or her past decisions is something that must be meaningful within the social subsystem of psychiatry. Similarly, a family member's account of their relationship with a loved one and the degree to which the investigators are esteemed may be regarded as understandings formed in the social systems of intimacy and morality respectively.[5] A significant aspect of an investigation, however, is oriented towards confirming whether the past decisions of those called to account were consistent with the health of the patient and others around him or her. Social systems of communications, therefore, enable accountability relationships to have meaning and to maintain the expectation that the inquiry is predicated on tranches of functional (autopoietic) authority. Social systems of communication, such as medicine, provide an overarching structure of meaning that those involved (eg, inquiry panel members, account givers) – in their systemic plurality as living and thinking beings – participate in as incomplete 'persons'. Yet, the socially available meanings that are produced in the investigatory space are wholly separate from the beings that step into their production. Conventional concepts of accountability, therefore, overlook important detail and conceal the operation of medical, scientific and psychiatric communications behind procedures of apparent information transmission by humans for the purposes of truth seeking.

A. Role Bundles and Character Masks

It is pertinent to transition to the issue of how communicative moments between the parties involved in an investigation are created to make what is, on the surface, a straightforward accountability relationship. An investigator interviewed for the present research explained how the questions she uses to hold witnesses to account during inquiries are formulated. She commented that these questions are formulated in accordance with psychology-based models:

> I tend to run a reasonably open interview style, so it'll be reasonably semi-structured. We don't go in with a long list of questions we want answering and then get out of dodge. I like the psychology-model, which is cognitive-based; so strong tell-all instructions – 'tell me about', 'describe', 'walk me through' – those strong, openly directed questions – 'tell me everything you can remember about', 'leave nothing out', 'no details too small'. **Investigator 2**

[5] See generally N Luhmann, *Love as Passion: The Codification of Intimacy* (Cambridge, MA, Harvard University Press, 1986). Luhmann explores the 'semantics of love'. Luhmann explains that love is not a feeling but a form of communication, used pursuant to a symbolic code of *love/hate* and encourages psychic systems to have feelings. See also N Luhmann, 'The Code of the Moral' (1992) 14(4) *Cardozo Law Review* 995, 999. Luhmann writes that 'the moral always concerns the question whether men esteem or disesteem one another'.

The investigator went on to explain that a psychology model was important for getting decision makers to 'embrace' their accountability:

> They needed to be able to embrace their accountability. So, I will use those kinds of techniques from peer group review rather than it being the investigation team against the practitioner, which I think is a very negative construct. You know, 'me against you', 'us investigators', 'you being reviewed', 'we're right, you're wrong'. That's not always the case because I've done it before where I've come out with a mixed bag … Had I run a traditional model we would have said 'you're wrong, we're right'. Again, that's counterproductive to learning in my view. Those are the kinds of things that when we've interviewed, that I will do. And, largely, it's worked well. **Investigator 2**

The reliance on psychology-based models for conducting questioning suggests that science is relevant to the questioning of witnesses. Drawing on themes discussed in Chapter 3, it may further be argued that scientific communications are enslaved. The psychology-based models referred to by the investigator are scientific because they were developed in accordance with scientific principles using accredited scientific methodology. The questioning carried out by the investigator in her investigations is, however, primarily concerned with establishing facts about the perpetrator's care and treatment. From the perspective of systems theory, it could be argued that science is enslaved by the social system of medicine and psychiatry; scientific communications are put to the service of clinical questions (eg, establishing what care and treatment was provided) framed by these other systems of communication. It may be tempting for readers to attribute these ways of investigating to the human agency of the investigator. It may appear that investigators are individuals in control of the production of meaning about health care services and homicide incidents. They ask questions. They obtain answers. They establish facts. They hold people to account. They seek truth. Systems theory prompts us to be more rigorous in our analysis.

Traditional notions of human agency accord primacy to one vantage point that is, on closer inspection, an irreconcilable space of systemic operations (ie, organic matter, thoughts, communication). Communications in particular (eg, science, medicine) are social systems which individuals, as biological and psychic systems, step into. As Lee points out, communication (ie, society) is not inside individuals, but between them.[6] Biological and psychic systems become part of society as meaningful constructs (eg, 'clinician', 'patient'). What is commonly regarded as a process of accountability, in which investigators conduct a line of questioning and elicit information with a view to establishing facts (a staple account of inquiries after homicide), is rather an autopoietic construction of meaning within social systems of communication. It involves the construction of role bundles

[6] DE Lee, 'The Society of Society: The Grand Finale of Niklas Luhmann' (2000) 18(2) *Sociological Theory* 320, 322.

and character masks.[7] The resources of agencies (eg, economic communications) will be communicated about. The consequences of treatment for the biological system of a perpetrator (eg, medical communications) will have meaning for investigators. Lines of questioning are similarly constructed. The answers given will, again, be constructions produced by social systems of communication – typically medicine and psychiatry – on terms that are validated by their internal binary codes. If, in response to an investigator, a doctor or organisational representative provides a defensive or unresponsive account of their conduct, the production of meaningful conclusions in an investigation will be stymied. From a systems-theoretical perspective, such accounts could be regarded as socially unavailable to society. Investigators step into certain social systems of communication, like medicine, when constructing the 'facts'. Conflict or disagreement is likely in cases where witnesses do not step into the same social systems of communication:

> [S]ervices that are open to comment, suggestion and learning are the services that you need to worry least about. One's that are closed, a bit inward looking, a bit defensive – in the inquiries, those are the ones that have the most concerns. **Investigator 7**

Chapter 4 explained that the patient homicide governance space involves conflict and disagreement. Accountability – as a space of social systemic communication – is similarly a battleground for conflict and disagreement:

> Health care professionals kind of have an implied duty to co-operate, to some extent, with investigations and also from the perspective of their employer, they are expected to. So, yes they are co-operative but they are also defensive … generally speaking, in industrial-type settings, the witnesses you interview are being interviewed very much as witnesses. Excepting a few, in a few unusual circumstances, there is not really any question of them being culpable in their own right, so you kind of get a level of co-operation, which is different where the investigation seems to try and do two things. Find root causation in corporate systems which I'm comfortable with, but there's also this trying to attribute accountability or blame to individual clinicians. That's a big tension there. That's difficult. **Investigator 5**

The investigator's comment shows that there might be a moral or ethical duty on health care professionals to cooperate with the investigation. While witnesses may express defensiveness towards the investigator because they do not regard themselves as having made decisions which diminished health care quality, the likely consequence is that the functions associated with the investigation become frustrated and conflict between the parties emerges. The frustration may reflect the prospect of a problem (ie, conducting a meaningful investigation) becoming resistant to a resolution. In such circumstances, these conflicts may become morally charged. The moral realities of investigations were discussed in the previous chapter. There, it was explained that moral communications emerge where

[7] See G Teubner, 'How the Law Thinks: Toward a Constructivist Epistemology of Law' (1989) 23 *Law & Society Review* 727, 741.

there are problems that lack a solution, prompting the parties to step into communications that enable others to be judged as (un)worthy of respect. In other words, there is tension between the moral duty to respect the investigation through cooperation (ie, acting with esteem as opposed to disdain) and the defensiveness exhibited on the grounds of having made clinically sound decisions.

The concept of accountability as communication helps us understand the dynamics of situations beyond the procedural relationship between investigation panels and health care professionals. NHS Trusts, for instance, are held to account after an investigation through recommendations and follow-up:

> There are some aims we've covered which are around what care was provided, but there are other aims. In particular, assurance: 'what's been put in place since?', 'how do we know it's not going to happen again?' … 'was the internal investigation robust?', 'were the [internal] recommendations reasonable, appropriate and have they been implemented?' **Investigator 8**

NHS Trusts will always conduct an internal investigation. A significant part of the independent investigation will be concerned with analysing the Trust's internal investigation report. More often than not, the independent investigation report involves criticising the internal report. NHS Trust internal investigations are usually not as rigorous as the independent investigations commissioned by NHS England. Judgements about the rigour of the internal investigation may be informed by a range of different communications: the independent investigation may consider that the NHS Trust circumscribed their remit too narrowly and NHS Trusts may exclude events in the relevant medical past from its investigations or fail to consider issues relating to resources. NHS Trusts will also be subject to subsequent review regarding what they have done since the investigation was concluded (eg, what changes in clinical practice have been made). Julian Hendy reported that subsequent review is welcomed by families:

> There's been quite a few follow-up investigations into how they've [the NHS Trust] done and what progress they've made which I think is actually quite welcome … it is a way of the investigators going back to see what progress has been made.

NHS Trusts are not passive in these situations however. They have been known to pose questions to investigators, challenge their findings and establish their own version of accountability:

> NHS Trusts are very sensitive to criticism and will make attempts to mimimise. In the end, they'll have to agree at least to the report's accuracy. They may not agree with the findings but they must accept the accuracy. And secondly, they have to accept the recommendations. And there may be some discussions about the recommendations that are in there before it is finally signed off. That is the leverage they have as an organisation to try and influence things. **Investigator 10**

The 'leverage' described by the investigator is sometimes used aggressively:

> Strongly worded letters telling us that the investigators have got it wrong. That there's a difference of opinion and that their version of the truth is the real truth. **Investigator 8**

The investigator was asked whether NHS Trusts support their objections with evidence. The investigator replied that they do not and acknowledged that the situation was pressurising. Families may also be involved in subsequent processes of review by investigators of NHS Trusts, in the form of seeking assurances about the safety of services. The issue of service safety is explained in more detail in the next chapter but it is relevant here insofar as families – as part of their tendency to communicate through a code of intimacy and morality – may also communicate about time and the desire for the future to be safer. Julian Hendy explains that families look to investigators to provide an assurance that services are safe and that families will be spared a hard time in the future:

> So we're trying to find out essentially, what the care was like, could it have been better, was there anything that could have been different that might have meant that someone didn't need to die and that's basically what we're after. And what could they learn to make sure it doesn't happen to anybody else. And I think a lot of families are not punitive. They are angry, they don't want to see heads on a pole, they're not looking for scapegoats particularly, they just want to know services are safe and that no other families are going to go through a hard time and I don't think that's unreasonable really … the families say 'we want to know what you've been doing in a year's time. Can we go back and ask?' … we're trying to get them to learn.

Progress may therefore mean different things in different contexts. For investigators, there will be an emphasis on progress in medical terms. Much of their focus will be taken up with checking whether services are benefiting the health of patients and minimising the possibility of future loss of life; accountability has a medical meaning. There might be economic considerations relating to the implementation of recommendations, however, and an accompanying politically driven reorganisation of services, alongside the interest of families in obtaining apologies and safety assurances.

The present section illustrates that there are many dimensions to accountability when systems theory is recruited as a framework for understanding it. It is a multi-varied concept. The conventional appearance of accountability as a process of asking questions, eliciting answers and making judgements obscures a constellation of observations within social systems of communications that make sense of their uniquely constructed environments. These observations are a multi-layered space of meaning. Different meanings may be produced about the same event (eg, a past decision) by different 'roles' involved in the investigation.

It is possible to further develop the present section's depiction of accountability by referring to Luhmann's ideas about how the political system constantly generates accountability through welfare state expansion. The NHS is a significant part of the British welfare state and it is possible to link up with Luhmann's ideas on politics with a view to enriching the present chapter's examination of accountability in the patient homicide governance space.

B. Accountability and Politics

The present chapter conceptualises accountability in the patient homicide governance domain as an observational space of meaning produced within society's function systems of communication. The observations of social function systems are self-made. They refer to their own communications when constructing their social environment. Accountability relationships are self-constructions within these systems about the relevant past, in the present. Accountability – as a sterile process of questioning and eliciting information – is not an incorrect portrayal. However, it is an incomplete and oversimplified one. It assumes that the positing of questions and the eliciting of answers is a straightforward relationship of sender–receiver information transmission. Luhmann's theory posits that the transmission metaphor is no longer relevant in a functionally differentiated society. From the perspective of the present chapter, these oversimplified versions of accountability are unable to serve as a reliable starting point of analysis of what accountability is. A fuller conceptualisation of accountability must take into account the tripartite distinction between biological, psychic and communication systems and consider communication systems as wholly resistant to replication or direct causal influence.

As a process of questioning, eliciting information and passing judgement, accountability must ultimately mean something for it to be realisable as accountability in a specific context. Accordingly, accountability relationships are possible but only as self-constructions of meaning within society's social systems of communication. Independent patient homicide investigations involve the self-construction of accountability relationships in the medical system (eg, enquiries made by trained health professionals into the quality of past medical decisions), legal system (eg, acknowledgement of the perpetrator's criminal culpability), economic system (eg, enquiries into the resource capacity of health services) and morality system (eg, the formation of judgements about a person's willingness to help the inquiry with its enquiries). A dimension of accountability that has yet to be explored here is the growing expectation within investigations and outside of them in other channels of health care governance to scrutinise a broader range of service elements beyond care and treatment provision:

> [T]he NHS … is a wide variety of providers and I think since Mid-Staffordshire, where a supposed quality assurance and oversight with SHAs [Strategic Health Authorities] and commissioning bodies – PCTs [Primary Care Trusts] – was found to be lacking, we are being required to look at the whole approach to health care. Not just the provision, but what was purchased and what scrutiny took place and checks and quality assurance of what was provided. **Investigator 8**

Health care provision, budgeting, purchasing and regulation are a few elements that investigations are increasingly expected to consider. Investigations are, furthermore, expected to investigate commissioning. Commissioning is an activity that is economic and financial, primarily and involves the allocation of health care resources over a specific geographical area by CCGs:

> My role is to carry out the independent homicide reviews, but also to expand our role into activities that are more proactive, for whoever needs them – CCGs, Trusts. **Investigator 1**

Commissioning requires medical expertise because the health needs of the local population must be reliably understood before the allocation of resources can take place. Commissioning is, however, a complex task that involves accounting and budgeting, in addition to clinical expertise. It is notable that independent investigations after homicide are increasingly expected to communicate about commissioning in the form of follow-ups after an investigation has been concluded. The expectation has been criticised by some investigators:

> I don't believe that the investigators are the best people to do that follow-on check six months on. We've got no management over them [CCGs]. We've got no leverage over them, badgering them over what was produced in the report. And, what's less clear to me is when we produce our six months report showing deficiencies, I'm not sure who's picking that up really and what seems evident is that there's a huge dearth of skills and talent in the CCGs to do this follow-up work and to do this challenge. I believe when it comes to the political stuff it goes back to that last major upheaval of the NHS, which saw SHAs go and PCTs go. There was a lot of structure, systems and experience which got lost. And often, when you look at CCGs … they're the people who've should have some leverage over it, with old money if they need to. But they'll say they haven't got the experience to do it, to challenge. They wouldn't know about it. **Investigator 10**

The investigator's comment illustrates how accountability, as a process of eliciting accounts from relevant health care bodies and personnel for the purpose of bringing about improvements, is meaningfully constructed by those with specific knowledge and expertise relevant to the task. The investigator identifies health care commissioners (ie, CCGs) as ideal candidates for the task because they should have the necessary organisational and economic expertise, in addition to their medical expertise. The investigator, however, describes the undesired consequences of politically driven 'upheaval' of the NHS (ie, political change has irritated the social system of economics in the form of resource scarcity), with the result that commissioners lack the resources necessary to form accountability relationships and communicate about tranches of expertise associated with commissioning. Independent investigators are thus expected to step into the breach and do the job that commissioners are ideally best placed to do. For the investigator, a difficult burden is placed on investigators. They are expected to expand their role and create accountability relationships in different areas of health care services. They are expected to step into specific modes of communicating. The modes of communication the extended role requires (eg, economic expertise) constitute systems of meaning (ie, the economy) that investigators do not easily step into.

It may be argued that the expectation placed on investigators to hold a broad range of actors to account for their decisions and conduct after an inquiry has been completed is part of a broader assumption of accountability by the social subsystem of politics. The NHS, as a publicly funded institution that delivers a variety of health care services, forms part of what is commonly referred to as the welfare state. Central to the welfare state's purpose is the provision of social help.[8] It has emerged in tandem with the growth of civil rights and an explosion of 'opportunities for successful assertion of rights by outsiders, dependents, and subordinates against society's managers and authorities'.[9] Higher expectations of institutional performance by society's elite members are generated.[10] These rising expectations to tackle social problems (eg, poverty, illness) have been addressed by governments with political measures that seek to ambitiously solve these problems with results-oriented measures.[11] The NHS is regulated by a host of institutions on behalf of the political system, in the interest of welfare. For example, NHS England forms part of a complex network of political institutions. It regulates the financing of health care services. It commissions independent homicide investigations and it is inextricably linked to how the political system functions as an autopoietic communication subsystem of society. Investigations apply political power along the diffuse chain of political power and they carry out a series of tasks (ie, decision making, investigating) mandated by those who exercise political power (ie, the Department of Health, NHS England).

C. The Political System

Luhmann's theory of politics is introduced now to explain the growth in political accountability for welfare problems and in particular how the growth relates to the patient homicide governance space. Luhmann's theory of politics is positioned in the broader context of his general social system theory. His theory departs from mainstream political theories in a fundamental respect: it rejects the notion that politics, in the form of 'the state', is a definitive location where social stability is ensured.

For centuries, the state has been designated as a centrepiece of society. It is looked upon to solve a range of problems in different areas, from health to the economy. For Luhmann, 'the state' is a semantic construction of the political system.

[8] N Luhmann, *Political Theory in the Welfare State* (Berlin and New York: de Gruyter, 1990) 21.

[9] See M Galanter, 'The Turn Against Law: The Recoil Against Expanding Accountability' (2002) 81(1) *Texas Law Review* 285, 287. The expansion of law in the United States at least has led to the enlargement of accountability among society's elites.

[10] ibid.

[11] See ibid.

It is a convenient fiction constructed within the political system to give the latter recognisable order.[12] The need for the welfare state fiction arises in a functionally differentiated society. Politics, once under the omnipresent authority of God, is now a functionally differentiated social system of communication that is justified using concepts like 'democracy' and 'the state'. As an autonomous function system unable to look outside of itself for justification, politics is left to justify itself.

Politics, like all other social systems, is paradoxical. It may be argued to be a self-referential system of communication that lacks objective legitimacy. Luhmann's concepts of social autopoiesis and operational closure precludes the replacement of political operations with the operations of another system. The semantics of 'the state' play a vital role in obscuring the paradox. They frame the political system as a distinct site or location where power is applied. Luhmann's theory of social systems, however, wholly rejects the idea that social systems occupy sites or locations. Granted, the author of the present book refers to the patient homicide governance 'space' throughout, but the reference to 'space' is not a subscription to the view that social communication systems occupy a finite space, as such. Social communications are diffuse. They emerge everywhere. They have no specific location as such. It just so happens that they, too, emerge when patient homicides occur and that the communications produced about these events and the health care provided to the perpetrator form complex structures of life that constitute a diffuse governance space. To depict vital social functions as occupiers of contained locations and, under certain conditions, removable by external forces (ie, individuals or other social systems) is impossible under Luhmann's theory.

The political system under Luhmann's theory is autopoietic. It produces political communications about its politically relevant environment.[13] Its function is to enforce collectively binding decisions. These decisions are enforced through the provision of power. Power, therefore, is the crucial communicative medium for the political system. Politics does not communicate in any other way. For Luhmann, the political system is only capable of applying power (eg, regulations, decisions, legislation, circulars) and is identifiable as the political system because of the power currency it autopoietically trades in. Power differentiates politics from other social systems of communication that do not concern themselves with power. Applying power in a functionally differentiated society, however, is a complex affair. Applying it in a functionally differentiated society is unpredictable because society's social systems – medicine, law and economics for example – do not recognise power. Yet, the political system has built up a sufficient level

[12] See M King and C Thornhill, *Niklas Luhmann's Theory of Politics and Law* (Basingstoke, Palgrave Macmillan, 2005) 78.

[13] Luhmann, *Political Theory* (n 8) 73.

of internal complexity to deal with the unpredictable arrangement of society. Producing fictions about itself (ie, 'the State') in order to create communicative possibilities is an example. It also reduces social complexity through making distinctions that originate in a primary distinction of *power/no power*.

When power in society was first distinguished from what lacks power, the political system has since continued to make further distinctions (eg, *government/governed*, *government/opposition*, *left-wing/right-wing*) that reproduce the initial distinction between power and no power.[14] Power is diffuse and endlessly distributed along highly complex networks that include ministerial departments, committees and small administrative entities.[15] Take, for example, the NHS. Not only do government ministers and political parties communicate power, but so too do lobbyists, patient groups, NHS Trusts and a range of other bodies (eg, independent regulators, non-departmental executive bodies). These actors reproduce political communications (among other communications) and trade in power.

Moreover, in reducing social complexity, the political system has differentiated into autonomous subsystems that rely on the existence of each other to operate (ie, they are structurally coupled). These are politics (ie, the formation of premises for future decision making; political rank), administration (ie, the implementation of decisions) and the public (eg, voters who are subject to political power and who exercise it during elections). What appears to be a demonstration of legitimate democracy is, rather, the recursive communication of power within the political system between the three political subsystems. The subsystem of politics generates the premises for decisions (eg, manifestos, parliamentary debates) by the administration (eg, statutes), which the public accept or reject by voting and campaigning.[16]

The political system is extremely limited in what it can do. It communicates power and nothing else. Political authority is generated politically. It may rely on the existence of other social systems, such as law (ie, through legally constituted parliaments), but these systems are incapable of directly replacing political communications. To do so would frustrate the function of the political system. Political legitimacy is constructed from within, expressing itself symbolically in the form of political declarations and democratic justifications.

The political system may therefore be regarded as inherently paradoxical but it is generally regarded as capable of intervening in other function systems of society and managing crisis. For Luhmann, the idea that politics is society's superintendent is a myth that the political system requires to understand itself. He adds, however, that the myth is dangerously put into practice. It is a dangerously-practised myth because most problems that society encounters are irresolvable through a sole

[14] See King and Thornhill, *Niklas Luhmann's Theory* (n 12) 120.
[15] ibid 123.
[16] ibid 60–61.

appeal to power. For instance, the provision of medical treatment is bound to fail or cause untold harm if power is used to regulate it. Indeed, there were instances during the twentieth century (eg, Nazi Germany, Soviet Russia) where medicine was put to the service of power, resulting in traumatic experiences. A key aspect of Luhmann's theory of politics, however, is the argument that the myth of state primacy underpins the emergence of the modern welfare state. As will soon be discussed, there is a tendency for politics to dedicate resources to helping the welfare state grow. For Luhmann, however, the welfare state is also a fiction that politics constructs and uses to organise itself. Faith is placed in the welfare state, of which the NHS is a part, by politics in response to public opinion. In particular, these responses may involve decisions being made to address the protection of citizens from dangerous mental health patients and the risks posed by certain activities that are regarded as requiring strict oversight.[17] It is important to note that the myths of state primacy and the welfare state conceal the excessive assumption of accountability for welfare problems as an expression of recursively generated political power.

Luhmann would designate the creation of the NHS as an example of an excessive assumption of accountability. The assumption of excessive accountability by politics in the form of a decision premise (eg, that the population's health must be improved) is translated by the subsystem of administration (eg, the Department of Health) into decisions (eg, statutes, regulations, instructions) that aim to discharge accountability. A burgeoning of bureaucracy then ensues:

> In all these regards, political action in the welfare state has to begin from the fact that the circumstances towards which it directs its efforts are changed in unexpected ways by the effort itself. Politics already is in a position where it constantly has to deal with *self-created realities*. The needs, unpleasantries, the almost unsolvable problems that it faces are partially of its own work. One only has to consider the topic of bureaucracy. In the long or short run, the consequence will be a fractured relationship with its own goals.[18]

Resources are devoted by the social subsystem of politics to manage themes originating in other function systems, such as medicine. According to Luhmann, political management leads to the problems of 'overtax' and excessive inclusivity; the social system of politics creates an unwieldy bureaucracy, to the extent that its function (ie, to make collectively binding decisions through power application) is interrupted by a growing need to manage the bureaucracy created to manage society's welfare. Power becomes ill-suited to solving economic or medical problems and the political system may compromise its own function if it regards welfare (health) problems as political issues. These problems are most suitably addressed by other systems (eg, medicine), but politics – in the guise of the welfare state

[17] N Luhmann, *Risk: A Sociological Theory* (New Brunswick, Aldine Transaction, 1993/2008) 163.
[18] Luhmann, *Political Theory* (n 8) 24.

(ie, the NHS) – performs in areas not relevant to its own operations.[19] It extends tasks and creates new bureaucratic links at the interface of system relations.[20]

The excessive assumption of accountability by the political system is predicated on the general assumption that the welfare state occupies a supreme vantage point in society from which to steer the latter.[21] A structure of inclusion is created and affirmed by decision premises (ie, politics), decisions (ie, administration) and relevant feedback (ie, public opinion). The entire population's welfare needs are constructed as politically relevant. They *must* be addressed through the medium of power.

According to Luhmann, however, politics may cease to function properly in such circumstances. The political system, instead, engages in performance:

> This means that too many decisions are accompanied by further decisional necessities relative to the success that can be attained through them. Thus 'bureaucratization' is the direct consequence of increasing political performance in domains where one can attain success not simply or even primarily through the production of binding decisions.[22]

Political performance – defined by Luhmann as the political system managing its own complexity – includes the latter's excessive assumption of accountability for all welfare problems. It leads to an 'astonishing expansion of competence in the welfare state' and necessitates 'gigantic and uncontrollable' bureaucratic machinery.[23] For Luhmann, an uncontrollable bureaucracy is a consequence of the political system's inclusivity. Like all social systems in a functionally differentiated society, the political system is necessarily inclusive and leads to an extensive assumption of accountability for all welfare problems, leading to overtax:

> The concept of inclusion means the encompassing of the entire population in the performance of the individual function systems. On the one hand, this concerns *access* to these benefits and, on the other, *dependence* of individual modes of living on them. To the extent that inclusion is achieved, groups disappear that do not or only marginally participate in social living.[24]

For Luhmann, social systems encompass the entire population insofar as the former are functionally relevant to the population's mode of living.[25] We do not live in just one social system. We step into many when we visit a doctor (ie, the medical system), pay for groceries (ie, economic system) and vote in elections (ie, political systems). Inclusivity is a precondition for the modern political system. The political system, however, has interpreted the condition of inclusivity as

[19] King and Thornhill, *Niklas Luhmann's Theory* (n 12) 84.
[20] Luhmann, *Political Theory* (n 8) 76.
[21] See King and Thornhill, *Niklas Luhmann's Theory* (n 12) 84.
[22] Luhmann, *Political Theory* (n 8) 76.
[23] Luhmann, *Risk* (n 17) 145.
[24] Luhmann, *Political Theory* (n 8) 34.
[25] ibid 35.

essential for democracy. Needs and interests, be they medical, economic or legal, are constructed as political themes by politicians for the purposes of attaining office and maintaining power.[26] Luhmann's depiction of the welfare state is one of excessive inclusivity, potentially undermining the ability of other function systems to discern themes relevant to their own operations. In brief, the political system may politicise other function systems and bring about functional de-differentiation.

D. Patient Homicide: An Expansion of Accountability

The present chapter's detour into Luhmann's theory of politics serves an important purpose. It provides a framework on which the expectations placed on investigators to investigate broader swathes of health services in their investigations – from provision, to commissioning to quality assurance – may be analysed. The claims of investigators that independent investigations are increasingly expected to examine health services generally, as opposed to discrete areas of provision well suited to their experience, may be explained as a symptom of the political system's impulse to assume accountability for everything that occurs within health care services. Investigators, after being delegated the task of investigating services by NHS England, are expected to assume the responsibility of ensuring that tranches of welfare state activity – from provision, to commissioning and quality assurance – are operating satisfactorily after a homicide investigation has been concluded. It could be said that these expectations constitute political performance (ie, investigating the bureaucratic machinery of commissioning set up by the political system):

> The first ones that I did was very much about the Trust, but now when looking at what care and treatment was provided, we're looking at what was commissioned and what was the cluster and pathway that was expected to join. So it's not just about what the NHS provided but also what they were expected to provide and who checked that they were providing it properly. **Investigator 9**

The same investigator described independent investigations as ruffling feathers throughout the whole system of care:

> As the nature of the investigations has changed, you have to understand the whole system – the care pathway, the agencies involved, the commissioning processes – you start to ruffle some feathers elsewhere. **Investigator 9**

Another investigator described a growing expectation on investigations to hold those in senior positions to account:

> [W]e are being asked to question systems of assurance and commissioning. Increasingly, people at a very senior level who are meant to offer assurance and who are

[26] ibid 36.

> meant to commission process are often taken aback that we could dare question what is going on. **Investigator 8**

These statements support the argument that the patient homicide governance space is embroiled in political performance. Granted, the governance space is predominantly constituted with communications in the social systems of medicine and psychiatry, but not exclusively. It is also an economic structure of life for investigators, especially on the issue of costs, for instance, and it is furthermore constituted by structures of political life also. The political system delegates power through the subsystem of administration (eg, NHS England) and from there new bureaucratic tasks are created for investigators, such as holding different aspects of services to account. The expectation on independent investigations to conduct a foray into the NHS bureaucratic machinery is a central example.

The present chapter has developed a systems-theoretical concept of accountability that has different dimensions. One dimension relates to the communicative essence of accountability. It is correct to view accountability as a procedure of asking questions and eliciting answers, but it is not enough to completely capture the accountability concept. The process must have meaning and meaning is argued here to be dependent on the social system of communication that generates the meaning. An accountability relationship may have a medical meaning in the medical system or a legal meaning in the legal system in a range of moments (eg, witness identification, questioning, eliciting information, follow-up). Crucially, however, accountability has a uniquely political dimension in independent investigations. It may assume the form of political performance. Some of the investigators interviewed explained that they are increasingly expected to hold broader areas of health services (eg, commissioning) to account through their investigations. The chapter thus far engages Luhmann's theory of politics in order to analyse these developments. Luhmann argues that accountability expansion in the context of the population's welfare needs is a consequence of the over-inclusive and 'democratic' qualities of the political system. The welfare state is the political system's way of securing democratic conditions, by interpreting society's inclusiveness as an essential condition for democratic power. In framing a multitude of population needs and interests as political themes and to assume accountability for them however, the welfare state overtaxes itself by resourcing large bureaucratic machinery. A central argument advanced by the present section is that investigators are caught up in the bureaucratic overtax. They are increasingly burdened by the political system (eg, the power exercised by NHS England) to investigate broad swathes of public health services after a homicide has been committed.

The following section transitions to the issue of time because time is yet another important conceptual aspect of accountability, systems theory and the patient homicide governance space. The concept of time and its significance for systems theory is explained, followed by its relevance to inquiries and the concept of accountability developed in the present chapter. The aim of the transition now is to advance the book's thesis that the patient homicide governance space is a diffuse set of observational structures of communication – provided by social systems of communication – in society.

III. The Concept of Time

'Intuitively, everyone knows very well what time is, but its mystery becomes impenetrable when we try to explain it'.[27] Time is elusive. We are familiar with linear conceptions of time, particularly those relating to astronomy, physics, history or the clock. Yet, time varies historically, culturally, socially and theoretically.[28] It is 'social, plural and rhetorical'.[29] It refers to 'a specific human ability to work on the experience of change, to react, to organise and confer meaning on the experience'.[30] It refers to social activities imbued with a distinct 'rhythm'.[31] For example, holidays, working days and elections punctuate social life with rhythmic intervals. The view that time is rhythmic has a long pedigree. It is traceable back to Durkheim's view that reality is produced in the beliefs, practices and activities of their subscribers.[32] Social beliefs, practices and activities provide the conditions under which the present and the future come to be meaningful.[33] These conditions enable social coordination and create premises for distinct forms of future action.[34]

The relevance of meaning to the concept of time is important. Luhmann provides an account of how meaning is produced in society and time is equally important to his description. For Luhmann, time is one of three dimensions of meaning in which social systems operate. The other two dimensions relate to the material covered in Chapter 3: the material (or factual) dimension and the social dimension.[35]

[27] S Tabboni, 'The Idea of Social Time in Norbert Elias' (2001) 10(1) *Time & Society* 5, 6.

[28] See R Nobles and D Schiff, *Observing Law Through Systems Theory* (London, Hart Publishing, 2012) 8–12. See also H Nowotny, 'Time and Social Theory: Towards a Social Theory of Time' (1992) 1(3) *Time & Society* 421, 421, 423.

[29] J Harrington, 'Time as a Dimension of Medical Law' (2012) 20(4) *Medical Law Review* 491, 491.

[30] Tabboni, 'The Idea of Social Time' (n 27) 6; N Elias, *Time: An Essay* (Oxford, Blackwell, 1992) 46: 'the word "time" is a symbol of a relationship that a human group of beings biologically endowed with the capacity for memory and synthesis establishes between two or more continua of changes, one of which is used by it as a frame of reference or standard of measurement for the other or others'.

[31] Nowotny, 'Time and Social Theory' (n 28) 422; JM Domingues, 'Sociological Theory and the Space-Time Dimension of Social Systems' (1995) 4 *Time & Society* 233, 236.

[32] E Durkheim, *The Division of Labour in Society* (New York, The Free Press, 1964) 79–80.

[33] See H Nowotny, 'Time Structuring and Time Measurement: On the Interrelation Between Timekeepers and Social Time' in JT Fraser and N Lawrence (eds), *The Study of Time II* (Berlin, Springer, 1975) 326.

[34] Nowotny, 'Time and Social Theory' (n 28) 433.

[35] Luhmann, *Risk* (n 17) 51; Luhmann, *Social Systems* (n 2) 80.

The three dimensions of meaning 'can be described as forms of observing the world with the aid of certain distinctions'.[36] The material (or factual) dimension is concerned with the distinction between system and environment (see Chapter 3). In other words, a system's existence is established through the drawing of distinctions by its own operations. For example, the social subsystems of medicine and psychiatry will distinguish an event on the basis of its relevance to physical and mental health. The social dimension of meaning, on the other hand, draws a different set of distinctions. It refers to asking of every meaning produced whether another experiences it in exactly the same way.[37] As a realm of perception and anticipation of the perception of others,[38] Luhmann refers to the social dimension as the drawing of a distinction between ego and alter.[39] For example, the semantics of competition are an aspect of the social dimension.[40] Competition involves the continual anticipation of others' experience of thinking (ie, psychic systems), the pursuit of resources (ie, social system of economics), the expansion of power (ie, social system of politics) and academic progress (ie, social system of education).[41] The present monograph has thus far been concerned with the material and social dimension. The present chapter, however, shifts the emphasis to the temporal dimension and its relevance for understanding the patient homicide governance space. The temporal dimension is used when something is to be observed with the aid of the distinction drawn between 'before' and 'after'.[42]

Chapters 3 and 4 explained that social systems reduce complexity because their codes and programmes enable events (eg, social communication, the physical world) to be selected for their functional significance. Selecting all possibilities at one time is impossible however. Social function systems are unable to represent society's complexity in its entirety. God used to be an omnipotent observer that could represent such complexity, but social systems today have to make choices.[43] Making choices enables further choices to be made. Order begins to form. An initial choice forms a ditch in the dead, meaningless landscape, followed by a series of choices that firm up the ditch, creating a channel, after which a river is formed.[44] Choices cohere over time into a system of communication and form a fabric of time for that system. Social systems – and therefore society – may even be regarded *as* time.[45]

[36] Luhmann, *Risk* (n 17) 51.
[37] Luhmann, *Social Systems* (n 2) 80.
[38] ibid 306.
[39] ibid 80.
[40] ibid 382.
[41] See ibid 383.
[42] Luhmann, *Risk* (n 17) 51.
[43] M Tada, 'Time as Sociology's Basic Concept: A Perspective from Alfred Schutz's Phenomenological Sociology and Niklas Luhmann's Social Systems Theory' (2018) *Time & Society* at 9 (forthcoming).
[44] ibid.
[45] ibid 10.

Time, as a dimension of meaning, consists of many variables.[46] On the one hand, social systems of communication exist in the present only. As soon as communication is produced, it disappears and is then replaced with another communication. Communication is therefore always present. One crucial variable of time is the irreversibility of the present.[47] Events occur in the present in what is perceived to be an inevitable and irreversible flow of time. Examples may include the passing of a train or the falling of an apple from a tree. These events take an inevitable degree of time to happen and they are eventful because they are differentiated from what preceded them.[48] The example of a passing train is preceded by a train approaching. An apple falling from a tree is preceded by its motionless state when attached to the tree branch. According to Luhmann, the present as an irreversibility is one kind of present. It is symbolised as a certainty.[49]

Luhmann contends, however, that the concept of the present as a certainty is accompanied by a second version of the present that relates to the production of meaning by society's function systems.[50] Luhmann writes that 'the present becomes the turning point which switches the process of time from past into future' and 'the relevance of time … depends upon the capacity to mediate relations between past and future in a present'.[51] Mediating the link between the past and the future is, for Luhmann, crucial to understanding time as something constructed in the present by autopoietic communication systems.

Luhmann develops these ideas by claiming that nothing in the past or future is open to experience.[52] The present is either the present past or the present future. The past and future are always out of reach. Social systems construct 'their own boundaries of relevance in the directions of the future and the past and their own rules (which must always be practiced in the present) for linking future and past (their own and the environment's) events'.[53] The past and the future are, therefore, horizons of reference that social systems use to self-construct their distinct realities:

> The essential characteristic of a horizon is that we can never touch it, never get at it, never surpass it, but in spite of that, it contributes to the definition of the situation. Any movement and any operation of thought only shifts the guiding horizon but never attains it.[54]

To illustrate, a surgical operation may be understood as a series of movements learned by surgeons during their time at medical school. The operation begins

[46] Luhmann, *Social Systems* (n 2) 185.
[47] ibid 42.
[48] ibid 288.
[49] ibid.
[50] ibid 78.
[51] N Luhmann, 'The Future Cannot Begin: Temporal Structures in Modern Society' (1976) 43(1) *Social Research* 130, 133 and 137.
[52] ibid 78.
[53] Luhmann, *Social Systems* (n 2) 186.
[54] Luhmann, 'The Future Cannot Begin' (n 51) 140.

when the surgeon picks up the scalpel and ends when he leaves the theatre.[55] The social subsystem of medicine structures the operation by referring to past communications on what surgical movements benefit the health of the patient. Here, the medical past contributes to what the situation means for the surgeon and others involved in the operation. In contrast to the first version of the present described by Luhmann as irreversible, the second version of the present is reversible. Chapter 3 explained that social systems of communication are autopoietic and self-referential. They refer to their own operations (ie past communications) in order to produce meaning about their uniquely constructed environment. Luhmann writes that 'Self-reference enables one to return to earlier experiences or actions, and it continuously indicates this possibility: a thing is still where one left it; a mistake can be undone'.[56] Social systems, therefore, refer to their own operations for the purposes of reversing events. The social system of medicine may provide for corrective surgery if previous surgeries are deemed unsuccessful. Science may (and indeed has) revisited scientific theories and replaced them with new ones. The legal system strives to place claimants in negligence cases in the position they were in before experiencing loss (eg, physical injury) by awarding compensation. Social systems of communication, from Luhmann's perspective, reverse events.

A. The Construction of Time in the Patient Homicide Governance Space

Independent patient homicide investigations play a crucial part in constructing time. Here, time is constructed with meaning. Meaningful time, from the investigator's point of view, begins from when the first contact was made between the perpetrator and mental health services. Subsequent contacts are identified right up until the last one prior to the incident occurring. These contacts are meaningful from a psychiatric perspective and are placed within a chronology of time, enabling a meaningful concept of time to emerge for the investigation. Each contact is situated in relation to what contact was established before and after it. The initial identification of the first medical contact is comparable to the etching of a small ditch into the meaningless landscape, after which further choices are made to identify relevant past events of medical significance, all the way up until the final contact of medical significance. A specific channel of time is formed:

> We created a timeline. Then we looked at the contact the service user had with key people prior to the event. It was clear that there was a key worker that was responsible

[55] See Nobles and Schiff, *Observing Law* (n 28) 134 and 135.
[56] Luhmann, *Social Systems* (n 2) 79.

> for co-ordinating … there were two in fact that had spanned time so we knew that we would need to interview those. And also, within the health care professions, there is the issue of supervision, clinical supervision. So, we also interviewed the management, the clinical management of these people to discuss that and also the team manager because one of the issues was timely close-out of actions and being proactive with service users and so on. **Investigator 5**

Investigators refer to case chronologies when generating knowledge about past decisions. They identify the consequences these decisions are perceived to have had on the health condition of the perpetrator and services in general. They identify the effects of decisions to administer medication and the degree of dialogue entered into about the perpetrator. These events are framed as having specific consequences, ranging from their effects on the perpetrator to the ability of services to operate in conformity with clinical policies. A distinct construction of time as a sequence of relevant events within the social function systems of medicine and psychiatry is formed.

The inquiries conducted in the 1990s and earlier emphasised legal expertise when constructing case chronologies. The case chronology for the Ritchie Report was provided by Clunis' solicitor[57] and two lawyers were recruited by *The Falling Shadow* inquiry to examine documentary material dating back over a decade. These experts were chosen for the task of examination on the basis that they possessed 'able and astute eyes'.[58] The phrase 'able and astute eyes' does not mean that the chronology constructed in these cases identified events that were meaningful solely from a legal perspective. Yet, one of the criticisms aimed at *The Falling Shadow* was its overemphasis on legal expertise, as opposed to other types of expertise (eg, psychiatric expertise). Legal expertise is considered to be overly reductionist, excluding non-legal perspectives (eg, medical, morality).[59] It tends to look for breaches of the law and past conduct that would attract legal accountability:

> If I'm doing an investigation from a legal framework point of view, you're looking for causality, you're looking for duty of care, you might be looking for negligence, but also in the legal field you may be giving too much attention to detail. That is the nature of their work. **Investigator 2**

In equal measure, investigations may acquire legal significance and form an aspect of legal time. Judicial review proceedings, in particular, may be initiated against an investigator if the investigation's findings are disputed by a party with legal standing. Judicial review is used to scrutinise the procedural integrity of decisions carried out by public bodies. It is based on a body of legal principles developed

[57] JH Ritchie et al, *The Report of the Inquiry into the Care and Treatment of Christopher Clunis* (London, HMSO, 1994) 1.

[58] L Blom-Cooper et al, *The Falling Shadow: One patient's mental health care 1978–1993* (London, Duckworth, 1995).

[59] See G Adshead, 'Root Cause Analysis' (2005) 29(2) *The Psychiatrist* 71, 71.

over time. Investigators are understandably keen to avoid having their investigation reviewed by a judge. An investigator interviewed by the author described his experience of being targeted for judicial review by the police. He commented that a police force disputed his finding that the force could have – and should have – predicted and prevented the homicide incident occurring. Prior to the killing, the perpetrator – who had been showing signs of mental disorder – had been in the company of police officers at the entrance to a hospital. According to the investigation's finding, the police officers failed to prevent the perpetrator leaving the scene. A short time after leaving, the perpetrator committed the homicide. The police disputed the finding and initiated judicial review proceedings against the investigator company responsible for the investigation and producing the report. The communications produced by the inquiry panel in their final report acquire legal significance in such circumstances. The disputed finding in question may be regarded as a communication produced by the social system of science; the finding related to causation, reached through RCA and verification through the consideration of evidence (ie, surveillance video recordings of the scene outside of the hospital). For the legal system, however, the investigation's finding is relevant to the question of whether the investigation's conclusions are lawful (ie, whether they conform to the principles of 'natural justice', 'rationality' and 'reasonableness'). After legal argumentation, the judicial review action was settled out of court. If the matter had reached the courts, a legal judgment would have been produced in accordance with previous legal communications (eg, judicial review principles) and perhaps previous court judgments involving the review of independent homicide investigations. Legally relevant facts would be distinguished from non-legally relevant facts (ie, the factual dimension of meaning). Those involved in the proceedings would anticipate what others similarly involved are likely to contribute (ie, the social dimension of meaning). The investigation – and perhaps previous investigations that acquired social significance for the legal system – would become part of the legal system's experience of time.

Investigations are meaningful in the time dimension of the political system also. Chapter 3 described the occasional relevance investigations have to politics. The relevance extends to the way in which investigations are occasioned. The communications of, say, a government department or NHS Trust regarding marked increases in mental health homicide rates and the findings of investigations have constituted past events of political significance. One investigator described the importance of political dynamics to a thematic investigation prompted by the Secretary of State for Health and Social Care:[60]

> We did a review of about forty homicide cases for NHS London and that was … regarded as a scandal at the time in that it was discovered that there had been a number of cases

[60] Independent thematic homicide investigations are carried out when a cluster of homicides have been committed by service users treated by the same NHS service provider, usually within a short time period. The cluster is assessed with a view to identifying themes and similarities (if any) within it.

> of homicide which had not been investigated. The commissioning of these, rather than being routine or formal, was regarded as quite ad hoc. Some got commissioned, some didn't … The Minister of Health said at the time 'tell me this same problem is not happening elsewhere?'. So everybody scrambled. **Investigator 10**

These experiences were echoed by other investigators:

> There's another political dynamic you get from the thematic inquiries that sometimes mental health Trusts are looking to protect their own back so that they can say 'we've had a run of these problems, but we've taken care of it and had it reviewed. We know where the problems are'. Or in one case, this chap was due to appear in court following a conviction for murder in a road rage incident and the Trust was hoping to say 'well, actually, we've got it all under control because the review is in place'. It won't work out quite like that. It rumbled on and they got all of the opprobrium of the press and all the rest of it and the report came out some time later. That was commissioned partly by the Trust and partly by NHS England. That went up to Ministers in the end. **Investigator 11**

These comments show that investigations may, on occasion, form an aspect of political time for the political system. The homicide incidents that trigger investigations and the investigations themselves may become events that the political system will select as events relevant to the application of power (eg, policy changes, political debates, criticising the government) in the present.

Independent investigations therefore involve a range of time constructions. Medical and psychiatric constructions of time are more dominant in these investigations today, but other versions of time (eg, legal time, political time) may be constructed also. Investigations may acquire legal or political significance in the social function systems of law and politics and form an aspect of time in these systems. There are, undoubtedly, other constructions of time. Investigations involve the production of moral and economic communications and they will acquire significance in social subsystems as events that exist in time as determined by those systems' operations. The illustrations above, however, showcase the argument that the patient homicide governance space is made up of multiple versions of time constructed by social systems of communication. Luhmann's theory of social systems provides the tools to theorise the governance space as temporalised complexity. In other words, different versions of time are self-constructed within society's function systems throughout the governance space.

B. Time and Change

A prominent theme in Luhmann's work is the argument that direct influence and control in the world, pursuant to predefined goals, is impossible. Luhmann's theme stands in opposition to conventional philosophical and political theories that suggest that direct influence is possible and that humans possess the ability to execute it. Luhmann's scepticism about societal steering links up with his conception of time. He writes that there is no point-for-point correspondence between a social system and its environment.[61] Rather, 'the environment of a system always exists simultaneously with the system … [and] it can never happen that the environment gets stuck, as it were, in the past, while the system becomes the future of the environment (or vice versa)'.[62] The prospect of controlling or influencing other social systems or understanding the complexity of the world is impossible owing to the simultaneity of all communications.[63] Law is an environment for medicine, but medicine will not wait for law to communicate about the legality of these advancements.[64] Society, as a functionally differentiated world system, is chaotic and contingent. There is little harmony in the rate and speed at which social systems communicate about their individual environments.[65] For instance, the time it takes for the legal system to respond to an industrial accident is far greater than the time it takes for the system of medicine to respond to it.[66]

Luhmann's depiction of society is one of disharmony and contingency. It helps further develop the concept of time in the present chapter. A panel's recommendation for services to revise medication protocols today may be tomorrow's discarded mistake. Communications produced by the social system of economics (eg, cuts in hospital funding) may mean that protocol revisions are shelved later or delayed. An all-important distinction between system and environment is thus underscored here. Systems produce their own identity through communication and, inevitably, structure time in unique sequences that reduce the complexity of their environment.[67] Recommendations may be made by investigators that are informed by their construction of the medically relevant past but the economic past (ie, the resource history of services and their future budgetary concerns) may irritate the clinical ambitions of recommendations. Resources may be lean, thus making the implementation of recommendation more difficult.

These observations on time enable new understandings to emerge about familiar challenges facing investigators and policy makers generally. These challenges were neatly summed up by an investigator. He described difficulty in coping with elapsed periods of time between the way health services were configured at the time of the homicide and the investigation itself:

> I think it [the delay] is significant for the staff as it hangs over their head for a long time, doesn't it? We had a patient who committed a homicide. We had an inquiry and

[61] Luhmann, *Social Systems* (n 2) 43.
[62] Luhmann, *Risk* (n 17) 35.
[63] See ibid 106.
[64] See Harrington, 'Time' (n 29) 496. See also J Paterson, 'Trans-Science, Trans-Law and Proceduralization' (2003) 12(4) *Social & Legal Studies* 525, 534. Writing on the legal regulation of risks, Paterson claims that 'It is true that when tasked with the regulation of risks law does face a significant challenge and that the apparent absoluteness of the norm in such circumstances can rapidly dissolve into the provisional in the light of the ongoing evolution of scientific knowledge'.
[65] See Luhmann, *Risk* (n 17) 165.
[66] For example, a legal claim for damages through the courts is a lengthy process, whereas conducting disciplinary proceedings or compiling reports about costs after an accident are much shorter.
[67] Luhmann, 'The Future Cannot Begin' (n 51) 133.

> just heard that NHS England had reviewed it and are opening it up and having another inquiry. Well, that was five years ago and it was hanging over your head and now you'll be answering questions about something that happened so long ago. So, for the staff, the longer it goes on, the more stressful it is for them. As I already said, people move on. In terms of the learning, I don't think it makes that much difference to the information you glean. But I suppose the fresher it is in people's mind, the better. I don't think the time-lag is that significant in terms of getting information, apart from people who have moved away and stuff. **Investigator 7**

The investigator's statement demonstrates that institutional change and the passing of time may irritate the psychic systems of staff members, in the form of memory recall difficulties and stress. They may also raise difficulties in conducting a meaningful investigation where proceedings are hampered by delay. Past communications (eg, medical documents, notes) relevant to the case that the investigation, in the present, requires in order to conduct a meaningful investigation are sometimes inaccessible because they are missing. In these circumstances, there is no relevant past that can be gauged for the purposes of, say, communicating medically in the present:

> I can think of one case where no-one was left from the original care team in the organisation. People couldn't remember the perpetrator. Notes got lost. It was almost irrelevant that you made recommendations because it is a completely different organisation now. It has to be fairly close to the incident to be meaningful. **Investigator 8**

An investigator explained that, during delays, legal and economic circumstances change and investigations – once commenced – are problematic:

> This Trust had changed status, had merged with other Trusts and had become integrated with social care and health care, whereas previously it was split between council and the NHS. And so, all of those changes were quite problematic and pinpointing all the people involved was quite challenging. **Investigator 5**

The same problem was echoed in other interviews conducted with investigators:

> We've had situations where people have emigrated, doctors working in Australia. So that's one problem. Second, there may be external reorganisation but also internal reorganisation within Trusts. They have their own shake ups at regular intervals. So you're looking into a service from five years ago, the Home Crisis and Intervention Service, which no longer exists. The Trust will say, 'this body no longer exists. How relevant is this going to be?' So, some of the difficulties you get are … people's memories. You'll interview and some people will say, 'well I met him once five years ago and, to be honest, I don't recall much about it'. **Investigator 11**

Overall, delays between the incident and the inquiry diminish the perceived quality of an investigation:

> [To] be honest, that is probably the main factor that made it difficult and technically challenging – the elapsing of time … The more delay there is in commissioning the investigation, it's always going to be poorer, whether it's an air crash, a health care homicide or whatever. The longer you leave starting an investigation, the worse it's going to be. **Investigator 5**

Significant delay between the homicide incident and the independent investigation weakens the prospect of a meaningful conclusion to the investigation. It produces undesired consequences for those involved, particularly families:

> It's appalling. A politician talked about 'double whammies' and 'triple whammies' and all the rest of it. And you think of it from the family's point of view, you're going through the internal inquiry, the inquest, the report and these things are dragging on for four years on average. That is terrible for the families. And if the government is not speaking out about it, all it's doing is saying 'we've done these reports, these legacy reports'. What a choice of words. What they mean is these outstanding reports that they finally got pushed to produce and it was all so long ago that everyone has lost the will to live. So, there's no enthusiasm for it. **Investigator 6**

The investigator added that he was one of the first to ensure that investigation reports were published six months after the incident. Recent investigations, however, are less timely and the investigator expressed frustration at the tardiness:

> Probably the most frustrating thing here is that this is supposed to be about learning lessons, but this is not happening at the top. **Investigator 6**

A concept of time informed by systems theory helps develop the argument that the patient homicide governance space is constituted by moments of social systemic observation about time, at different rates. The argument provides a new frame of understanding for the common problems that patient homicides raise, such as obtaining accessible and meaningful information and institutional change. Concluding investigations and advancing convincing recommendations is challenging. The patience of those involved in investigations and those who await their findings is tested because social communication never ceases.

The present chapter has, thus far, sought to reposition a series of existing concerns about the challenges time presents for investigations. These concerns are often advanced in order to identify the procedural flaws in inquiries and to provide a platform for correcting these flaws. Luhmann's ideas on social systems and time enable a richer picture to emerge about time in the patient homicide governance space. The different versions of the past that Luhmann's theory allows for and the idea that change in society involves social systems continually communicating at different speeds opens up a new way of appreciating the difficulties, reported by investigators, of investigating the past, communicating in the present and recommending future change to services.

C. Hopes and Fears

Communicating about the future is fraught with uncertainty. The future is a horizon that 'can never begin'.[68] Gaining sufficient knowledge of the future is

[68] ibid 130.

impossible because everything occurs in the present, guided by a past. The future cannot exist in the present.[69] The future is, rather, a projection screen for present hopes and fears.[70] It is also a focus for social systems of communication when they operationalise their unique binary codes.[71] Hopes and fears may have a legal quality (eg, the fear of future legal liability) or a religious quality (eg, the fear of God's judgement). For the patient homicide governance space, these hopes and fears are varied but they are primarily, although not solely, of a medical and psychiatric quality (eg, the fear of patients and citizens sustaining death or injury).

These hopes and fears may extend to performing the onerous task of ensuring that clinical improvements are made after an investigation has ended. Recommendations are commonly made by investigators after the conclusion of an investigation. They are suggestive; they usually suggest that the NHS Trust must introduce changes to services:

> A more recent requirement that has crept into the terms of reference is about not just producing the report but making a judgement six months after the report about how the Trust have implemented the recommendations. So, they ask us to examine that six months hence. On the ones we've done, I have to say that it has been a tortuous process. In the sense that, what you're saying to them is 'give me your evidence, here are the recommendations'. 'What have you done? Where's your evidence that you've done it?' We think that the requests are fairly straight-forward … It can take a lot of chasing. Weeks, months. What we've discovered more recently is that they're saying to us 'well when we looked at it we don't accept the recommendations so we're not going to do it'. We say 'hang on, you've signed this off. You've told the public you're going to do all this when you had the press spotlight on you. We come back six months later and you have changed your mind'. **Investigator 10**

In equal measure, as demonstrated in Chapter 3, investigations may project the fear of future loss in monetary terms and hence communicate about economic risk (eg, limiting the financial costs of investigations). More general is the acknowledgement that investigators instigate defensiveness and anxiety about what the investigation will mean for others' futures.[72] Fear and anxiety link up with political and economic communications about the future in relation to potential losses of jobs (eg, the potential for a loss of decision-making authority, ministerial criticism and board sackings in response to a finding that services are woefully inadequate) and resources (eg, the imposition of fines). For example, an investigator commented that he had previous experience sitting as a non-executive director on an NHS Trust. He referred to a recent high-profile instance of mismanagement by an NHS Trust, commenting that health care providers often

[69] ibid. See also Luhmann, *Risk* (n 17) 12–13, 35.
[70] Luhmann, 'The Future Cannot Begin' (n 51) 145.
[71] ibid.
[72] J Warner, 'Inquiry Reports as Active Texts and Their Function in Relation to Professional Practice in Mental Health' (2006) 8(3) *Health, Risk & Society* 223, 233.

fear the potential economic and political consequences of an independent investigation report. The fear is particularly acute if the report highlights inadequacies in the services targeted for investigation:

> NHS Southern just got fined £2 million. They had two cases. One only reported two or three weeks ago. The second was an in-patient suicide. So, the consequences for them were that most of the Board went. The Chief Executive went. The Chairman went. Most of the non-executives went. Reputation was shot at. Southern Health is a byword. 'Don't go near it'. **Investigator 10**

The future for investigators is potentially one of reduced economic resources and sullied reputations in the network of political power and economic scarcity.

The possibility of future loss is conceived within the patient homicide governance space in legal and moral terms also. Inquiry panels conduct interviews with health professionals connected with the perpetrator. The latter often express the fear of future legal liability and moral blame.[73] Witnesses sometimes express fears of bullying and harassment after interview.[74] Investigators themselves may express fears of legal liability. The spectre of a judicial review looms large. Investigators are always keen to avoid it:

> [B]ig companies rather than I are better off at doing that because they have a longer reach, bigger resources at their disposal. It's not the sort of stuff that floats my boat. I much prefer to work with incidents where I'm working with a cluster of organisations or local agencies and looking at it with them. Things like judicial reviews … I just wouldn't put myself in the line for those, even if I was doing it in partnership with one of my competitors. **Investigator 2**

The prospect that a judicial review action may be taken against an investigator was framed by others as worrying:

> We've been around long enough to know that relatives can threaten to take people to judicial reviews and I think that's not happened for a while, so people don't realise now how serious this is. I think something will happen soon, that an investigation has not been thorough enough or has not been wide enough. **Investigator 3**

The fear of judicial review is quite pervasive. The fear is understandable. It was noted in Chapter 3 that investigators struggle to feel comfortable when embroiled in judicial review proceedings:

> It was very worrying for us. We, as a company, felt quite isolated with this … it could have gone a number of ways. It could have been financially ruinous for us, because of the costs involved. It's an expensive process. Even if in the end, we won the argument, the criticism was just unfair. **Investigator 10**

[73] ibid 232. See also K Walshe and J Higgins, 'The Use and Impact of Inquiries in the NHS' (2002) 325 *British Medical Journal* 895, 897. See generally J Peay, 'Themes and Questions: The Inquiry in Context' in J Peay (ed), *Inquiries After Homicide* (London, Duckworth & Co, 1996) 26.

[74] H Waldock et al, *Independent Investigation into the Care and Treatment provided to Mr AT* (NHS South West SHA, Health and Social Care Advisory Service, November 2009) 42.

The legal and economic fears that investigators have are well founded.

Communicating about the future is therefore demanding, especially when it comes to making decisions to do or not do something in response to health care safety concerns. There is a dilemma. For inquiries, making recommendations for health services to undergo change in some way or to refrain from recommending change at all is a source of unease. Recommendations aim to reduce the prospect of fatal incidents occurring again and to ensure that health services are adequate. These aims denote an ambition to directly influence services and their future orientation. The complexity of health services and the uncertainty of a functionally differentiated society raise doubts, however, over whether such ambitions are achievable.

As far as Luhmann's theory of social systems is concerned, the prospect of realising lofty policy ambitions assumes that a privileged seat of observation within which these ambitions may be framed exists. Fate is no longer fate in the traditional sense. It is, rather, a matter of self-constructed meaning within social systems, as opposed to society leaving the matter to religion.[75] To accept otherwise would be to accept that change in society can be engineered from outside of it. Luhmann is clear that society is all of communication. Nothing can exist outside of communication and communications are functionally differentiated. Advancing recommendations to change health care policies and to modify the behaviour of hospital staff is fraught with difficulty because of operational closure (ie, autopoiesis). From psychiatry to economics, different and opposing expectations, opinions, fears and concerns reflect unique modes of social communication about health care services. Exacting desired change pursuant to predefined goals is immensely difficult. Furthermore, the simultaneous production of communications in society and the different speeds at which they are made means that any attempt to manipulate or control complex areas of society, like health care services, will yield unpredictable and uncoordinated consequences in different communication systems (ie, perturbations). An investigator commented during interview that advancing recommendations in the hope that services change for the better is difficult because of service complexity and their tendency to be in a constant state of flux: 'services are re-organised. The complexity I think makes it hard' [**Investigator 7**]. Inquiries strive to understand a 'complex, real world that is in a continuous and dynamic flow'.[76] An investigation conducted in 2012 captured the problem in concise terms: '[a] culture of flux in staff members, ambiguity over boundary issues and changing nursing management styles affected and impacted on the environment'.[77]

[75] Luhmann, *Risk* (n 17) 51.

[76] E Munro, 'Mental Health Tragedies: Investigating Beyond Human Error' (2004) 15(3) *Journal of Forensic Psychiatry & Psychology* 475, 479.

[77] G Roberts et al, *An Independent Investigation into the Care and Treatment of Mr R* (Niche Health & Social Care Consulting, February 2012) 36.

The state of flux referred to above extends to the recruitment of new concepts and terminology (eg, safeguarding) in services. Some inquiry reports acknowledged that once introduced, these concepts would need time to become embedded in the staff culture:

> 'Safeguarding' was a new concept in teams at the time of the homicide and was not yet embedded in team culture. The safeguarding lead said: 'I think possibly nationally and not just within ourselves, I don't think people fully appreciated and valued the identification of safeguarding from an adult perspective'.[78]

Against the background of complexity, it is difficult for an inquiry to advance a set of recommendations to initiate well-intentioned change to services because of communicative complexity. Services change considerably and present new areas of concern that were not previously recognised. The meanings produced across services within social systems of communications occur simultaneously, rendering these areas of concern uncontrollable from any one perspective. Independent investigators, however, appear to attempt an exercise of direct influence over health services or an element of them, albeit tentatively. The expectation that lessons are learned, services are improved and risks to public safety are minimised all point to the expression of ambitions which, from a Luhmannian perspective, are problematic. Whatever hopes and fears are harboured about an investigation, they are bound to be based on different or irreconcilable meanings.

IV. Accountability and Time

It is prescient to draw a series of explicit links between the concepts of accountability and time. In brief, these two concepts are connected because they overlap (ie, accountability is concerned with looking into the past). It is more important, however, to note that these two concepts are connected because they are both constructions of meaning within social systems of communication. The construction of case chronologies and the questioning of witnesses, for example, involve the construction of time within social systems of communication. By way of illustration, past decisions to administer treatment to a perpetrator are meaningful within the function system of medicine. The consequences of treatment for a perpetrator's mental and physical health are relevant to an inquiry panel because they are constructed as meaningful within the function system of medicine. Previous detentions under the Mental Health Act 1983 are relevant (ie, the social subsystem of law). The past may be constructed by inquiries economically (eg, past resource issues adversely affecting care). These observations

[78] T Hussain et al, *An Investigation into the Care and Treatment of Service User Y* (Verita, February 2012) 51.

show that the past is constructed into a series of meaningful versions. At the same time, investigators construct the past by eliciting accounts from professionals and other witnesses, for the purpose of constructing a meaningful investigation of health services. Medical communications are produced in the present and refer to previous medical communications so that sense is made of the present. Producing understandings in the present about a person's response to medical treatment requires drawing on communications about what that treatment is, its effect on the human body and its purpose. Understanding why a particular individual was detained against their will in hospital will require drawing on previous legal communications regarding the lawfulness of such a decision. Time and accountability are, therefore, connected.

Accountability relationships may be regarded as constructions of time. The formation of these relationships means something to investigators and at the same time constitutes a moment (ie, the present) from which the horizon of the past and the future is observed. The moment produces a distinct understanding of the past for the purpose of communicating about the future. It provides a basis for decision making (eg, advancing a recommendation). Accountability relationships, as constructions of time, reduce the complexity of society. They reduce the past to a series of socially relevant events.

The accountability relationships that are formed by investigators during an investigation may be said to create future occasions for new accountability relationships to be formed. Consistent with the arguments developed earlier in the present chapter, accountability is expansive. It relates to the dynamics of political accountability for welfare problems, but also to social systems communicating about each other in the form of new decisions and the assumption of new responsibilities. The findings and recommendations of independent investigations tend to be directed towards senior authorities and officials in the public health care hierarchy, such as NHS management or the Department of Health. The latter may be regarded as points of power application within the political system that are expected to respond to the feedback of investigators. These responses may take the form of expressing concern about the welfare issues raised in an investigation or complaining about the investigation's findings. Mass media communications (see Chapters 3 and 6) and protest communications (see Chapter 6) may be produced about senior NHS and political figures, placing an onus on them to render accounts of how they will act on the issues raised by investigators. Managers will be recommended to implement new arrangements, such as staff training programmes, extra recruitment, resource improvements and an increase in the frequency of inter-team meetings. Investigation findings may become socially available to politics for the purposes of holding government to account.[79] The most

[79] See HC Deb, 29 June 1993, vol 227, col 822. After the publication of the Ritchie Report, the Prime Minister at the time was explicitly challenged on the issue of remedial action: 'In view of the revelations at the trial of Christopher Clunis, who stabbed and killed Jonathan Zito, will the Prime Minister

common developments to happen after an inquiry's closing involve instigating changes to local health services. The services provided by an NHS Trust may be found by an inquiry to have high staff attrition rates or reduced resource allocation, which recommendations may attempt to address.

All of these points show that the patient homicide governance space creates a vast series of future occasions, across a range of different areas and fields, on which accountability for welfare issues is assumed. What is more, accountability in these instances may not necessarily be concerned with bringing about radical change through decisions. Accountability may range from a senior official making claims that something will be done to remedy the problems highlighted by an investigation or review, for the purposes of retaining a position of influence within the welfare state hierarchy. Or, it may involve making medically justified decisions to change the way local health services are delivered with a view to minimising risks to mental and physical health. It may simply be an occasion for affected parties (ie, families, the public) to lodge grievances. As Luhmann remarked, 'we feel it increasingly appropriate to complain about and to attack decision makers, in particular those responsible (and therefore attracting attribution) at high levels'.[80]

Accountability is better conceptualised as a meaningful construction of the past, in the present, that creates future possibilities for social communications (eg, political, medical communications). Further contingency and uncertainty is the result. Inquiries perform a crucial epistemic function however. A central aspect of their work involves penetrating the complex medical and psychiatric detail behind adverse incidents, which traditional systems of authority (eg, law, politics) would struggle to do.[81] It is acknowledged that 'regulation and legislation frequently lag behind the dynamic forces of the health care market'.[82] Health care practices evolve rapidly and dynamically. Inquiries appear to play a crucial role in minimising the uncertainties associated with these evolving practices but only up to a point. After all, governance mechanisms, like independent patient homicide

accept that although most people suffering from schizophrenia are not dangerous, the failure of the Government's care in the community policy means that dangerous mentally ill people are walking the streets? What does he intend to do about that, and will he now order a public inquiry into the case and its implications for community care, as requested by Mr. Zito's widow?'.

[80] N Luhmann, 'Technology, Environment and Social Risk: A Systems Perspective' (1990) 4 *Industrial Crisis Quarterly* 223, 226.

[81] The ability of legal reform to transform society has been rigorously doubted since the 1970s (see Galanter, 'The Turn Against Law' (n 9) 296). See also AJ Wistrich, 'The Evolving Temporality of Lawmaking' (2012) 44 *Connecticut Law Review* 757, 784.

[82] LG Pawlson and ME O'Kane, 'Professionalism, Regulation, and the Market: Impact of Accountability for Quality of Care' (2002) 21(3) *Health Affairs* 200, 204: 'for example the recent spate of "patients' rights" bills at a time when HMO have improved their practices and their influence is in decline. While there have been attempts to create regulations that are more responsive to consumerism, there has been no concerted effort to examine current regulations in light of the evolution of the health care market and its forces'.

investigations, solicit 'input from those to be regulated and the public before creating rules to govern future conduct'.[83] Adverse events in particular, especially in complex and technical areas, expose the fallibility of science and law in addressing society's problems. Luhmann's work underscores the difficulty. The attempts made by inquiries to minimise risks and uncertainties associated with delivering health care treatment to mentally disordered persons are bound to encounter resistance. Health care providers may reject their recommendations. Senior officials may judge their findings to be embarrassing or politically inconvenient. Their findings may create occasions on which family interest groups may lambast NHS organisations and push for change.

Chapter 2 referred to the idea of the 'inquiry industry'. A more abstract version of the idea advanced in Chapter 3 may be advanced here. The occasions for conflict, disagreement and dispute which independent investigations create are – in a sense – the fuel which keeps the industry alive. Luhmann's work provides the conceptual vocabulary with which to articulate the idea. The continual drive towards change and occasional crisis is the 'natural' condition of a functionally differentiated society:

> 'reducing differences always requires producing differences. You never get a system which no longer deviates from expected values. By reducing unemployment you may produce inflation. By reducing pollution figures you may increase bankruptcy figures dramatically'.[84]

The patient homicide governance space, through the independent patient homicide investigation, appears to be a self-sustaining 'business'. There will always be an occasion to investigate:

> [T]here is no safe way to achieve the desired results without running the risk of consequences that may lead to post-decisional regret or, even more likely, to the risk of not achieving the intended results in spite of high costs, including opportunity costs.[85]

V. Conclusions

The present chapter adds complexion to the main theme of the book in general. Terms like 'inquiry' and 'investigation' sound straightforward but they conceal a reliable account of society's complexity in these instances. Society's complexity relates to social systems communicating about their environment (eg, each other) in a variety of different ways. The patient homicide governance space acquires significance for a host of social function systems (eg, law, politics, economics, medicine) that are unable to communicate with each other,

[83] Wistrich, 'Evolving Temporality' (n 81) 785.
[84] Luhmann, 'Technology' (n 80) 226.
[85] ibid.

but are able to communicate about each other on their terms. The present chapter develops the book's thesis further. It argues that accountability is yet another social self-construction within social systems of communication. On the surface, accountability is a process of answering questions and eliciting answers; an over-simplified conception arguably from which to begin a reliable and novel analysis of accountability in the patient homicide governance space. Rather, accountability is more accurately understood through the prism of Luhmann's concept of communication. Accountability is a meaningful construction to investigators. Persons, in their role as doctors, patients, nurses and other clinical staff, are constructed as relevant to the social system of medicine and psychiatry. Persons, in their role as politicians, are constructed as relevant to the political system. The notorious resource constraints that investigators often cite are, in similar fashion, meaningful as resource problems because the social subsystem of the economy provides the overarching framework of life required for making such an observation. The lines of questioning, the responses elicited and the subsequent analysis of evidence are rendered into meaningful constructions of reality within these function systems.

Accountability, as the construction of meaning by social systemic communication, is also a construction of time. The past is selectively observed within social function systems in the present for the purposes of communicating about the future in the form of decisions. Holding witnesses to account includes identifying past decisions that resonate in certain social subsystems of communication. Decisions of a medical and psychiatric nature are particularly relevant and are packaged together into uniquely meaningful chronologies of time. Indeed, the past may have relevance from an economic (eg, funding issues) or political (eg, a recent policy declaration) perspective.

A further aspect of accountability is the notion that the political system assumes decision-making responsibility for a greater number of welfare matters. The NHS is part of the United Kingdom's welfare state and is communicated about politically on a regular basis. The present chapter draws on Luhmann's theory of politics to argue that investigations after patient homicide have relevance for the social subsystem of politics insofar as they are relevant to political power application. In other words, they are relevant to a growing number of issues identified as amenable to investigation by decision-making elites (eg, NHS England, Department of Health). Investigators are compelled to assume investigative responsibility over a growing range of welfare-related matters (ie, commissioning) beyond the immediate purview of health services. The patient homicide governance space, it is argued, involves expansions of accountability by the political system.

Overall, the purpose of the present chapter has been to reappraise important elements of patient homicide governance (ie, accountability and time) by re-conceptualising them through the lens of systems theory. Truth finding, factual accuracy and procedural accountability inform common understandings of independent investigations. These investigations, however, are reappraised here as communicative constructions that reduce social complexity, while at the same time creating complexity because producing objective understandings of and conducting direct influence over health services is impossible. There is, rather, an ever-increasing likelihood of disagreement, objection and unintended consequences.

The following chapter develops these themes in more detail by exploring the idea that communicating about health care after homicide involves making sense of risk. Whereas investigations are occasions on which to assume accountability for a variety of problems in health care services and to express concern about welfare issues, the following chapter explores the idea that communicating about health care after homicide involves communicating about risk. For Luhmann, risk is a form of communication about the possibility of future loss. In a functionally differentiated society, risk communication is the rule as opposed to the exception. Polycentric social systems appeal to themselves in the present, rather than appealing to an objective source of authority, when communicating about the possibility of future loss. Social systems – as autopoietic systems – rely on their own operations to construct reality, including their version of time. The systems-theoretical concept of time developed earlier is one that depicts inherent uncertainty. The future, especially, is an unreachable horizon constructed by society's social function systems. All communication occurs in the present and its consequences are unpredictable. 'Risk' is the norm and it is communicated about within social function systems in unique ways, particularly throughout the patient homicide governance space. Independent investigations seek to minimise potential future loss and elevate safety standards in services and it is apposite to explore these ambitions further and to consider how the possibility of future loss in these circumstances is communicated about. The concept of risk occupies a central focus of the next chapter.

6

Risk and Protest

I. Introduction

The author conceives the patient homicide governance space as closed communication systems that resonate in society. These systems observe their uniquely constructed environment on their own terms, by referring to their operations. Social function systems of communication couple with biological, psychic, interaction and organisation systems and they produce distinct meanings about patient homicide within society. Social function systems distinguish themselves as systems from their environment. Society's function systems (eg, medicine, psychiatry, law, science) produce unique meanings about their respective environments (eg, other social systems, organic matter, consciousness) on terms which they themselves create. As explained in the previous chapter, social function systems produce unique versions of accountability. Events are sequenced in ways that enable account renderings to occur, accountability relationships to form and a semblance of time to be created for that system. Independent investigations involve constructions of time (eg, past and future), albeit medical time (eg, the perpetrator's treatment and contact with health services, future service provision), economic time (eg, past economic constraints, the economic viability of an investigation in the present) and legal time (eg, instances where a perpetrator has been lawfully detained, the fears of being exposed to judicial review) to name a few.

Luhmann makes claims about time in his work on risk. Risk is related to time because it is associated with the future. The risk of something happening is generally linked to the possibility of loss arising out of one's decisions in the present. Independent inquiries relate to risk, too. Investigators analyse risk assessments conducted by professionals. They advance recommendations. These recommendations encounter the risk of failure or rejection. Risk is a relevant concept and deserving of closer scrutiny in the present book from a systems-theoretical perspective.

For Luhmann, risk refers to the possibility of future loss. Unsurprisingly, he avoids imbuing the risk concept with ontological qualities (ie, as an objective condition that we may bring about or a concept that, once defined, enables humans to make the world safer). The belief that risk is objectively verifiable, according to Luhmann's concept of risk, implies the existence of a privileged observational standpoint from which risk may be understood, addressed and avoided through steering mechanisms. The utopian ideal of the risk-free society is, however, a solid aspect of conventional intellectual wisdom. The concept is often placed in a relationship *with* society rather than being a construction of meaning produced *in* society's social systems of communication. For example, an actuarial risk analyst uses the methods of his or her profession to analyse risk for the purpose of reaching an objectively verifiable conclusion about the level of risk involved in an investment. The actuarial analyst would regard his or her conclusion as a superior one to other types of risk calculations. For Luhmann, both the analyst's role and the conclusion reached are products of the social system of science. As Chapter 4 demonstrated, science – like our minds – is a closed system. Science may perturb society but its ability to directly manipulate society and exact precise change through scientific intervention is impossible. Science is unable to represent the whole of society in all its systemic complexity. Science simply communicates about its environment scientifically. At the same time, investing in the stock market is a communication in the social system of economics. Investing is a risk, albeit an economic one (ie, a future possibility of a bad return). Administering medical treatment (ie, a medical communication) may lead to medical risks. Unwanted side-effects may occur in the future, sometimes years later. In general, risks are constructed differently in social systems of communication but they are generally communications about the possibility of future loss.

The present chapter argues that the roles (eg politicians and health care managers) and organisations (eg, hospitals) that acquire significance for society's function systems form the patient homicide governance space. Persons step into social communications about potential future loss on a regular basis and organisations acquire social significance for a slew of communicational domains. For instance, medical communications may be produced to recommend the implementation of certain service arrangements in order to prevent the future deterioration of a patient's health. NHS Trust managers may express political or economic concern about their future position in the NHS power complex in response to a homicide. An investigator's findings may invite a legal challenge; potential future loss may involve having to follow a court order to reinvestigate services (ie, legal risk) and incurring huge costs in doing so (ie, economic risks).

Luhmann's ideas on risk enable the development of important themes raised in Chapter 3. There, it was explained that investigators attempt to fulfil a range of ambitions (eg, improving public safety) that, from a systems theory perspective, are impossible to realise. These ambitions are prone to disappointment. The concept of a functionally differentiated society typified by polycentric spheres of communication does away with the notion of direct causal change and the realisation of safety in particular. Independent investigations and health services generally will, accordingly, be unable to fulfil many of the goals and ambitions that they lay out (eg, learning lessons, improving safety). Nevertheless, later stages of the present chapter introduce Luhmann's ideas about protest communications. They demonstrate the relevance of these ideas to the governance of patient homicide aftermaths. In particular, the chapter draws on Luhmann's view that social movements have emerged as a newer and distinct type of social system. Furthermore, these types of social system acquire meaning in the form of protest communications. Protest communications are often produced about patient homicide and health care. The present chapter examines the dynamics of protest in the patient homicide governance space, the importance of these dynamics and why they are fraught with difficulties and challenges.

The chapter begins by outlining the concept of risk, followed by a close examination of its relevance to decision making and protest.

II. The Concept of Risk

'Time is intrinsically connected with risk'.[1] Risk means different things depending on the context but it may be said to describe the possibility of future loss. Risk is, therefore, a description of time. Yet, descriptions of time come in different forms.[2] Economists and actuarial analysts may use statistical calculation to construct these descriptions.[3] Health care services are increasingly understood in risk-based terms also. For example, discharging a psychiatric patient with a history of violence poses a risk to public safety.[4]

For patient homicide investigations, risk is very much in the foreground too. A dreadful event has occurred. Something must be done to ensure that the event does not happen again. The measures taken to do something, however, create a unique set of expectations. Will the measures work? Will services truly be safer as a result of their implementation? What lessons can be learned? Who should learn them? Learning lessons means different things. It may have medical significance in the form of minimising the adverse consequences of mental illness on patients and limiting the possibility of future loss of human life. Learning lessons may have legal significance; a civil claim against a health care provider for negligence may prompt learning for the organisation in the form of staying on the right side of the law. In developing a systems-theoretical conception of risk further, the meaning of 'learning lessons' for the future is dependent on the mode of communication utilised to learn them. The possibility of future loss may also be described in the

[1] N Luhmann, *Risk: A Sociological Theory* (New Brunswick, Aldine Transaction, 1993/2008) 124.

[2] See C Hood and DKC Jones, 'Introduction' in C Hood and DKC Jones (eds), *Accident and Design: Contemporary Debates in Risk Management* (London, UCL Press Limited, 1996) 2; A Philippopoulos-Mihalopoulos, *Absent Environments* (Oxford, Routledge-Cavendish, 2007) 119; Luhmann, *Risk* (n 1) 6.

[3] See generally P Bernstein, *Against the Gods: The Remarkable Story of Risk* (New York, Wiley, 1998) 229. See also P O'Malley, 'Uncertain Subjects: Risks, Liberalism and Contracts' (2000) 29(4) *Economy and Society* 460, 645.

[4] See E Baker, 'The Introduction of Supervision Registers in England and Wales: A Risk Communication Analysis' (1997) 8(1) *The Journal of Forensic Psychiatry* 15, 21. See also R Castel, 'From Dangerousness to Risk' in G Burchell et al (eds), *The Foucault Effect: Studies in Governmentality* (Hemel Hempstead, Harvester Wheatsheaf, 1991) 281, 282.

form of blame, moral and otherwise, for an adverse event. The clinical personnel responsible for services and targeted for independent investigation frequently occupy the focus of blame and criticism from many quarters. The possibility that a member of staff could undergo damage to their career or reputation through opprobrium from the victim's family or the media is a fear that is not uncommon. NHS managers and even political officials may fear the loss of their jobs. There are different ways in which the possibility of future loss emerges in the patient homicide governance space. Despite the ambiguity of the phrase 'learning lessons', one thing is clear: it may be regarded as indicating an attempt to reduce the likelihood of future loss in the present.

A. Risk and Society

Decision making is perceived to have consequences involving future gain or loss. Future gain or loss is an inescapable perception. It is an essential aspect of decision making. Luhmann's theory of social systems is, however, non-normative.[5] It avoids making judgements about whether decisions and their consequences are inherently good, bad, risky or safe for society. His theory sidesteps debate about whether risks objectively exist and whether certain ways of addressing them are adequate. Luhmann's concept of risk – like his general theory of social systems – is concerned with observing observers. How observers observe, make their decisions and produce discourse about the possibility of future loss informs his theoretical outlook. Luhmann's ideas on risk lie in stark contrast to mainstream ideas about risk. Law and politics are frequently looked upon to provide answers to risk problems. One possible explanation for the growing primacy of law and politics when it comes to addressing risk issues may lie in the growing uncertainty surrounding scientific knowledge. Whether it is in the area of health care services, industrial safety or environmental regulation, the scientific understandings that underpin these areas – and that were once afforded unquestionable status owing to their truth value – are now burdened with unanswerable challenges to their authority.[6] For example, the courts have demonstrated a greater willingness to question medical expert authority and even to declare it illogical.[7] Medical scandal and error have played a part in heightening tension between patients and doctors, fuelling concerns that medical professionals construe the needs of patients more narrowly than patients themselves.[8] Science has given up some ground to law, policy and administration as the seat of truth and progress.

[5] N Luhmann, *Social Systems* (Stanford, Stanford University Press, 1984/1995) 325.

[6] See generally J Paterson, 'Trans-science, Trans-law and Proceduralization' (2003) 12(4) *Social & Legal Studies* 525, 527.

[7] *Bolitho v City & Hackney Health Authority* [1997] 3 WLR 1151.

[8] JP Davies et al, 'The Problems of Offenders with Mental Disorders: A Plurality of Perspectives within a Single Mental Health Care Organisation' (2006) 63 *Social Science and Medicine* 1097, 1097.

Luhmann writes that law in particular appears to provide a unique guarantee: the elimination of risk. Law guarantees that complying with law ensures one's conduct is considered free of future recrimination.[9] The appearance of risking nothing through an adherence to law, however, does not mean that conduct is risk free.[10] Even if the law is proved to be incorrect because new advances in science require a different regulatory approach to be taken, law remains valid as long as it is valid. Even if repealed or replaced, law requires new law to change it.[11] No matter what developments happen outside of law, legal norms will arguably immunise society against the anxiety of an unknown future. Law, it seems, renders the unknown future less risky, albeit in *legal form*. Legal communications about human rights (ie, Article 2 of the ECHR) and fairness (ie, natural justice) justify the independent investigation process in particular and inform it as a process grounded in the pursuit of truth and certainty. Security is provided. Patient homicide investigations are legally mandated procedures that, in addition to improving health care safety, are invested with legal qualities that make them 'safe' in other ways (eg, providing legal protection). Yet, law itself is questionable. For instance, a legal decision to ban the sale and use of a noxious industrial chemical may be made according to what previous legal communications have been made about similar issues. Indeed, these types of decisions make sense from a legal point of view (ie, that protecting people and the environment is a legal duty,) but it may have unexpected ramifications in other social systems that are unable to speak to questions of law. At most, social systems, such as the economy, are irritated by legal communications in such situations. Furthermore, they are irritated in unpredictable ways. A legal decision to ban the use of certain chemicals may irritate the economy in the form of firms being unable to do business. Legal communications therefore may be risky to make.

These points underline the extent to which societies are defined by unique logics of risk. Conventional theories of risk situate the concept in ontological categories (eg, technological risks, the risks of globalisation, power).[12] Beck famously attributed risk to technological progress and the pursuit of wealth. He argued that risk is an explosion of unforeseeable hazards that call for the 'discovering, administering, acknowledging, avoiding or concealing such hazards with respect to specially defined horizons of relevance'.[13] The unintended 'side-effects' of technological progress (eg, genetic mutations from the use of pesticides, accidents on oil

[9] N Luhmann, *Law as a Social System* (Oxford, Oxford University Press, 1993/2008) 66, 471–73.

[10] See M King and C Thornhill, *Niklas Luhmann's Theory of Politics and Law* (Basingstoke, Palgrave Macmillan, 2003) 187.

[11] Luhmann, *Risk* (n 1) 54; *Law* (n 9) 469. Luhmann writes that 'Norms, and the validity that supports them, are no longer based on the constants of religion or nature or an unchallenged social structure, but are now experienced and dealt with as time projection. They are valid until further notice'. See also Paterson (n 6) 533.

[12] See U Beck, *Risk Society: Towards a New Modernity* (London, Sage Publications, 1992/2005); Burchell et al, *The Foucault Effect* (n 4).

[13] Beck, *Risk Society* (n 12) 19–20.

platforms) have defied scientific expertise. Science reacts, however, by mounting attempts to control the side-effects.[14] Science, therefore, is an 'expansion of research possibilities and of knowledge itself'.[15] The result, however, is an uncontrollable explosion of side-effects resulting from scientific attempts to control a previous set of side-effects. Science, as a result, loses its standing as an unquestionable authority.

For Beck, non-scientific voices are now seen as carrying equal, if not more, weight when it comes to judging how hazards should be controlled, monitored and addressed. The promises of science to ensure technological safety have been broken on many notable occasions. More doubt has been expressed about the abilities of science to make the world safer. The mass media and interest groups are particularly vocal. These doubts have led to the reaffirmation of scientific promises 'through cosmetic or real interventions in the techno-economic development'.[16] These interventions become the focus of objection and suspicion by non-scientific voices; chief among the non-scientific voices that have gained wider currency are law, politics and morality.[17]

Like science, however, non-scientific voices are unable to resolve doubt and solve risk-based problems in a functionally differentiated society.[18] Man-made disasters and responses to them illustrate the point. The Thalidomide scandal and the dangers of asbestos have undermined society's faith in scientists to protect people. Scientific discovery is inherently unstable.[19] The ambition of making the future of society safe through science is open to dispute.

The logic of risk and its disputable quality in independent investigations is difficult to escape:

> I think years ago, people would say 'it's rare, but occasionally, someone's going to go out and do something awful and there's probably not a lot we can do about it'. I don't think anyone would dare utter those words now. Everything is seen as predictable and preventable. We see it all the time, on the news. We see it with baby deaths.

[14] ibid 49.

[15] ibid 28.

[16] ibid 19–20.

[17] See AM Weinberg, 'Science and Trans-Science' (1972) 10(2) *Minerva* 209, 215; AJ Wistrich, 'The Evolving Temporality of Lawmaking' (2012) 44 *Connecticut Law Review* 757, 783; SP Hier, 'Risk and Panic in Late Modernity: Implications of the Converging Sites of Social Anxiety' (2003) 54(1) *British Journal of Sociology* 3; N Luhmann, *Ecological Communication* (Cambridge, Polity Press, 1989); M Douglas, *Risk and Blame: Essays in Cultural Theory* (London, Routledge, 1992) x. Risk, according to Douglas, is 'the regular coinage of exchange on public policy'.

[18] See Luhmann, *Risk* (n 1) 61–62; Paterson, 'Trans-science' (n 6) 526; King and Thornhill, *Niklas Luhmann's Theory* (n 10) 27–29, 155; Philippopoulos-Mihalopoulos, *Absent Environments* (n 2) 127–29; R Nobles and D Schiff, *Observing Law Through Systems Theory* (London, Hart Publishing, 2012) 131.

[19] K Popper, *The Logic of Scientific Discovery* (London, Hutchison, 1972) 111. Popper writes that 'The empirical basis of objective science has nothing "absolute" about it. Science does not rest upon a solid bedrock. The bold structures of its theories rises, as it were, above a swamp. It is like a building erected on piles. The piles are driven down from above into the swamp, but not down to any natural or "given" base; and if we stop driving the piles deeper, it is not because we have reached firm ground. We simply stop when we are satisfied that the piles are firm enough to carry the structure, at least for the time being'.

> Unfortunately, there are some horrible nasty manipulative cruel people who will go out and harm babies and children. Are they all predictable and preventable? Probably not, but nobody dare say it. **Investigator 3**

Risk embodies the 'limits of ignorance'.[20] It is the rule in a functionally differentiated society rather than the exception. A functionally differentiated society is inherently uncertain and contingent because it lacks a superintendent. It lacks a system for all other systems to follow for the purpose of dissolving identified risks into safety. There is simply disagreement, objection and regret. A risk of something happening is resistant to certainty because the event lies in the future. We already know from Luhmann that the future is always out of reach. It is inaccessible. Risk is yet another aspect of the future that is unreachable: 'When we seek definitions of the concept of risk, we immediately find ourselves befogged, with an impression of being unable to see beyond our own front bumper'.[21] Yet, a risk ceases to be a risk once the future becomes known in the present and is converted into the past.[22] The possibility of future loss is pervasive in society's (ie, social systems) descriptions about itself and its future.[23]

B. Luhmann's 'Risk'

The points discussed thus far link up with Luhmann's concept of risk. He understands risk as a form of communication produced by society's social systems. There is, however, more to Luhmann's concept of risk. Luhmann's conceptual framework is built in a way that enables the argument that 'risk is everywhere'. In other words, risk is pervasive. It relates to a diverse set of conditions in modern society. It relates to the possibility of future loss. It is irreducible to a single category or observation. For Luhmann, risk relates to decision making and meaning in three dimensions of social reality in which society's function systems operate.[24] These dimensions were explained in the previous chapter: the time dimension, the material dimension and the social dimension. Risk as a description of loss which society produces and applies to its future resonates in all three.[25] Communications have implications for the experience of time (ie, time before a communication is made and after it

[20] Philippopoulos-Mihalopoulos, *Absent Environments* (n 2) 120.

[21] Luhmann, *Risk* (n 1) 6.

[22] Philippopoulos-Mihalopoulos, *Absent Environments* (n 2) 119: 'Any definition of risk simultaneously tries to negate the subject matter of definition: the fear of risk renders obsolete the need for a definition of risk per se'. '[W]e define risk by defining the initial steps of any method of prevention, which are the calculation of probability and of consequences'. See also Luhmann, *Risk* (n 1) 7: attempts to define risk have been said to 'delimit, [and] not adequately describe (let alone explain) the object under investigation'.

[23] Luhmann, *Risk* (n 1) 33.

[24] Philippopoulos-Mihalopoulos, *Absent Environments* (n 2) 122. See also KD Japp and I Kusche, 'Systems Theory and Risk' in JO Zinn (ed), *Social Theories of Risk and Uncertainty: An Introduction* (Oxford, Blackwell, 2008) 85. 'Decision making integrates past and future in a selective way, which means always contingently or according to criteria themselves fixed by decisions'.

[25] See Japp and Kusche, 'Systems Theory and Risk' (n 24) 83.

is made), the physical world (ie, the condition of the material environment and objects within it) and other people, groups and societies (ie, social effects). Risk may, then, be analysed through systems theory and explained as a form of communication that relies on decisions that have implications for the three dimensions of reality.

Chapter 3 explained that decisions are a building block of organisational communication. Decisions to locate an organisation, admit members to it and plan activities all make up an organisation. Decisions are an organisation. Organisations are outside of society under systems theory however. Conceivably, decisions are made whenever an organisation or a sentient being selects a possibility over others. A decision, in itself, does not mean anything socially, however, until it acquires significance (ie, meaning) for one or more of society's social function systems. To reiterate, socially available meaning is produced by social systems of communication rather than the decisions of an organisation.[26] Yet, decisions are an important aspect of Luhmann's general theory of social systems and they are central to his concept of risk.[27] Decisions emerge as dilemmas also, in addition to being a necessary element of organisations. Decisions are, then, a choice between alternatives.

Social systems, as self-referential systems of communication, self-create reality because their operations are irreplaceable and non-replicable. The reality of a social function system is concerned with selecting self-constructed possibilities over others using recursive operations, moment to moment. Decisions are crucial for enabling these selections. What decisions mean is a matter of social communication but the selection of a possibility necessitates a decision to be made out of a range of possible others. Decisions are typified by making choices over others. Social systems, through their operations, structure how decisional choices are made as opposed to choices made on behalf of social systems by psychic, biological or other social function systems. Social systems of communication are the architects of their own reality and consequently must attribute their fate to themselves as opposed to external sources of authority. Decisions replace fate as self-directed choices among possibilities, which is a defining moniker of a functionally differentiated society, in addition to being a building block of organisations.

Public (health) services are made up of decisions. They involve an ever-increasing differentiation of expertise (eg, psychiatry, nursing, social work, probation services), competing orientations of time and different local rationalities.[28] Independent investigators are tasked with examining patient homicides, making judgements about the decisions made within services and making

[26] See J Jalava, *Trust as a Decision: The Problems and Functions of Trust in Luhmannian Systems Theory* (Helsinki, University of Helsinki, 2006). Jalava argues that the decisions of organisations form the necessary programmes for social systems of communication, enabling the application of their binary codes.

[27] Paterson, 'Trans-science' (n 6) 526.

[28] See E Munro, 'Mental Health Tragedies: Investigating Beyond Human Error' (2004) 15(3) *Journal of Forensic Psychiatry & Psychology* 475, 479.

recommendations. Making sense of and hence reducing service complexity through investigation and recommendation inevitably requires selecting certain approaches and judgements (ie, decisions) over others. As one investigator interviewed explained:

> [T]he NHS is like a large whale, but what happens when you get closer to it is that it is a large shoal of fish instead. It's very fragmented and there are lots of different organisations in it. **Investigator 5**

Each individual fish may be said to represent a different rationality, a different way of doing things and a different way of making decisions. Taking advantage of a possibility to change service delivery (eg, through making a specific set of recommendations) is nonetheless risky because the effects of deciding on a particular recommendation may produce unintended consequences in areas governed by decisions informed by opposing aims, rationalities and system logics.

Many voices resonate throughout the patient homicide governance space and they place a series of demands on investigators. These voices and demands operate within structures of legal, political and moral communication. Inquiry recommendations, investigative lines of questioning and contact with families are all risky in the sense that they may attract moral criticism, are subjected to newsworthy exposure by the mass media and invite resistance from families. They are a risk. These dynamics capture Luhmann's ideas about risk:

> One demands more information, better information, complains about the information being withheld by those who wish to prevent others from projecting other interpretations or making greater demands on an objectively given universe of facts – as though there were 'information' available that one could have or not have as the case may be.[29]

Decisions constantly have to be made because trust is hard to come by. As Luhmann put it, 'we feel it increasingly appropriate to complain about and to attack decision makers, in particular those responsible (and therefore attracting attribution) at high levels'.[30] It is not surprising, therefore, to see those on the periphery of an investigation (eg, families, the media) disagree and object to its findings or for there to be objection to the decision that an investigation is necessary at all. It is common for claims to be made that a superior decisional possibility should have been taken by a decision maker (eg, investigator) on a particular issue but was not.[31] For Luhmann, regrets are expected in a functionally differentiated society; 'there are so many causes for things going wrong in improbable ways'.[32] Much speculation and concern is generated about what could have been achieved had a different decision been taken. Decisional dilemmas, indeed, have a long pedigree.[33]

[29] Luhmann, *Risk* (n 1) 21.
[30] ibid 226.
[31] See King and Thornhill, *Niklas Luhmann's Theory* (n 10) 184.
[32] Luhmann, *Risk* (n 1) 12.
[33] See Aristotle, *Poetics* (London, Penguin Books, 1996) 48. 'So much for tragedy and epic, the number and variety of their forms and component parts, the causes of their success and failure, and criticisms and solutions'.

Luhmann's systems theory, however, revolutionises how we understand decisions and risks. It rejects the idea that there are risks 'out there' that we, as human beings, identify and tame to the point of safety for the purpose of making society a better a place. Consistent with his general theory of social systems, Luhmann argued that risk is communicated about within social systems of communication on their own terms. Risk is defined here as a description society applies to the possibility of future loss:

> Risk can be defined as the possibility of future damage, exceeding all reasonable costs, that is attributed to a decision. Risk is the hopefully avoidable causal link between decision and damage. In other words, it is the prospect of post-decisional regret.[34]

For Luhmann, risk involves communicating about decisions the consequences of which may involve future loss and which could always have been decided differently:

> At the present moment we cannot know how they [decisions] will turn out. But we can know that we ourselves and other observers will in a future present know what the situation is, and will then judge differently from the way we do now – although differences of judgement among us might arise.[35]

Decisions make society's descriptions of future loss possible. Decisions would not, however, be recognisable as decisions if the future were regarded as certain.[36] That decisions exist means that there are possibilities, only one of which may be taken up and others passed over. Put another way, making decisions means foregoing other possible decisions that could be made instead. Furthermore, decisions are not verifiable externally. Social systems are unable to refer to an external source of authority, such as religion, to verify society's fate. Decisions, therefore, rely on the authority of the social system that they are significant for. Otherwise, a social system of communication would not need decisions. Only internally, within social systems, are decisions rendered meaningful through self-referential communications. Contrary to popular assumption, no matter what methods and safeguards we use to respectively analyse and control the future before making a decision, decisions are experienced everywhere as a self-attribution of consequences for what we choose to do.[37] Decision making is itself contingent in a functionally differentiated society. The methods, techniques and routines we use to create the illusion of security are themselves subject to decisions that are inherently risky and contingent. Advantages are only enjoyable if a decision has actually been made:

> The apparently 'safe' alternative then implies the double certainty that no loss will occur and that the opportunity will be lost that one would possible [*sic*] have been able to take

[34] N Luhmann, 'Technology, Environment and Social Risk: A Systems Perspective' (1990) 4 *Industrial Crisis Quarterly* 223, 225.

[35] Luhmann, *Risk* (n 1) 16.

[36] ibid 107.

[37] Japp and Kusche, 'Systems Theory and Risk' (n 24) 81.

> via the risky variant. But this argument is deceptive, for the lost opportunity was in itself no certainty. It thus remains uncertain whether by forgoing the opportunity one has lost out on something or not; and what remains is an open question of whether one ought to regret preferring the 'safe' variant or not.[38]

Causation in accidents ranging from nuclear power to homicide committed by those receiving health care treatment for their mental disorder share one thing in common: in each instance, something could always have been done to alter the course of events and perhaps prevent the fatal occurrence. It remains uncertain, in both cases, whether by foregoing the opportunity one has lost out on something or not.

C. Decisions, Risk and Causation

Luhmann, in many areas of his work, addresses the issue of causation. His theory rejects that society is amenable to direct causative influence and control. Yet, causation is important to the patient homicide governance space. Making recommendations to improve health care services is a crucial task of the independent patient homicide investigation. The task assumes that recommendations can precisely address a diverse range of complexities in health services. There would be no point in making recommendations if the assumption was not held. Luhmann's concepts of communication and time prompt us to question these assumptions. The previous chapter explained that social systems conduct their operations at different speeds and construct time in different ways. There is no prospect of fulfilling goal-oriented improvements in health care services because of fragmentation and complexity. Projected outcomes (eg, safety reductions) arguably exist dynamically in time.[39] New events come into view as communications and decisions in society are continuously made. The 'successes' of risk reduction or elimination are, under Luhmann's theory, a communicative self-construction. A 'success' implies that there is a pre-ordained plan to improve society. Luhmann's sociology dismisses the idea that promises to eradicate risk or reduce it are viable. These promises assume that society is open to improvement and steering through a particular set of perspectives. Society is too complex to be represented in one particular perspective. Luhmann's views, therefore, prompt a rethink about what we can expect from the patient homicide governance space and the attempts of elites to influence it directly through recommendations and policy changes.

Compounding these issues around influence and control is the notion that decisions informed by one social system must be repeatedly made because other decisions in that system's environment are, unexpectedly, being made also.[40]

[38] Luhmann, *Risk* (n 1) 20.
[39] See S Burris et al, 'Nodal Governance' (2005) 30 *Australian Journal of Legal Philosophy* 30, 35.
[40] Luhmann, *Risk* (n 1) 189. Luhmann posits that 'To be a decision, a decision requires other decisions'.

The future is uncertain and increasingly contingent because the dynamic flow of decisions and communication – insulated in their operational closure – never ceases. The flow of change makes what seemed correct yesterday appear erroneous today and in need of modification. A perpetual need for social systems to communicate about their environments and drive future decision making in the face of continual change has emerged. The future, as a horizon that never can be grasped in the present, is continually communicated about in the form of decisions that have anticipated effects, but which are beyond what is really knowable. Communicating about the future means acquiring more knowledge, but it also means becoming more ignorant:

> [T]he more we know, the better we know what we do not know, and the more elaborate our risk awareness becomes. The more rationally we calculate and the more complex the calculations become, the more aspects come into view involving uncertainty about the future and thus risk.[41]

Error, disappointment and surprise about risk call for more communications to be made about the future, especially in the form of decisions. Attributing causes to decisions for the purposes of communicating about the future and making decisions is therefore not straightforward. For example, legal communications traditionally emphasise individual culpability when it comes to ascertaining causes. Theories of causation developed in criminal and civil law are well known for the simple causative link they draw between defendant and damage.[42] Yet, even legal causation is beginning to struggle with the growing complexity of society.[43] The pace of change, inequality of resources, new industrial dangers, public service fragmentation and occupational uncertainties mean that other advanced social systems of communication (eg, medicine) equally encounter uncertainties relating to causality. Decisions to create new ways of doing things create an 'excess of options'.[44] For instance, independent investigators are given the task of understanding and judging the complexity of options that face psychiatrists and other clinical staff when treating a patient. The task is rendered all the more uncertain because staff conduct is, primarily, based on skills rather than non-human influences (eg, laboratory conditions or equipment).[45] There is, therefore, bound to be greater questioning and regret after certain decisions, or decisions not to make a decision, have been made about a patient who goes on to commit a homicide.[46] There is blame and accusation.[47]

[41] ibid 28.

[42] Legal scholars, however, have sought to draw attention to the apparent shift in law from a philosophy of individual responsibility to group responsibility. Barach Bush maps the shift by exploring the implications of vicarious liability, which allows the imposition of legal liability on a group for the actions of its members (see RA Baruch Bush, 'Between Two Worlds: The Shift From Individual to Group Responsibility in the Law of Causation of Injury' (1986) 33 *UCLA Law Review* 1473, 1477).

[43] See *Fairchild v Glenhaven Funeral Services Ltd and Others* [2003] 1 AC 32 at 43.

[44] Japp and Kusche, 'Systems Theory and Risk' (n 24) 81.

[45] See Luhmann, *Risk* (n 1) 226.

[46] ibid 20.

[47] G Szmukler, 'Homicide Inquiries: What Sense Do They Make? (2000) 24 *Psychiatric Bulletin* 6, 9.

For independent inquiries, learning meaningful lessons from the medically defined past with a view to improving care and treatment in the future involves eschewing strict models of causation and attributing events to wider systems of care. An investigator commented during interview that causality is far from simple. It is fraught with tension and confusion:

> There's too much tension between the root causation determination and lesson learned and the individual culpability. You've got to do one or the other and I think the professional bodies probably need to concentrate on individual culpability. I think these investigations, which are meant to be about improving service-user's care, should be about the organisation. And personally, I don't think you can do both. That's not unique because if you look at, say, marine accidents or shipping accidents you've got a regulatory function in the UK anyway, the maritime and coastguard agency and the marine accident and investigation branch which has an explicit role not to apportion blame. Its role is to discover root causation of shipping accidents and making maritime safety better … If you just deal with immediate causation, which some organisations do, you can kind of address very tactical sort of issues, but you've no confidence that you're going to prevent the same things happening again. **Investigator 5**

Attributing causes to events within investigations is therefore difficult. It involves many possibilities, including the attribution of root and contributory causes. Likewise, Luhmann indicates that causal attributions proliferate as society becomes more functionally differentiated. The causes of events become untraceable among the chains of decisions already made. These causality problems are clearly visible in independent investigations and they are emblematic of causality problems more generally as 'long-term remote effects and an incalculably high number of contributing causes'.[48] Luhmann continues that assigning causes to decisions becomes increasingly complex but it is obvious to those attributing the causes that decisions are responsible:

> [I]n the accumulation of the effects of decision making, in long-term consequences of decisions no longer identifiable, in over-complex and no longer traceable causal relations, there are conditions that can actuate considerable losses or damage without being attributable to decisions – although it is clear that without decisions having been made such detrimental effects would never have occurred.[49]

Luhmann goes on to write that 'the occurrence of a disaster is often not attributable to any particular individual decisions'.[50] 'Decision trees' emerge that 'actuate losses without being attributable to decisions'.[51] Decisional complexity is managed in a variety of ways within the patient homicide governance space, not least

[48] Luhmann, *Risk* (n 1) 169.

[49] ibid 26.

[50] ibid.

[51] ibid. Luhmann cites the example of the decision to start car engines and the effects of car exhaust fumes. He contends that 'it would not be possible to classify starting up a car engine as a risky decision'. The conditions of loss in Luhmann's example are created by 'a vast accumulation of decisions' as opposed to an isolated instance of decision making.

through the creation of incident decision trees that shift the assessment of adverse incidents away from attributing blame and more towards systems and processes.[52] 'One can relate everything to everything else' and 'Everyone is cause *and* effect, and thus *non*-cause. The causes dribble away into a general amalgam of agents and conditions, reactions and counter-reactions, which brings social certainty and popularity to the concept of system.[53] For Luhmann, however, risk is communicative. For scholars like Beck, it is technological. Although both thinkers share similarities in their arguments, they are fundamentally different. One is anti-humanist (Luhmann) and the other is ontological (Beck) in outlook. Indeed, there is a major benefit to Luhmann's approach that Beck's position fails to provide: its applicability 'to every instance of decision making', rather than its confinement 'to the realm of technology or health or to aspects of globalization'.[54]

Luhmann's theoretical arguments about decisions and causation connect to current concerns about the patient homicide governance space. Investigators are tasked to consider a raft of evidence relating to past decisions. Munro explains that independent investigations involve a process of attribution of causes to events, but there is nothing linear about how events are understood to happen in complex systems of care:

> When investigating a homicide after the fact, we are tracing a chain of events back in time to understand how it happened. We are not, however, dealing with a closed system with linear causality (where it can be relatively simple to identify the causes of an outcome) but with the complex, real world that is in a continuous and dynamic flow.[55]

An investigator commented that their investigations open up many opportunities to causally attribute events to past decisions:

> [T]he link between failings and harm was a bit less tangible perhaps than machinery guarding accidents or something like that … we basically found them extremely challenging, both technically and commercially … Historically, failures in industrial settings were largely omissions rather than deliberate acts and here you've actually got someone who has committed murder or manslaughter. And then you're looking at the organisational performance around trying to prevent that event and that's quite different I suppose. **Investigator 5**

Another investigator expressed an aversion to using causality as a reference point:

> I don't ever approach an investigation with causality in my mind because it maybe that I'm interpreting the use of that word differently from the way you're intending it, but for me causality is 'I'm looking for the one thing'. And I'm never – I never look for one thing because I know, 99 percent of the time, I won't find one thing. I know there will be multiple factors. There will be multiple pieces of Swiss cheese that I am going to find

[52] NHS Improvement, *A Just Culture Guide* (NHS Improvement, 2018).
[53] Luhmann, *Risk* (n 1) 31–33.
[54] Japp and Kusche, 'Systems Theory and Risk' (n 24) 80; JO Zinn, 'A Comparison of Sociological Theorizing on Risk and Uncertainty' in Zinn (n 24) 174.
[55] Munro, 'Mental Health Tragedies' (n 28) at 479.

> that produce a group of contributory factors. So for me, the word causality, it jars a bit. **Investigator 4**

One investigator expressed the view that causality has lost meaning within investigations:

> I don't understand what is meant by causality. What I was trying to do was to get an honest account of what happened … that 'had things been done differently the outcome would have been different' is such a hard call. You could say 'had they detained that person, they would be in hospital and the homicide would not have happened'. It's crazy. It's not true at all. That person could have killed someone in the hospital. They could have escaped from hospital. They could have been discharged early and still killed that person. We just don't know. **Investigator 6**

Independent investigations encounter a myriad of potential causes of homicide that obfuscate linear lines of causality. Causes, in these terms, appear as constellations of missed opportunities, combinations of proximal factors and 'suboptimal processes' consisting of organisational factors, patient factors, communication factors, education factors, working conditions, team and social factors.[56] There is no hierarchy of causes, as such. There is simply 'an accelerated dynamic of information and knowledge' that obscures any real sense of direct cause and effect.[57] One inquiry report described the care failings identified by the investigators as cumulative, impacting one another over many years 'in a snowball effect':[58]

> Often, it is rarely easy to find a particular cause. What happens a lot is that you pick up a lot of service delivery problems that may not have particularly contributed to the incident. It's not very often that you identify a specific causative factor, if something could have been done very differently and you're sure the incident would not have happened. It tends to be much more 'this didn't happen', 'that didn't happen', 'the person wasn't followed up for their depot'. So, you tend to pick up a lot of service delivery problems that are not directly causal I think. **Investigator 7**

As knowledge expands, particularly in complex areas such as health care services, so does manufactured uncertainty; there are always ongoing attempts to understand why risks materialise, leading to the creation of new bodies of knowledge about the risks associated with dealing with other risks. Our perceptions of risk thus change often.[59] Governance in many areas tends to view an incident 'as an outcome of what has come before' and 'that we will inevitably get it "wrong"

[56] See L Wilson and S Wicks, *An Independent Investigation into the Care and Treatment of JMcF* (Niche Health & Social Care Consulting Ltd, October 2011) 87; M Dineen et al, *Independent Investigation into SUI 2006/8119*, 63.

[57] See Japp and Kusche, 'Systems Theory and Risk' (n 24) 81.

[58] A Johnstone, *Independent Investigation into the Care and Treatment of Mr X by the Lincolnshire Partnership NHS Foundation Trust and the Avon and Wiltshire Mental Health Partnership NHS Trust* (Health and Social Care Advisory Service (undated)) 15.

[59] See N Eastman and J Peay, 'Law without Enforcement: Themes and Perspectives' in N Eastman and J Peay (eds), *Law without Enforcement: Integrating Mental Health and Justice* (Oxford, Hart Publishing, 1999) 4.

to some extent'.[60] More, not less, contingency is invited into the present. The complexity of decision chains also makes it unclear as to what consequences belong to a particular decision.[61] There are instead complex interactions between many decisions, omissions and their consequences. Further courses of action and omission occur in relation to a range of decision-making responsibilities that 'overlap, occur sequentially or merely run parallel to, possibly in ignorance of, one another'.[62] Decisions are individually abstracted, described, mulled over and commented upon in detail.[63] Yet, conclusions are rarely firm. It is understandable that limits are placed on answering questions of causation in inquiries.[64] In theory, they may investigate all manner of causal possibilities that impact on other causal factors:[65]

> A thorough examination of a patient's history could include a study of society in general and how public attitudes to mental illness or racial, social, and economic factors affect someone's mental well-being and how these, in turn, limit the beneficial effects of psychiatric treatment.[66]

There is, therefore, no end to what an inquiry may potentially explore. Independent investigations have gone as far to apply 'stop rules' in order to moderate their inquiry. Lines of questioning are thus circumscribed. The evaluation of patient care is moderated against accepted policies on 'best practice'.[67] The accumulation of past decisions surrounding a perpetrator is reduced to manageable proportions for the purposes of establishing meaningful conclusions.

The lengthy time period between a homicide incident and the completion of an investigation has presented 'a number of challenges' for investigation panels also.[68] A series of 'significant positive changes in policy, standards, systems and processes' occur during that time.[69] The past may become inaccessible for investigation purposes. The attribution of consequences to certain past decisions made by

[60] Burris et al, 'Nodal Governance' (n 39) 35.

[61] See Luhmann, *Risk* (n 1) 26, 41. For example, disastrous events are often precipitated by a conglomerate of decisions that are resistant to direct connection with such events. Yet, without these decisions, the disastrous event would not have occurred. Luhmann writes that 'Observers may well continue to fight about shares, for example in the question of whether and to what extent automobile exhaust fumes are responsible for the death of forests; but even then, it would not be possible to classify starting up a car engine as a risky decision'.

[62] J Peay, Introduction' in J Peay (ed), *Inquiries After Homicide* (London, Duckworth & Co, 1996) 2.

[63] D Carson, 'Structural Problems, Perspectives and Solutions' in Peay, Inquiries After Homicide (n 62) 124.

[64] See, however, C Parker and A McCulloch, *Key Issues in Homicide Inquiries* (London, MIND, 1999) 2.

[65] Munro, 'Mental Health Tragedies' (n 28) 479: 'it is logically possible to ask why it [the factor deemed to have a causal effect] itself occurred and so continue tracing events further and further back in time'.

[66] ibid 480.

[67] ibid.

[68] M Rae et al, *Report of the Independent Investigation into the Circumstances Surrounding the Care and Treatment of Mr A* (NHS London Strategic Health Authority, Caring Solutions UK, February 2012) 8.

[69] ibid.

professionals about the patient is, potentially, infinite in some circumstances but also impossible in others. Indeed, it may not be possible to produce a meaningful finding in an investigation if information is socially unavailable due to inadequate memory recall or missing documentation.

D. Decisions and Dilemmas

The idea that decisions are dilemmas is an important theme of the present chapter. Risk is, in simple language, a dilemma. Dilemmas pervade the patient homicide governance space. Alongside the problems of counterfactual reasoning, bias and mutating foreground events,[70] investigations have been known to advance hypotheses of alternative, possible pasts that never actually materialised.[71] A series of judgements, made in the present and based on these hypotheses, is subsequently formed on what to do next. A series of possibilities therefore opens up for investigators (and others). Recommendations may be selected over possible others. Decisions are made to attribute adverse consequences to past decisions and new occasions for decision making are taken up. Decisions and dilemmas typify the investigation process as well as the care and treatment provided to the perpetrator. They necessitate occasions for fresh decision making about previous decision making.

The circularity of decision making connects with Luhmann's description of decisions to address perceived risk as risky to take.[72] For example, risk assessment is common practice in mental health services. It involves calculating the likelihood of a patient becoming violent in the future. During an independent investigation, the inquiry panel itself will decide to subject a past decision to conduct a risk assessment to scrutiny. It will consider whether the assessment made was adequate for the purposes of reaching a conclusion about the quality of care provided and making a recommendation. The panel are communicating about past risk communication. In the process, the panel feeds its determination into a new set of communications about the future which, through second-order observation, is a risk too:

> You would always look at the risk assessments, whether they had been updated, you'd always ask people how they saw the risk, how they considered the risk. But I think that risk assessment is an inexact science. Often, the real tendency is to have hindsight bias

[70] See Szmukler, 'Homicide Inquiries' (n 47) 8; A Grounds, 'Commentary on "Inquiries: Who Needs Them?"' (1997) 21 *Psychiatric Bulletin* 134, 134; D Reiss, 'Counterfactuals and Inquiries After Homicide' (2001) 12(1) *The Journal of Forensic Psychiatry* 169, 171–77.

[71] See generally JM Olson et al, 'Psychological Biases in Counterfactual Thought Experiments' in PE Tetlock and A Belkin (eds), *Counterfactual Thought Experiments in World Politics: Logical, Methodological and Psychological Perspectives* (Chichester, Princeton University Press, 1996) 296.

[72] Luhmann, *Risk* (n 1) 30. 'The additional and relief risk can consist in the preventive measures proving quite unnecessary: we toil day after day round the lake to keep fit only to meet our end in a plane crash. Or prevention proves to be causally ineffective'.

> and to say that he was always risky, he was always a murderer, but actually at the time in hindsight … so risk is one … people will look at that in a great level of detail and perhaps give undue emphasis over it. **Investigator 7**

Another investigator was more explicit about the impulse to assess the safety of risk assessments in health services:

> My role is to carry out the independent homicide reviews but also to expand our role into activities that are more proactive … 'are our risk assessments safe as they could be?'. **Investigator 1**

Risk communications in the patient homicide governance space therefore involve reflecting on past decisions and their consequences for the purposes of making decisions in the present. Decisions could be taken differently, granted, and a possibility not taken could have produced greater advantages if taken. During the perpetrator's care and treatment and then after in the context of an independent investigation, there are decisions, dilemmas and contingency. Investigators are very open about the contingency of decision making in health services and its relevance to their work:

> When we do an investigation, when you look, you can always find something that could have been done better. That's always the case. **Investigator 3**

Looking back into the past with a view to reaching conclusions in the present for the purposes of making decisions about how health services should operate in the future is about referring to past decisions and creating a decisional chain in the present so that meaningful change can be brought about:

> What I'm looking to find out is what was informing their decision making? Why did they think that was okay? Why didn't they think differently? **Investigator 2**

It is rare for investigators to form the belief that no other decisional possibilities were realisable by professionals involved with the perpetrator's care and treatment. One investigator commented that, after reviewing 60 investigations conducted by his company, only one reached a conclusion that nothing could have been done:

> We analysed 60 reports and there was one report that we found where there was nothing that could have been done. There are no recommendations. One report out of 60. All the others go from 'something could have been done' to 'this incident could have been predictable and preventable' … The vast majority in the middle was that staff could not have predicted and prevented but the standard of care wasn't fantastic. The medication wasn't given in the way it should have been. The diagnosis was off. **Investigator 1**

Those interested parties beyond the investigation (eg, families) frequently implore investigators to examine past decisions and to consider the decisional possibilities that were available to clinical staff at the relevant time. Julian Hendy explained the point in the following terms:

> They [families] just want to know what went wrong. What went on? Were there any problems, could anything have been done differently? Are they going to do anything about it in the future?

The dilemma of decision making (ie, that decisions forego other decisional possibilities that are different and arguably better) even applies at a much broader policy level where changes in how investigations are conducted have been instituted. Chapter 2 explained the degree to which investigations have evolved into a process that is now informed by clinical expertise. Following the implementation of the amendment to HSG(94) in 2005, independent mental health homicide inquiries ceased to be chaired by a senior lawyer or judge. The amendments created scope for those close to health services (eg, psychiatrists, nurses, social workers) to step into the spotlight and change the way these processes were managed. The change, ultimately, came about because a decision was made that inquiries could be conducted better and more reliably:

> [T]here were new kids on the block like me who saw new ways of doing things and thought this can be done differently. You know, this does not need to be done like this. You know, you don't need a lawyer to do a constructive analysis of a case management for a patient. **Investigator 2**

The contingency of decision making – an important element of Luhmann's work on social systems and more specifically on risk – is a far-reaching concept that is relevant to understanding the dynamics of the patient homicide governance space. Luhmann's approach encourages us to step back from complex governance processes and to appreciate that they, too, are part of a chain of decisions that originate in the care and treatment of a perpetrator. Decisions form an opportunity to communicate about decisions in an ongoing cycle of decisions where contingency and dilemma are perpetual.

E. The Need for Caution

The decision to recommend modifications to health services after a homicide incident is something that investigators want to see lead to successful improvement. The option of recommending a complete overhaul of services is, in theory, possible although these types of recommendations are, unsurprisingly, rarely tabled. The risks associated with incremental change are less visible than those of structural reform.[73] Knowledge of the future, in the form of risk – combined with a broadening horizon of possibilities – makes attempts to establish more certainty very difficult. A tendency towards conservatism is therefore cultivated.[74] The decision to investigate homicides, interview witnesses and make recommendations are all made with an eye on their future consequences. The utmost caution is practised, however, because, as some investigators openly acknowledge, health care services are vital and complex and it is considered unwise to recommend radical change to them. Unpredictable consequences are likely even if conservative

[73] Japp and Kusche, 'Systems Theory and Risk' (n 24) 82.
[74] See King and Thornhill, *Niklas Luhmann's Theory* (n 10) 198.

recommendations are implemented. Health care services undergo continual change and are sensitive to external intervention. Introducing yet more change leads to further complexity:

> I think it's the capacity of people, if you're in a day-to-day frontline service, there's a lot going on, people can only concentrate on so many things, people move on, the organisational memory drops a bit. There was a crisis six months ago, there's something else going on now. The amount and complexity of the task. It's actually quite hard to keep your eye on all the plates spinning. **Investigator 7**

The investigator added that the complexity of health care services makes it difficult to articulate precise recommendations:

> Sometimes there are specific things that you can identify but a lot of it is around the interfaces between services and about communication with GPs, families. These are slightly softer things. It is not something specific you identify has to happen. So I think the recommendations tend to be a bit more general really. **Investigator 7**

Conservatism as opposed to radicalism appears to be the preferred approach for investigators. Some investigators perceive the root of many care inadequacies in health services to be located in culture, which is an issue too complex for successful intervention:

> The themes of the findings tend to be the same sort of things. The recommendations tend to be the same, so they tend to be around supervision of staff, awareness of policies, documentation of risk. They tend to be in those sorts of groups. The problem or the underlying issue is always one of culture. It is actually quite hard to make recommendations that address culture. **Investigator 7**

Conservatism manifests itself in other ways:

> In response to one-off aberrations, we'll set them [health services] with a directional recommendation rather than a 'do this to mend it' recommendation. The latter is quite traditional … If it's an isolated issue and it's not normal in the field, sometimes there is no value in making a recommendation. We don't want to change things on the back of one slip up. **Investigator 2**

The investigator's comment demonstrates that there is a threshold for advancing recommendations. There is a general reluctance to try and 'fix things' in precise terms, but rather to steer services in a preferred direction.

F. Risk and Danger

Luhmann's argument that observing observers brings about a paradigm shift in how society's problems are understood and acted upon is crucial to his understanding of risk. The counter-condition to risk in mainstream social and intellectual life is safety. People, organisations and institutions aim to minimise risks in all walks of life. Being as safe as possible is the norm. Statistical calculation, actuarial projections and risk assessments in complex industries all work towards instituting a set of safe conditions or as safe as one can make these conditions. People may take an alternative route home after working late at night because it is well lit and less attractive to criminals; the alternative route is considered a safer option than our usual route, which we may regard as less safe. At the level of law as a social system, Article 2 of the ECHR and the independent investigations carried out pursuant to it are part of an effort to maintain the expectation that health services are safe and the legal rights of patients secured.

According to Luhmann, the concept of safety in mainstream social life is an oversimplification. The notion that there is an attainable condition of safety or a set of attainable conditions that are safer than what is currently experienced is arguably utopian and ignorant of society's complexity. The belief that safety is achievable or that improvements in areas of safety can be made is a notion that sits close to the purpose of an independent patient homicide investigation however.[75] The notion is supported by an investigation's ability to organise the diversity of views and opinions about patient homicides, what led to their occurrence, whether they could have been prevented and what should be done to improve services for the future. The views of families are particularly relevant here. Relatives are given forums to request information[76] and ask questions.[77] They advance an assortment of perspectives and demands. They express views that past decisions are regrettable and that other, more advantageous decisions could have been made.

The trouble is, however, as Luhmann pointed out, that the advantages of alternative decisions can never be realised unless decisional alternatives are taken up. First-order observational perspectives do not recognise these alternatives as advantages not yet selected. For example, professional safety experts regard risk as an objectively quantifiable condition. It is a condition considered to be achievable through the exercise of knowledge and skill. Similarly, second-order observation operates along the same lines. Most function systems may be said to involve the observation of internal observations (eg, science may observe itself observing in the form of scientific publications).[78] Independent investigators conduct second-order observation because they utilise their knowledge of clinical practice to investigate clinical practice. They produce a final report that produces more clinical knowledge about existing clinical knowledge and practice. The main difference between second-order observation within function systems and systems theory (which is, itself, a communication in the social system of science) is that the former claims to be superior or at least claims that there is a way to exercise steering, control or manipulation in society. The difference between the two strands

[75] D Tidmarsh, 'Psychiatric Risk, Safety Cultures and Homicide Inquiries' (1997) 8(1) *The Journal of Forensic Psychiatry* 138, 145.

[76] For example, see M Dineen et al, *Independent Investigation into the Care and Treatment Provided to SU* (NHS London Strategic Health Authority, Consequence UK, February 2012) 29.

[77] ibid 7, 8, 30, 79, 82.

[78] See HG Moeller, *Luhmann Explained: From Souls to Systems* (Chicago, IL, Open Court, 2006) 76.

of thinking – systems theory and independent investigations – may be neatly captured by drawing on Moeller's view that 'second-order observation is also a kind of first-order observation, but one that has to pay for its increase in complexity with the loss of ontological certainty of data, essentials, or contents'.[79] In other words, second-order observation seeks to provide an essential truth that systems theory claims is impossible to provide. The observer conducting the observation is not taken into account (ie, the observer's blind spot). Social systems are therefore unique because they observe their respective environment as an Archimedean point of reference.[80]

Independent inquiries also involve a type of first-order observation. Patient and public safety is a main priority. Individual investigators acknowledge their scepticism about their ability to secure these aims, however, because of the challenges involved. Nevertheless, investigations are carried out for a purpose. As explained in Chapter 3, many of the investigators interviewed commented that investigations introduce objectivity and legitimacy into the quest for answers and learning post-homicide. Luhmann's concept of risk, as part of his general theory of social systems, prompts a radical questioning of such an approach.

Systems theory, at its core, is a theory of observation that describes society as a self-referential construction of meaning. These constructions, however, are produced through autopoietic observations that have blind spots.[81] Observing systems that observe in order to establish truth, objectivity or safety reveals these blind spots. Systems theory embraces blind spots and accepts that a 'final' blind spot is unobservable. As a theory of observation, Luhmann's systems theory rewrites the 'Old European' intellectual rulebook. It leads to the conclusion that safety – as a final destination for those preoccupied with minimising and eradicating risk – is unachievable because it too has its blind spot. From a systems-theoretical perspective, the only way in which a decision could be proved safe is if all decisional possibilities could be taken at once. Of course, observing both sides of a distinction at the same time is impossible (eg, a person cannot communicate legally and economically simultaneously) and we can only take up one decision-making possibility at a time. It is impossible to know whether another decisional option would have been more advantageous.

Luhmann therefore argues that it is more precise and reliable to contend that the counter-condition to risk is danger, rather than safety. The *risk/danger* distinction is, for Luhmann, a second-order distinction that a social system uses to attribute events in its environment to decisions (ie, risk) or as occurrences that are not attributable to one's decisions (ie, danger). Luhmann's approach is to understand how risk is observed rather than working out a final answer to what risk

[79] ibid 72.
[80] ibid.
[81] See ibid 74.

actually is. He therefore designates danger as a more accurate description of risk's opposite:

> The potential loss is either regarded as a consequence of the decision, that is to say, it is attributed to the decision. We then speak of risk – to be more exact of the risk of decision. Or the possible loss is considered to have been caused externally, that is to say, it is attributed to the environment. In this case we see speak of danger.[82]

Luhmann's conceptual distinction between risk and danger presupposes 'that uncertainty exists in relation to future loss'.[83] Once risk has been designated from that which is a danger, a host of possibilities to describe the possibility of future loss emerge:

> On the side of decision making ('inside' the form) we can look for ways to improve things, we can thus rationalize, carry out more complicated calculations, or introduce computers; or we can take the perspective of those affected (the other side of the form); we can, for example, round off sharp edges or deploy appeasing communication. This does not change the form in any way, nor does it lead to a dialectical 'cancelling out' of the distinction. Affected involvement remains the other side of the form, and the affected party sees the decision (even if the constraints thereof are thought about) differently from the way the decision maker does. It is an irrevocable duality – which does not necessarily constitute a conflict.[84]

Risks (eg, moving to an earthquake-prone area) and dangers (eg, having one's home destroyed by an earthquake) are contingent categories and dependent on observation. A risk or a danger is only realisable if an observer drawing that distinction is observed by a second observer (ie, second-order observation). The distinction between risk and danger, furthermore, resonates in the material dimension (ie, the distinction between system and environment) because it relates to the attribution of events to decisions, allowing for the construction of facts. So, changing one's occupation might be considered a danger if regarded as a response to unavoidable economic catastrophe and conversely having one's home devastated by an earthquake could be regarded as a risk because a decision was made to remain in an area of potential earthquake activity.

A homicide committed by a mentally disordered perpetrator may be attributed as a danger which health professionals have no control over. On the one hand, the high-profile Ritchie Report appeared to attribute Clunis' behaviour to his penchant for knives as a youngster.[85] On the other hand, the victim's family may regard a homicide as a risk that should have been better addressed by the decisions of health authorities.[86] Although most inquiries completed in 2017 were concluded

[82] Luhmann, *Risk* (n 1) 21–22. cf Philippopoulos-Mihalopoulos, *Absent Environments* (n 2) 136.

[83] Luhmann, *Risk* (n 1) 21.

[84] ibid 106.

[85] See generally J Warner, 'Inquiry Reports as Active Texts and Their Function in Relation to Professional Practice in Mental Health' (2006) 8(3) *Health, Risk & Society* 223, 231.

[86] N Wolff, 'Risk, Response and Mental Health Policy: Learning from the Experience of the United Kingdom' (2002) 27(5) *Journal of Health Politics, Policy and Law* 801, 802.

on the basis that the homicide incident was not predictable and/or preventable, all of them have produced findings that express some form of objection, regret or disagreement in relation to the expert decisions made prior to the incident occurring.[87] There will always be clashes of understanding, ongoing disputes and continual objection about what an event should be attributable to. These tensions, of course, provide the ground for further decision making (eg, decisions to launch judicial review actions).[88] Decisions are self-perpetuating.[89] Decisions inevitably have a distinct meaning within social systems of communication also and they enable systems to self-construct the past and the future. Decisions, then, acquire different levels of meaning and significance.[90] Decisions to assess homicide and suicide risks in hospitals using specific methods of assessment are, despite their scientific rigour, selective ways of dealing with possible future loss and causal attribution.[91] They are a risk to those making the selections, while a danger to others (eg, patients, local people) who do not make those selections.

Families and investigators, in particular, will attribute mental health homicides to different decisions or at least have different ideas about how these dreadful

[87] See Niche Patient Safety, *Safeguarding Adults Review and a Mental Healthcare Related Homicide Independent Investigation into the Care and Treatment of B and A* (Niche Patient Safety, 2017) 7; D Hunter and P Cheeseman, *Domestic Homicide Review Incorporating an NHS Independent Investigation [Mental Health] Overview Report Post Quality Assurance Panel: 'Nina' and 'Jenny'* (Sefton Safer Communities Partnership, November 2017) 16; N Moor, *An Independent Investigation into the Care and Treatment of Mental Health Service Users (F and Maureen) in County Durham* (Niche Health and Social Care Consulting, September 2017) 49; T Thompson et al, *An Independent Investigation into the Care and Treatment of a Mental Health Service User (Mr EF) Provided by Barnet, Enfield and Haringey NHS Trust* (Caring Solutions (UK) Ltd, August 2017) 15; N Ibbs, *An Independent Investigation into the Care and Treatment of a Mental Health Service User (Mr H) in Sussex* (Niche Health & Social Care Consulting, September 2017); K Hyde-Bales and E Ewart, *An Independent Investigation into the Care and Treatment of Mr J* (Verita, November 2017) 51; N Ibbs, *An Independent Investigation into the Care and Treatment of a Mental Health Service User (Mr L) in London* (Niche Health and Social Care Consulting, August 2017) 10–11; Iodem, *Independent Investigation into the Care and Treatment of Mr S* (Iodem, June 2017) 6; S Denby, *An Independent Investigation into the Care and Treatment of a Mental Health Service User Mr S in TEWV and BHFT* (Niche Health & Social Care Consulting Ltd, November 2017) 54; J Wigmore, *An Independent Investigation into the Care and Treatment of T, a Mental Health Service User in Camden* (Niche Health & Social Care Consulting Ltd, July 2017) 56; C Rooney, *An Independent Investigation into the Care and Treatment of a Mental Health Service User (Miss B) in Rotherham* (Niche Health & Social Care Consulting Ltd, October 2017) 25; C Rooney, *An Independent Investigation into the Care and Treatment of a Mental Health Service User (S) in Liverpool* (Niche Patient Safety, July 2017) 35; Iodem, *Independent Investigation into the Care and Treatment of Ms Z* (Iodem, June 2017) 30; G Jenkins and N Moor, *An Independent Investigation into the Care and Treatment of P in the West Midlands* (Niche Health & Social Care Consulting Ltd, June 2017) 65.

[88] See generally N Luhmann, 'Ecological Communication: Coping with the Unknown' (1993) 6(5) *Systems Practice* 527, 531; Japp and Kusche, 'Systems Theory and Risk' (n 24) 83, 84. See also Carson, 'Structural Problems' (n 63) 139 and A Buchanan, 'Independent Inquiries into Homicide: Should Share Common Methods and Be Integrated into New Quality Systems' (1999) 318 *British Medical Journal* 1089, 1089.

[89] See Philippopoulos-Mihalopoulos, *Absent Environments* (n 2) 120–22 and 136. Philippopoulos-Mihalopoulos advances a reading of Luhmann positing that risk is all there is. If risk and danger were only visible at the level of second-order observation, according to Luhmann, then social systems would not perceive dangers. The latter would be external to the system.

[90] Luhmann, *Risk* (n 1) 16. See also Japp and Kusche, 'Systems Theory and Risk' (n 24) 85.

[91] For instance, risk assessment (such as the Violence Risk Appraisal Guide (VRAG)) is just one form of assessment psychiatrists use.

events should be attributed. Julian Hendy described in detail how families in some cases demand greater rigour within the investigation:

> I've had a couple cases, you know, where families will say they want something published in the reports. That's sort of happening, a bit like a victim impact statement. With the case on Friday, NHS London is not allowing, for various reasons, the family statement to be in the report. But it will probably be issued as a press release. They don't agree, the family doesn't agree with the report because they don't think the findings are correct. So, in this case where the report found fault with the police, it didn't really investigate the circumstances of this woman's release in the first place. She previously killed her own mum, was let out in questionable circumstances and was in a position to go and kill somebody else. And the family found that wasn't investigated properly enough in the report ... the report was essentially looking at low-hanging fruit. So they blamed the police and the last nurse to see them rather than the more fundamental issues.

An investigator reported, in one case he managed, receiving a suicide threat from a member of the victim's family. The investigator had compiled a draft of the final report that concluded the police were at fault for not preventing the perpetrator leaving the area prior to the homicide being committed. The victim's family vehemently rejected the finding, to the extent that one member threatened to commit suicide if the investigation's conclusion went unchanged. Family members attributed the incident to a patient discharge decision within health services and refused to accept the investigation's conclusion.

G. Decision Makers and Affected Parties

Social systems of communication observe risk and a central task of systems theory is to observe social systems observing risk (ie, second-order observation). Its task involves introducing important distinctions (ie, *risk/danger* and *before/after*) that bring into view the observations social systems make of their own factual and temporal reality. Decisions are a defining element in these social systemic observations. Function systems structure life and make sense of possibilities using their own operations when making decisions rather than drawing on an external, a priori, source of authority. The patient homicide governance space is constituted by functionally differentiated social systems communicating. In order to make sense of their unique environments, they must author their own reality by selecting decisional possibilities over others. They causally attribute events to decisions, reducing complexity. Yet, in doing so, further decisions are necessitated. Decisions are, furthermore, unable to be final in the sense that they solve all risk problems once and for all. Decisions are unable to represent society's complexity. Society and its problems are too complex to be reduced to clinical, mathematical or legal decisions. A first-order distinction drawn between risk and safety is blind to the observer who draws the distinction.

An important aspect of Luhmann's concept of risk is its relevance to the *social* dimension. In the social dimension, risk emerges as a distinction between decision makers and those affected by decisions. Whereas the *risk/danger* distinction is relevant to the material dimension, Luhmann goes on to argue that risks are assumed by decision makers and those affected by decisions are exposed to danger. The two positions of observation of decision maker on the one hand and those affected by decisions on the other are explained by Luhmann. He writes that 'distinct forms of social solidarity develop differently depending on whether the future is seen from the angle of risk or from the angle of danger'.[92] Therefore, risk is an attribution possible only through decision making. Danger, however, is something that one is exposed to without making a decision that causes the exposure:

> In brief, risks are attributed to decisions made, whereas dangers are attributed externally. From a sociological point of view this would be relatively unproblematic if these matters could be kept meticulously separate. An analysis of decision making and affected involvement indicates that this does not occur. It shows that the risks the decision maker takes and has to take become a danger for those affected. Within the decision making process itself, one cannot avoid attributing consequences to decisions (otherwise the decision would not be recognisable as a decision). Thus one can also not avoid an attribution of future loss and has to accept it as risk where it cannot be entered under costs. The affected party finds himself in a quite different situation. He sees himself as endangered by decisions that he neither makes himself nor controls. Self-attribution is not possible for him. He is dealing with dangers – even when he sees and reflects that, from the point of view of the decision maker (perhaps himself!), it is a matter of risk. We are confronted by a classical social paradox: risks are dangers, dangers are risks – because it is a matter of one and the same content observed in the medium of a distinction requiring differing sides.[93]

Luhmann's argument focuses on the intractable conflicts that typify risk issues. Risks are constantly disputed. Attempts are often made to reach consensus by appealing to the specific qualities of the persons or organisations involved in a dispute. In mainstream social and intellectual life, risk issues are constructed as an opposition of interests and values that, through certain mechanisms (eg, law, science), may be reconciled. For Luhmann, the idea that conflicts over risks are reconcilable conflates risk with human values and questionable sources of authority, making for an unreliable starting point for a study of risk. Luhmann argues that mainstream constructions of risk are semantic descriptions that frame risk debates as an opposition of values and beliefs. These descriptions conceal the paradox of risk: that one man's risk is another man's danger.[94] The paradox is inescapable. A decision maker always remains polarised to those affected by the decision maker's decisions. Polarisation may be subjected to reconciliation and consensus-building efforts but Luhmann's point is that these processes are unable to escape the inevitability that one party is responsible for a decision and its consequences and one side is affected by it. Even if a decision maker is a valued expert who bases

[92] Luhmann, *Risk* (n 1) 102.
[93] ibid 107.
[94] ibid 108–09.

their decision on rigorous evidence, they – as a decision maker – stand in opposition to those affected by their decision. The polarisation of decision makers and affected parties, as a mainstay of functional differentiated societies, is enough for the latter to question or reject the decision and for the decision maker to question or reject the rejection.[95]

Luhmann's concept of risk captures, in unique terms, the perpetual conflicts that often occur between decision makers and those affected by decisions. It also accounts for widespread distrust of elite decision makers, such as politicians, by those considered to be affected by their decisions. Elite decision makers are often viewed with suspicion by affected parties, not necessarily because the issue at hand is complex or resistant to consensus, but because of the different ways in which decision makers and those affected by decisions attribute consequences to decisions. Elites may go to considerable lengths to earn the trust of those affected by their decisions. They may involve affected parties in decision-making processes or publish the minutes of their meetings as a gesture of transparency. For Luhmann, however, such efforts are unable to escape the inevitable distinction between decisions and those affected by decisions. Earning trust necessitates decision making. Earning trust in these ways reintroduces the distinction between decision makers and those affected by decisions. Further suspicion of decision makers by affected parties is bound to be produced:

> The decision maker is more likely to believe himself to be in a position to cope with future losses than is an affected party, has the possibility of taking into account his expertise, his self-confidence and his collateral when making his decision; whereas the affected individual has to be content with believing that others will keep the situation under control. Such confidence in experts, in technologies, in the promises and scrupulosity of others is being progressively undermined; it is being ruined by the rigour of the difference between the perspective of risk and that of danger – and is dwindling in proportion to the danger not being due to natural events (for example, the impact of a meteorite) but to decisions made by others. We accordingly find that the general public evaluates risk and the possibilities of averting it differently from the way this is done in the political arena; that the layman takes a different view from that taken by the expert.[96]

Luhmann explains the emergence of protest movements in these terms.[97] The proliferation of suspicion in society about decision makers has brought with it proposed remedies of hope, dialogue, comprehension and the willingness to compromise.[98] Risk – as the distinctions *risk/danger* and *decision makers/affected parties* – is veiled with topics that become occasions for further communication. These distinctions are alerted to more systematically by social system programmes (eg, the 'cause' being championed, the aim to be achieved). According to Luhmann,

[95] Japp and Kusche, 'Systems Theory and Risk' (n 24) 91.
[96] Luhmann, *Risk* (n 1) 113.
[97] ibid 138. See also Luhmann, 'Ecological Communication' (n 88).
[98] Luhmann, *Risk* (n 1) 114.

these distinctions enable a new distinction to emerge between protesting and not protesting.[99] Decisions made within different function systems inevitably create a set of conditions in which social systems of communication (ie, the social system of protest) are able to form about the contingency of political decisions (ie, differences in attribution). Once indicated, a marked side of a functional code (ie, *protest/issue*) combines with a programme (ie, a topic) 'and the two of them together set off a process of reproducing related communication, thus permitting the system to distinguish between relevant and irrelevant activities'.[100]

Independent investigations are no stranger to the type of conflict regularly seen in contexts of protest. Different understandings are reached about the homicide event, the health care services provided to the perpetrator and the scope for prevention. Conflict emerges out of a polarisation between decision makers and affected parties. Various parties (eg, investigators, health care providers, commissioners) select decisions between different possibilities that are structured by the operations of particular function systems. An example would be the decisions exercised by clinical experts to make certain judgements about health care services. These decisions are regarded as having consequences for certain parties, such as families:

> I think it really highlights the difference between professional judgement … and the family point of view which is 'well, he said he was going to do something awful, therefore it was predictable and preventable'. That's not the same thing. I think there's quite a gap. **Investigator 12**

The differences between professional judgement and family viewpoints were elaborated upon in detail by other investigators. One investigator expressed the view that families often made the incorrect assumption that decision makers (ie, clinical staff) have omniscient control over patients:

> Some people seem to have the view that if you're dealing with a mental health patient, then they're permanently under the control of qualified staff and that they've got 24/7, 365 days a year oversight over that individual. So, that if they're going to do something bizarre, they can then be immediately whisked off the streets and brought back into detention. **Investigator 11**

Investigators furthermore describe families and staff as assuming the role of victims:

> We talked a bit about the families as victims. I think sometimes the staff are victims as well. We've had interviews with staff where they're extremely upset … you sense from some of the press reports that these people [staff] don't care, that they're not doing their job. They're just swanning along but actually its very rare that they're not affected badly. **Investigator 12**

[99] ibid 126 and 128.
[100] ibid 126–27.

The patient homicide governance space, it appears, has its victims too:

> It's not uncommon to have people very distressed. Staff, family, the perpetrator themselves. It is not uncommon to come across traumatised people in that whole process. **Investigator 1**

The difference between badly affected staff members and families, however, lies in the levels of anger and distress experienced as a result of losing a loved one. Curiously, the reactions by families prompt investigators into differentiating themselves from families by further delineating their role as decision makers:

> I think sometimes they're [families] very angry, they feel that they weren't listened to at the time. Sometimes, I think they find it hard to distinguish between you as an external panel and services in general, so you try and be careful and try to maintain that distinction. **Investigator 7**

Families often engage in intractable conflict with investigators. Families may feel helpless in their position *vis-à-vis* the position of investigators as expert decision makers:

> [T]he police inspector who did the homicide investigation for the court case was there and he said 'I've been in homicide for 20 years and this is the most difficult family I've ever had to deal with'. And, in the process of going through court, they got through three different liaison officers because they've sacked them or fallen out with them. We knew what we were getting into. As we've gone on, they've [the family] had expectations. For the first time ever, we appointed a victim support officer to work with the family knowing that things were going to be difficult. When we got close to finalising the report, we were preparing the way, saying 'this is the way we're envisaging handling the report to the family'. 'When would you like to receive it?' 'How would you like to receive it?' 'Would you like to meet up and talk about it?' They were very specific on how they wanted it delivered, when they wanted it delivered. On a Friday afternoon, couldn't be after 3pm. So they were very precise in the details. And then, as a footnote, saying 'if it doesn't say what we want it to say, then I'm going to take my life' which was the direct statement in it. We had to speak to the Trust and everybody else, saying, 'we've got somebody threatening to take their life if we report and we don't think it's going to say what they want it to say.' And we had a horrendous reaction. **Investigator 10**

Furthermore, both the police and the family expressed unhappiness with the investigation's findings in the case above. They presented as affected parties to a decision made by investigators to reach a particular set of findings. They brought a unique and complex set of interests to the table. The police brought legal concerns and the family brought a strong familial concern to vindicate their loved one. Both groups diverged in their reasons for their disagreement, but shared the trait of affected involvement; a complex decision was made that affected them.

The conflict between decision makers and affected parties materialises in other ways within the patient homicide governance space. Julian Hendy expressed frustration at what he perceived as the inertia of NHS decision makers on the issue of patient homicides:

> I go to a lot of meetings with NHS people and they've all got very long titles. I've got no idea what these people do. And it's all 'quality assurance' and you think, what does it actually mean? There's a lot of rhetoric around it and it's not clear. I'm sure they're very nice people and people in the NHS say nobody comes through here to do a bad job. I perfectly understand that, but I go to a lot of NHS meetings where it's all about process. It's like meeting for a meeting's sake but, practically and pragmatically, stuff doesn't get done.

Julian Hendy further explained that families often dispute the decisions of investigators to withhold information on the grounds of medical confidentiality:

> [S]ometimes you'll go to a Trust and say 'we'd like to see your internal investigation' and they'll say 'we'd love to give it to you but we can't because of patient confidentiality reasons'. And so the families are thinking 'hang on, this bloke has just killed my dad and his rights to confidentiality trump my rights to know? Why should the offender have more rights than the victim?' And I think that a lot of people just don't understand. I think members of the public would think that if you kill somebody you don't get much right to confidentiality. And I understand there are reasons for confidentiality, but there are other reasons for the running of efficient public services which mean that the right to confidentiality can be breached and, particularly, can be given to a grieving victim's family. I don't think there's anything wrong with that. I think that the law potentially allows for it. There are ways and means of giving it to victims' families and I don't think the perpetrators' right to confidentiality should trump the victim's rights to know.

Julian Hendy went as far to say that the decisions taken by investigators to withhold information on the grounds that disclosure would breach the legal duty of confidentiality were alienating for families:

> It's distancing, it's distancing and it's inhumane and I'm not sure, as I say and I've questioned people and they say 'well we've always done it like that' and I say 'well that's actually not good enough'. You know, you have to have a good reason for not doing it rather than 'this is how we've always done it'.

Family opposition to an investigation's conclusions is quite common. It was discussed earlier that the final conclusions of an investigation rarely designate a homicide as predictable and preventable. Investigations often conclude that nothing could have been done to predict the event or to prevent it. Julian Hendy, however, commented that families are sometimes unconvinced:

> Sometimes, the family will say the report will find a whole list of problems … and yet still find that the incident was not preventable or predictable. And I think most families will say that's a joke really. How can you say there are all these problems but that these problems didn't have any effect at all on the outcome? On paper they say with certainty it's not, but the evidence that these things were not preventable when there's a list of a whole range of problems – families will question that.

These responses help illustrate the argument that the fundamental difference in observational perspectives between decision makers (eg, NHS institutions and investigators) and those affected by decisions (eg, family members) places both sides in irreducible conflict. Each side is staunch in its view about the result. Investigators will argue that they applied the tools necessary to conduct a full and independent investigation. Families will often argue that more must be done (eg, broader investigation remits, greater information disclosure). Julian Hendy made his suspicions clear about NHS decision-making processes:

> I think there needs to be more transparency … it all goes a bit opaque and a bit dark and you start to think 'okay what's going on here then?'

It is noteworthy that one of the investigators interviewed highlighted an insoluble tension between what the families expect from investigations as affected parties and the expectation placed on investigators to make a decision on whether the homicide incident was predictable and preventable:

> What infuriates relatives … and the general public to some extent [is] we're asked to make a judgement. Was this predictable and was it preventable? To make a judgement on those two. And fairly recently we've worked on a definition of what is predictable and what is preventable. We've worked on a standard definition, which we include in all of our reports. The panel makes a judgement on what they gather on those two things. And invariably, in 90 percent plus cases, they come back with a view that the case wasn't predictable and wasn't preventable … the family and to some extent the wider public want someone to blame for this. We come back and tell them 'we can't provide that'. They find it infuriating that we don't find it predictable and preventable. They find it really unhelpful. **Investigator 10**

It is easy to assume that the source of the conflict between investigators and families lies at the doorstep of the issues at stake (eg, transparency, investigative remits) and that consensus is a possible antidote. Yet, systems theory reminds us that consensus in a functionally differentiated society is impossible. As Japp and Kusche point out, social systems are based on internal processes of a system (eg, a protest movement).[101] Observation is all there is and the observer is only able to take up one observation at a time as opposed to blending all observations into one omnipresent observation that will solve all of society's problems. An observer's blind spot will mean that taking into consideration others' perspectives is never fully realised.[102] Systems theory research has shown that where decision-making procedures are opened up to public participation, the arrangements become flooded with dense mixtures of arguments that are each informed by the distinct codes of different communication systems. The final decision made is unable to represent the variety of argument presented during the participation process. If the decision is, say, a legal one, then the contributions of protest groups, experts and citizens are

[101] Japp and Kusche, 'Systems Theory and Risk' (n 24) 94.
[102] ibid.

bound to be excluded – unless these groups step into legal communications during the participation process.[103]

These points bring the concerns of the family's representative regarding decision inertia into sharper focus. In the context of an investigation itself, the meetings between interested parties may be rather eclectic:

> When an investigation is commissioned, they'll call a meeting in a room. All interested parties are invited to attend. You get the Trust represented, the commissioners, us, the police will often turn up and others – probation, GP. It's a bit of a gathering. **Investigator 10**

It is understandable that at the end of a six month investigation process not all parties will agree with the findings produced and the conclusions drawn. One set of findings is simply unable to accommodate all perspectives and especially the perspectives of decision makers and affected parties. Luhmann's theory of risk is, therefore, highly suitable for capturing these dynamics and explaining why they exist.

III. Protest and Politics

Luhmann's work on protest appears, at first glance, far removed from the context of patient homicide. His work is relevant, however, because it is closely related to his work on risk and it is referred to here for the purposes of illuminating a specific issue of interest: the relevance of protest to the patient homicide governance space. Luhmann's ideas on protest help reinforce the theme that the patient homicide governance space is constituted by moments of observation produced by society's social communication systems. These communication systems observe a self-constructed environment (eg, biological systems, psychic systems, other social systems) through their internal operations. As autopoietic observation systems, social function systems distinguish between government and opposition (ie, politics), information and non-information (ie, mass media), legality and illegality (ie, law) and so on when making sense of their environment (eg, other function systems, biological systems, psychic systems). The present section draws on Luhmann's argument that protest communications are yet another form of social communication that society produces for itself. Protest communications are explained in the present chapter followed by an explanation of how they are relevant to the patient homicide governance space.

[103] See A Bora, 'Discourse Formations and Constellations of Conflict: Problems of Public Participation in the German Debate on Genetically Altered Plants' in P O'Mahony (ed), *Nature, Risk and Responsibility* (London, Palgrave Macmillan, 1999) 130–46.

A. Protest as Communication

Luhmann's examination of protest as a form of communication is set against the backdrop of ecological communication. He explains that ecological communication forms a separate type of social system: social movements. For Luhmann, social movements are a type of social system, alongside social systems of interaction, organisation and function systems. They are unlike organisations because they lack a structure of decision making whereby members are admitted and excluded and location and mission statements decided upon. They are unlike interactions because they do not rely on face-to-face contact between psychic systems coupled through language. Social movements emerge as a distinct type of function system that, like society's function systems, observe themselves and their environment. In particular, social movements distinguish between protest and issue but lack a focus on value consensus and internal change.[104]

Social movements protest on issues that are constructed as in need of an urgent resolution. It is, therefore, unsurprising that social movements have emerged as a new type of function system. Many issues in a functionally differentiated society go unresolved. Resolving issues is highly improbable given that society is too complex to be represented by a single perspective. Inertia on specific social problems is the norm. A defining moniker of protest communications is that they communicate about the inertia around social problems (eg, global warming, political corruption) in the form of campaigns, advertisements, boycotts and so on. Henceforth, social movements become rigid, inflexible and socially relevant (ie, relevance to society's function systems) in a manner determined by society's function systems. For example, a protest communication (eg, that fracking must be stopped) may acquire legal relevance in the form of an application to court for an injunction. In the economy, protesting may acquire social significance in the form of dedicating resources for campaign purposes.

Protest communications are commonly associated with anxieties about industrial technological innovation. These communications involve the admonition of elite decision makers (eg, politicians) for failing to do enough to minimise exposure to the dangers these innovations pose. Furthermore, these movements assume that dangers are out there waiting to be discovered and acted upon; they call for society's elite decision makers to adopt a more enlightened approach to technological and industrial problems and to eliminate them for the benefit of humans and the natural world.

Luhmann is sceptical of social movements and protest because they overlook society's complexity. These movements assume that society is amenable to improvement through action on industrial dangers. They are well known for their calls for action on important issues so that an existing problem can be appropriately

[104] See Luhmann, *Risk* (n 1) 143.

addressed and solved. Luhmann questions the assumptions held by social movements that appropriate action on society's critical problems can lead to a solution to the problem.

Writing in the context of ecological problems, Luhmann frames his scepticism in the following way: '[w]e can formulate the question of the ecological basis of and danger to social life much more exactly if we look for the conditions under which the states and changes in the social environment find resonance within society'.[105]

Ecological dangers, for Luhmann, are not objectively 'out there'. They are constructed as dangers within society, in communication. Society exposes itself to danger.[106] After all, according to Luhmann's general theory of social systems, society is what has meaning for its social function systems and what is outside of society lacks social meaning. Social movements have meaning for society as protest. Protest involves selecting a specific topic and using it to discover what is to be criticised in society.[107] The problems (eg, pollution) of the organic world (ie, society's environment) are constructed from within; ecological matters resonate in or perturb society's function systems.[108] Furthermore, society's function systems also perturb each other on ecological matters:

> [T]he internal dynamics and sensitivity of function systems like politics, economy, science or law are disturbed by environmental problems. Sometimes this happens directly as when resources dry up or catastrophes threaten. But it also occurs indirectly via socially mediated interdependencies when, for example, the economy is forced to react to legal precepts even if it would attain better results following its own ideas.[109]

For example, law may resonate with ecological problems *legally*, by passing laws that prohibit certain industrial activities. The economy may resonate with ecological problems *economically*, in the form of payments made to persons damaged by industrial pollutants. Politics may resonate with ecological problems *politically*, in the form of 'Green' pledges in a party manifesto. The social system of the mass media may resonate with ecological problems informationally, in the form of news items and documentaries about pollution and global warming. Social systems construct ecological problems in their own image, in society.

Fuchs, writing from a systems-theoretical perspective, identifies the central aspects of social movements: resistance, dissatisfaction, goals, hopes and wishes for change.[110] He combines these elements into a theoretical account of social movements as 'dynamic communication systems that permanently react to

[105] Luhmann, 'Ecological Communication' (n 88) 16.
[106] ibid 32.
[107] Luhmann, *Risk* (n 1) 127.
[108] Luhmann, 'Ecological Communication' (n 88) 36.
[109] ibid 48.
[110] C Fuchs, 'The Self-Organization of Social Movements' (2006) 19(1) *Systemic Practice and Action Research* 101, 110.

political and societal events with self-organized protest practices and protest communications'.[111] Social movements are 'an expression of fear and dissatisfaction with society as it is and a call for changes and the solutions to problems'.[112] Protest movements complain and demand action. As forms of social communication, they distinguish between protest and issues.

These theoretical observations pose a problem for protest movements. The problem is that in their reductionism they are unable to represent the complexity of a polycentric and functionally differentiated society. In calling for action on issues and demanding that society be improved, protest assumes that there is a superior approach through which society's big problems may be resolved. Protest generally calls for a 'better perspective', which, if adopted, will enable society to rid itself of, say, nuclear dangers, corrupt politicians and violent criminals. As explained in Chapter 4, Luhmann's theory rejects the idea that any one perspective can represent society and its complexity. For him, it is naïve to suggest that any one perspective occupies a privileged vantage point from which society can be represented, authoritatively understood and steered towards predetermined change. The actual existence of environmental problems is not an issue deserving of attention for Luhmann. These problems are, rather, recursively constructed within society.

The change campaigned for by social movements is difficult to realise because protest issues irritate – first and foremost – social systems rather than the primary focus of social movements (ie, the natural world, biological systems): 'Problems cannot be treated at their source. Instead, they have to be treated elsewhere'.[113] There is, then, too much resonance within social systems on ecological matters and very little on the ecological side of things (eg, cleaner air).[114] The impulse of protest to demand that elites 'get their act together' and change for the better is likely to result in failure.

Protest is, however, regularly perceived as successful. A primary focus for Luhmann in his work on protest is a pertinent example. He argues that ecological movements are constantly at the centre of political and media life. From a systems-theoretical perspective, however, success is, rather, systemic resonance; social systems form the structures of life in which environments (eg, protest issues) are communicated about and these may generate considerable resonance within those structures. For example, protest has been rather 'successful' in the social system of politics.[115] Political parties have formed for the purpose of giving *political* life to protest about environmental pollution and climate change. They have created manifestos to make society 'greener' and they have garnered popular support in elections. Despite the inroads of protest in politics, Luhmann argues that it is naïve to assume that the achievements of protest represent a success. Success merely

[111] ibid 101.
[112] ibid 113.
[113] N Luhmann, *Political Theory in the Welfare State* (Berlin and New York, de Gruyter, 1990) 58.
[114] See Moeller, *Luhmann Explained* (n 78) 106.
[115] ibid.

demonstrates that protest has assumed political form. The reduction of greenhouse gases or environmental pollution (ie, resonance with society's environment) is rarely, if ever, occasioned by these 'successes'.

B. Patient Homicide, Protest and Risk

Homicides committed by mentally disordered individuals appear removed from traditional ecological problems because they refer to homicide and health care primarily rather than pollution and climate change. Nevertheless, health care acquires relevance in a range of opinions and agendas.[116] It raises a series of similar issues to social movements. For instance, it involves the formation of protest communications about certain risks and dangers about mentally disordered health care patients.

Investigations and health care services attract protest from families in particular. The Zito Trust (see Chapter 2) and more recently Hundred Families assume the shape of protest for families. They embody a movement that champions improvements in public safety and victim support within the patient homicide governance space. Fear and dissatisfaction are often expressed by victims' families regarding the possible future occurrence of a homicide incident and the ability of families affected by these incidents to receive adequate support from the authorities. These fears and expressions of dissatisfaction are usually directed at NHS decision makers and politicians. Independent investigators, NHS Trusts, commissioners and politicians all make decisions about health services. Investigators make decisions to judge what was predictable and preventable. They make decisions about how health services are to be delivered. Politicians and government departments have an ability to affect changes in policy and to champion legal reform. It is clear that these decisions affect families. Families are anxious for many reasons but an important reason is that they are parties affected by the decisions of others. They play no part in the decisions of elites to set terms of reference for independent investigations and provide support to families. From a systems-theoretical perspective, families are affected parties to decisions. A stage is thus set for conflict and disagreement.

Families frequently regard investigators, NHS decision makers and politicians as deficient in addressing their concerns. For society's function systems, these consequences are unintended. From a systems-theoretical perspective, these unintended consequences occur because society is unable to reflect on its functionally differentiated condition. These unintended consequences are side-effects which, for Luhmann, are compensated for by protest communication.[117] Protest communications perform a function in society; they provide relief from the marginalising

[116] Wolff, 'Risk' (n 86) 802.

[117] See I Blühdorn, 'Self-description, Self-deception, Simulation: A Systems-theoretical Perspective on Contemporary Discourses of Radical Change' (2007) 6(1) *Social Movement Studies* 1, 8.

effects of functional differentiation.[118] Indeed, previous chapters demonstrate that social function systems, such as law, can be alienating for families. It is therefore unsurprising that health care campaigners and victim support advocates have continually struggled to get their concerns addressed by independent investigators. Whereas these campaigners and advocates urge action and demand change (ie, protesting), investigators regard themselves as wholly separate from these concerns. They 'get on with their job':

> Julian Hendy is influential in the process of these investigations with NHS England … He pushes much more for the families' voice to be heard and for them to receive support. That's an important thing, but it's not our job. Our job is to investigate. **Investigator 8**

Luhmann's work on protest communications opens up a theoretical starting point from which to accurately account for the anxieties that emerge around patient homicides. In particular, his ideas help depict resonance between society and its environment. Society is irritated into communication by psychic systems (eg, the command hallucinations of a perpetrator, the psychological needs of victim's families) and biological systems (eg, the physical movements that lead to fatal injuries) in different ways. In particular, independent investigations involve communication about NHS decision makers and their failure to do enough to prevent these events occurring. Julian Hendy, the family representative interviewed for the present book, plays a crucial role in the patient homicide governance space in England. It was earlier explained that he founded and registered a charity in the United Kingdom that represents victims' families. He set up the charity shortly after his father was killed by a mentally disordered NHS patient in 2007. It is through the charity that he campaigns for health service improvements on behalf of families and advises them on how to navigate the complexities of the independent investigation process:

> [W]e essentially try to do three things: we support and advocate for families who've been bereaved as a result of homicides by people with mental illness. We work with the NHS on a national, regional and, local level to try to embed learning. We also work with the police, family liaison officers, the Ministry of Justice, national funded management scheme service, victim liaison, victim support and others to try and assist families after they've been bereaved. We also do evidence of training, so we try and compile robust evidence because I think some of the statistics and some of the areas are a bit questionable. So we try and do that on the basis of solid evidence to try and help learning. We always say it's too late to help our relatives, but you don't want it to happen to anybody else … our organisation supports families who've been bereaved by homicides and we find that the amount of help provided to them is quite limited because people get sent to hospital as patients. They're not prisoners, which means the amount of information, again, is quite limited because of patient confidentiality.

[118] N Luhmann, *Die Politik der Gesellschaft* (Frankfurt, Suhrkamp, 2002) 318 quoted in Blühdorn, 'Self-description' (n 117) 10.

While Julian Hendy's work, in part, involves raising certain topics, opposing certain decisions and proposing change in his capacity as a campaigner and representative of families, it covers much more. His work resonates economically and legally. His work engages scientific communications (eg, statistical analysis) and legal communications (eg, making legal arrangements to set up a charity). It does, however, engage in protest in that it regularly castigates decision makers (eg, NHS managers, independent investigators) for failing to do enough to support families and ensure services are adequate. These protestations, under systems theory, will resonate significantly within society's function systems.

C. Politics, Public Opinion and the Mass Media

Protest resonates politically in the patient homicide governance space and indeed in society. Chapter 4 referred to the prominence of the Zito Trust – spearheaded by Jayne Zito – in the 1990s and its political resonance. Jayne Zito's views about the situation were, at the time, widely referenced in the media and in Parliament. In particular, the Prime Minister was openly questioned in Parliament about the political response to the killing of Jonathan Zito.[119] Jayne Zito campaigned for a reform of mental health law and campaigned vigorously for the institution of measures that would minimise future mental health homicides. The Zito campaign acquired political significance for politics and (eventually) for the legal system.

More broadly, it may be argued that the protest communications of the Zito Trust, and Jayne Zito specifically, were crucial to politics in the form of politically relevant public opinion. Public opinion, as a concept, was explained in Chapter 4 in relation to the social system of the mass media. It is also relevant to the social system of politics. It is apposite here to develop the book's examination of public opinion by exploring the relationship between the mass media, public opinion and protest in the context of patient homicides. Doing so will clarify the relevance of public opinion to the patient homicide governance space.

From a systems-theoretical perspective, the campaigns of the Zito Trust – and later Hundred Families – have continually resonated in the social system of the mass media because they have informational value. They form 'public opinion' on the topic of mental health homicide and facilitate the autopoiesis of mass media communications about the topic.

Public opinion is unable to assume its form for the mass media with redundant, non-information. The same news item about a patient homicide continually repeated, verbatim, is redundant and is unable to supply existing public opinion on a topic with the variety it requires for its continuance. Public opinion thrives only on information with informational value (eg, variety). For the social system of politics, however, protest communications about patient homicide irritate mass

[119] HC Deb, 29 June 1993, vol. 227, col 822.

media communications and are constructed politically; public opinion forms *politically relevant* public opinion.

The political system has, for a long time, constructed public opinion through the mass media.[120] Public opinion first began to be constructed in print form in the eighteenth century and has since developed to include television, radio and the internet. Whereas the mass media constructs public opinion on the basis of what has informational value, politics is interested in those mass media topics that have political value especially (eg, topics that improve electoral chances and aid questioning of the government). Politics produces communication by constructing what public opinion is for its purposes (ie, communicating power). The mass media is a distinct, operationally closed system of communication but its communications are cognitively open to the political system. The operationally closed political system constructs mass media communications as politically relevant for the purpose of constructing public opinion and responding to it in ways that create political reality (eg, passing laws, changing policy, debating in Parliament).

Jayne Zito's campaign demanded change but the change was reconstructed politically. The social system of politics identified her broadcast views in the media and elsewhere as a sign that public opinion required a political response to the issue of public safety and victim support. As demonstrated in the example above, the political response included initiating parliamentary debate about Jayne Zito's call for an independent public inquiry into the death of Jonathan Zito and, more recently, her appointment to the Strategic Board for Victim Commissioning with the Office of Police and Crime Commissioner and the Ministry of Justice Learning Group for Victims Commissioning.

In more recent times, protest communications have resonated politically with the appointment of Julian Hendy to NHS England's (South) Independent Investigations Review Group (IIRG). The IIRG makes decisions on whether serious incidents in the South of England meet the criteria for independent investigation under the NHS Serious Incident Framework. The NHS Serious Incident Framework lays down a series of principles (eg, collaboration, objectivity) to ensure that 'robust systems are in place for reporting, investigating and responding to serious incidents so that lessons are learned and appropriate action taken to prevent future harm'.[121] Julian also sits as one of the four lay members on NHS England's Independent Investigations Governance Committee. The task of the Committee is to ensure quality and learning after independent investigations.

Parallels may be drawn between Jayne Zito and Julian Hendy. While both may be said to have had modest political influence in different ways, their efforts illustrate the political resonance of protest communications in relation to patient homicide. The demands for action on safety concerns and victim support championed by both have, according to the argument advanced in the present chapter,

[120] N Luhmann, *The Reality of the Mass Media* (Cambridge, Polity Press, 1995) 105.
[121] NHS England, *Serious Incident Framework* (London, NHS England Patient Safety Domain, 2015) 9.

irritated the social system of politics in the form of parliamentary debate and political appointments.

Reaching a final resolution to the problem of public safety and victim support is, of course, a wholly different matter. Protest communications arguably create too little resonance and too much resonance. They resonate politically but rarely irritate society's environment (eg, the psychic systems of mental health patients) because 'there is nothing to suggest that protest movements know it [society's environment] better than other social systems of society'.[122] Luhmann elsewhere states that 'the protest movement is only the one half – and the other consists of those who seemingly impassively or at best slightly irritatedly do what they wanted to anyway'.[123] A protest movement 'does not burden itself with the responsibility of getting involved on the other side in order to practically achieve something there'.[124] There are two ways of applying these statements about protest to the patient homicide governance space.

On the one hand, the protest communications made in relation to mental health homicide incidents are just that; they do not actually do anything. They are confined to demands for action from the sidelines. For example, protesting at the failure of the Department of Health and NHS England to deal with public safety and victim support in relation to patient homicides may resonate politically in the form of new political appointments and parliamentary debates. It may resonate economically in the form of directing organisational resources to making these issues heard (eg, the payment of salaries, the financing of campaigns). Yet, patient homicides continue to occur occasionally. The families of victims continue to be adversely affected. However, the work of the Zito Trust and Hundred Families is clearly significant and it would be inaccurate to dismiss the work of these organisations as 'not doing anything'. They clearly do a lot.

On the other hand, it is possible to read Luhmann's statement as referring to the difficulty protest movements encounter when attempting to resolve a problem constructed within society. Protests by Hundred Families directed at decision makers' handling of health care services and independent investigations is, perhaps, less to do with producing resonance beyond society – in the form of making the psychic systems of potential perpetrators healthier and reducing rates of violence and attacks – and more to do with producing resonance in society's function systems (in particular the political system). Families understandably want patients to be well and homicide incidents to stop. A systems-theoretical analysis, however, showcases the difficulty in realising these specific ambitions. The intentions of families are to alleviate physical and psychological suffering for other potential victims and their families but the occasioning of intended and directed change by their representatives is hard to come by. Protest communications

[122] N Luhmann, *Theory of Society, Volume 2* (Stanford, Stanford University Press, 1997/2013) 165.
[123] ibid158.
[124] N Luhmann, *Protest: Systemtheorie und soziale Bewegungen* (Frankfurt, Suhrkamp, 1996) 191 quoted in Blühdorn, 'Self-description' (n 117) 9.

resonate too much within society's function systems. Societal resonance never yields results that those demanding action are happy with because the issues at stake are constructed within function systems in highly distinct ways, which result in unpredictable outcomes, unintentional consequences, and misunderstandings.

These points bring the discussion round to two final points. First, they link up with themes from Chapter 3 regarding the assumption, held by investigators, that directed change and manipulation by certain actors over others involved in mental health homicide investigations is possible. A notable theme raised in Chapter 3 was one investigator's depiction of family representatives and their recruitment by NHS England as illustrative of manipulation. In summary, the investigator expressed the concern that bringing a family representative and media figure 'into their tent' amounted to an attempt by NHS England to control media communications about mental health homicides and quell criticism both from families and the media. From the perspective of systems theory, the investigator's concerns are imprecise. At most, these concerns point to systemic resonance among protest communications, politics and the mass media. The protestations of Hundred Families have resonated politically through Julian Hendy's appointment to one of NHS England's committees and the appointment resonates in the protestations of Hundred Families in the form of a wider recognition of their complaints and demands.

Julian's appointment to one of NHS England's sub-committees reinforces the differentiation of protest and politics. Protest communications and political communications remain intact and distinct. A direct relationship of control or manipulation of politics over protest and vice versa is impossible. The same reasoning applies to the relationship between the mass media on the one hand and politics and protest on the other. The political and protest communications that emerge in the patient homicide governance space may irritate mass media communications in the form of press releases and news items but they are wholly unable to determine the selections made by mass media communications or steer these communications in a particular direction. Mass media communications remain mass media communications.

The second and final point to raise here is that Luhmann's systems theory underlines the difficulty families and family representatives have had in getting their concerns addressed by NHS decision makers and politicians. Julian Hendy, the trustee of Hundred Families, commented during interview that progress on improving health services, providing extra support for victims' families and reducing occurrences of mental health homicide is slow. It is telling that progress is slow because it speaks to the concerns expressed by Luhmann. Experience has shown that politics and the mass media resonate most acutely with the protests of families in the area of mental health homicide. There have been political appointments and newspaper columns about these incidents. Yet, the occasioning of intended and direct change in society, whether that is in health care services or politics, to a degree that would be satisfactory to families and their representatives is notable by its absence. Systems theory provides the tools with which to explain the conundrum. It is, on the one hand, a matter of politics reproducing communications about events in its environment in ways that involve the distribution of political power. On the other hand, it is a matter of the mass media reproducing communications about its environment in ways that distinguish information from non-information. It is also a matter of protest reproducing communications about its environment in ways that call for a better society through better decisions. Functionally differentiated communication systems are incapable of directly speaking to each other. A chaotic vision of society emerges that precludes the possibility of targeted and timely change from any one perspective. It is therefore unsurprising that the campaigns of both the Zito Trust and Hundred Families have been, and in some respects continue to be, arduous journeys.

IV. Conclusions

The present chapter represents another stage in the development of the argument that independent inquiries after patient homicides are spaces of meaning produced within different social communication systems. Medical and psychiatric communication systems are those that dominate the governance space. The present chapter argues, however, that the patient homicide governance space is constituted by social function systems that self-construct time (ie, past and future), risk (ie, the possibility of future loss) and protest. Risk communications, in particular, distinguish between before and after through decisions and they distinguish decision makers and those affected by decisions. They resonate medically (eg, the risk of a future loss of biological life) but they also resonate politically (eg, the possibility of a future loss of power in the NHS hierarchy) in the form of decisions and decision attribution. Decisions – from the recommendations selected by investigators to the implementation of them by health services – are selected from decisional possibilities. A clash of perspectives is likely. Furthermore, decisional possibilities that have certain advantages must be foregone. Decisional dilemmas typify social systemic risk.

Many challenging aspects of investigations (eg, the changing shape of services between the incident and investigation, the reluctance to stimulate too much change in health services) may be more precisely understood beneath the conceptual lens of risk provided in the present chapter. Family contestation, resistance to findings from NHS Trusts and media criticism typify the reaction to uncertainty associated with decision making. Deciding in the present is never without uncertainty regarding what the consequences will be. Independent investigators are inundated with potential lines of investigations regarding what may have been causally linked to a patient homicide and indeed other events surrounding it (eg, inadequate care provision). Causal attribution may have, at one time, been a relatively simple matter. Social complexity and functional differentiation have prompted communication about the past and the future in ways that avoid linear discernment in these situations. It is clear that for many involved in the investigation process many questions go unanswered that, ironically, enable society to function. Medicine, psychiatry, politics and law reduce complexity. They invite criticism and conflict but they occasion further decision making and they reignite possibilities for future change.

The present chapter, more broadly, enables a reliable analysis of the patient homicide governance space without atomising the concept of risk through emphases on risk calculations or technology.[125] Risk is everywhere.[126] Under systems theory, however, risk is a form of communication within society as opposed to an objective condition outside of society or a condition within society that is amenable to universal understanding. It is a systemic phenomenon, understood in ever more diverse ways in order to reduce society's complexity. Causal attributions of events to decisions are limitless in a functionally differentiated society, demonstrated most vividly by the shift from the semantics of individual blame and liability in independent inquiries to a focus on systems and processes.[127]

The present chapter also explores the argument that protest communications (ie, demands for action on health care improvements, public safety and victim support) are an important aspect of the patient homicide governance space. Protest communications are a specific response to anxiety and uncertainty in functionally differentiated societies. Drawing on Luhmann's concept of risk, protest may emerge when decision makers are regarded as making decisions that affect non-decision makers, thus leading to an inescapable polarisation of interests. Furthermore, protest is likely to emerge where the problems identified by those protesting (ie, affected parties) are unresolved; a final solution to such problems is inevitable in a society differentiated into different function systems that are unable to speak directly to each other. The present chapter illustrates that protest communications about patient homicides, like risk communications, resonate in the social subsystem of politics (eg, political appointments of family advocates) and the mass media (eg, news items, documentaries) in particular. It explains how the families of homicide victims and their representatives step into protest communications, among others, as a response to the dissatisfaction that usually follows from calling for action on issues relating to public safety, health care service inadequacy and victim support. The challenge facing families and their representatives is a tough one because protest communications are unable to speak directly to society's function systems. Drawing on Luhmann, the chapter argues that protest communications rarely resonate in those areas where the demands of protest are mainly focused. Rather, these communications resonate in society's systems (eg, politics) and are filtered through the binary codes of those systems, culminating in more divergence and disagreement about the issues that are the subject of protest.

[125] See T Seddon, 'Dangerous Liaisons' (2008) 10(3) *Punishment & Society* 301, 302.

[126] See R Sparks, 'Risk and Blame in Criminal Justice Controversies: British Press Coverage and Official Discourse on Prison Security' in M Brown and J Pratt (eds), *Dangerous Offenders: Punishment and Social Order* (London, Routledge, 2000) 128.

[127] Warner, 'Inquiry Reports' (n 85) 234. Mental health professionals may erroneously redefine potentially harmful defensive practice as 'good practice' or 'doing the job better'.

Conclusions

Patient homicide, health care and the relationship between both is complex. However, patient homicide – and the relationship between it and society – may be reliably understood as a self-construction within society's social function systems, by society and for society. What is more, the present research advances an original understanding of a governance space loaded with questionable policy ambition. Crucially, *Mental Health Homicide and Society: Understanding Health Care Governance* calls for readers to view these ambitions with scepticism through a wholly new paradigm of social theory.

Society *is* communication under Luhmann's general theory of social systems. The 'material' that exists outside of society (eg, thoughts, personal interactions) is unable to directly perform *social* functions. All types of system – biological, psychic and social – are essential for the existence of each other but they are operationally closed; thoughts are unable to reproduce biological material and social communication and vice versa. Moreover, the communication function systems that make up society are functionally differentiated and are unable to replicate or represent the functions of all social function systems. For example, law can only be law (ie, not the economy or politics or medicine) and it creates meaning (ie, the distinction between legality and illegality) on terms set by law itself, as opposed to terms set by other social function systems. Indeed, for a social function system to set the terms on which another function system operates (ie, produces communication) is a wholly inadequate proposition under Luhmann's general theory of social systems. To accept the proposition would mean abandoning the tripartite distinction between biological, psychic and communication systems. It would mean reverting to an imprecise humanist conception of society.

Understanding society as a world system of functionally differentiated, operationally closed function systems enables a new and original way of thinking about patient homicide governance to emerge. It enables a vision of homicide and health care being communicated about within society in highly distinct ways. What appears to be a conventional process of truth seeking, embodied in a final report on what actually happened in a case, is rather a chaotic series of observations produced within different social systems of communication. The book provided an original account of these observations in detail and illuminated their implications for common understandings of patient homicide. It is a crucial exercise that dispels the myths of progress and ambition that have become conventional routines within health care governance domains.

Common understandings of patient homicide turn, primarily, on the quest to learn lessons, improve services and achieve better public safety. The arguments set out by the author, however, question these common understandings through a theoretical lens that frames society as functionally differentiated communication. Homicide and health care are communicated about within polycentric social systems of communication. These systems communicate about each other, rather than communicating with each other. These systems communicate about each other on their own terms too, precluding the possibility that universal lessons may be learned. Social systems do learn. Function systems, however, learn on their own terms. The book rejects the idea that the predesigned aims and objectives of policy makers to instigate universal learning about adverse health care incidents, pursuant to predefined goals, are realisable. While issuing such rejection appears new, strange or even absurd to readers steeped in the Anglo-American tradition of social theorising, Luhmann's writings provide a platform upon which a more accurate, consistent and rigorous picture emerges of how society works and how homicide and health care resonate in it.

The author concludes that patient homicide governance emerges as a communicational space. The function systems that make up the space construct events, decisions and dilemmas in distinct ways. Indeed, decisions and dilemmas are unique to a functionally differentiated society. Decisions involve the selection of one decisional possibility over a range of others. The advantages of those other possibilities can only be realised, however, if they are taken up. The 'missed opportunity' is therefore inevitable and the missed opportunity is endemic in all of society's function systems. Decisions are made within these structures of life. Decisions are informed by the unique terms set by those structures through their unique codes. When attempts are made to substitute social system functions with others (the most well-known example being an all-consuming political dictatorship), society ceases to function.

The book performs the novel manoeuvre of applying these ways of theorising society to the patient homicide governance space. The patient homicide governance space is constituted by operationally closed social communication systems. These systems communicate about each other rather than with each other. The idea of learning universal lessons and initiating change in health care services with a view to achieving predefined goals underestimates the complexity of the patient homicide governance space; the space is too complex, functionally differentiated and chaotic for linear change or steering to occur. These dynamics may explain why there is tension within investigations between being too 'light touch' on the one hand and too radical on the other. Health care services are very sensitive to change and investigators are reluctant to interfere too much. Of course, patient homicide incidents call for a convincing response and investigators are part of the response. Responding to a homicide through an independent investigation involves navigating all other responses (eg, media responses, NHS Trust responses, police responses, legal responses) to the same event. Despite the best efforts of policy makers and investigators to bring about better care and safety in health care services following a homicide incident, these incidents continue to occur occasionally. The decisional cycle of legal, administrative and protest response starts once more. Decisions and events occur because other decisions and events occur. Patient homicide governance is inherently contingent. Making 'correct' decisions cannot be guaranteed or achieved because the future is inherently uncertain and prone to occasions of disagreement, objection, regret and misunderstanding in a polycentric communicational space of patient homicide governance.

The book develops an original concept of accountability as communication (Chapter 5) to support the novel contention that the patient homicide governance space is constituted by a series of moments in which communication is produced within social function systems on their own terms. In particular, the book draws on Luhmann's oeuvre and develops an anti-humanist concept of accountability. It posits that accountability is far more than a mere procedure of asking questions and eliciting answers. It is, rather, composed of social, material and temporal observations constructed within social systems of communication. These moments of accountability may take on a variety of communicational forms. In the present context, they principally involve the social systems of medicine and psychiatry communicating about the medical and psychiatric past, in the present. These moments of observations may be reconstructed anew within other social systems of communication however; accountability in the medical sense (eg, the question of whether a clinician made a defensible decision to discharge) may, at the same time, resonate in the social system of the economy (eg, the clinician may cite resource limitations as a reason for discharge). The book showcases how accountability can be reconceptualised and used to generate a novel, yet more reliable and highly rigorous, picture of the patient homicide governance space. Chapter 1 explained that Luhmann's work challenges the commonly held assumption pervading accountability theory that humans, as whole persons, are able to transmit information unchanged from sender to receiver. The book, however, contends that eschewing the transmission metaphor – as Luhmann's work does – opens up a new way of looking at accountability. Accountability, framed as communication, invites the conclusion that there are different types of accountability (eg, medical accountability, political accountability) being produced to make up the patient homicide governance space. Indeed, through the interviewing of independent homicide investigators, the research conducted for the book found that independent investigations appear to be sites of power application for the social system of politics. The performance of politics (ie, the dedication of resources and bureaucracy by politics for the purpose of managing the political system) encourages a greater assumption of accountability for health service-related problems (ie, service adequacy) through the investigation process itself. Indeed, the book shows that investigators are increasingly expected to go beyond their capabilities and examine broader swathes of health service activity (eg, commissioning). Accountability in the patient homicide governance space, arguably, is constructed politically by society's political system. A political assumption of accountability is, furthermore, expanded in the form of investigations being expected to investigate broader swathes of welfare state (ie, NHS) activity. Investigations are, then, an aspect of political performance.

The previous chapter demonstrated the relevance and importance of protest communications to the patient homicide governance space. Protest resonates across the governance space. It emerges as a moment of autopoietic observation and as a morally charged dispute between key figures (ie, families and investigators). Social communication systems, such as law, resonate in the function system of protest and morality in the form of victim support campaigns and demands for action to be taken to recognise families as a vital element of the patient homicide investigation. These campaigns and demands are often perturbed by inquiry report findings. These findings often stoke up disagreement between family representatives and investigators. NHS services may be lambasted for not doing enough to support families. The book framed these disputes as a clash of meaning. While investigators my reach conclusions that accord with a clinical or scientific understanding of cases, families often argue that these findings are ignorant of their interests in obtaining help and support.

Some investigators expressed the view that support for families is a good thing but some showed concern. They questioned the compatibility of protest on the one hand and the clinically oriented purpose of investigations (ie, to investigate the perpetrator's treatment provision and the adequacy of health care services) on the other. Moreover, investigators struggled with the traction that familial interests have obtained in the patient homicide governance space. The originality of the book therefore lies in its demonstration that the patient homicide governance space is far richer, more complex and more tense than the literature reviewed in Chapter 2 depicts. What is more, the book is novel in its conclusion that the patient homicide governance space is a space of communication in which socially available meaning is produced within society's autopoietic systems of communication. Precise attempts to reform services and minimise risk according to predefined aims and objectives are precluded if the author's conceptualisation of the patient homicide governance space is anything to go by.

The widespread concern patient homicide incidents trigger about the adequacy of health care services and public safety enlivens the health care governance space with morally charged communications. But in general, like many dreadful incidents that may happen during health care delivery, patient homicides are one type of adverse health care event. Adverse health care events may assume different forms (eg, deaths arising out of negligent medical treatment, patient suicides). All adverse events, however, share common themes: they are unintended; they provoke public concern; they attract emotional responses; they involve an investigatory response; and they create occasions on which interested parties (eg, those directly affected by the event and their families, the communities in which they occur, politicians, NHS Trust managers) step into certain systems of communication (eg, law, economics, politics).

The author's contribution is a far-reaching and novel one because it is equally applicable to other spaces of health care governance. The argument that spheres of social communication are resistant to linear processes of directed change from without is equally applicable to other areas of governance where crisis tends to occur. The present work therefore may stimulate new ideas about adverse event response in other areas. On the one hand, a recent review of the gross negligence manslaughter offence in England was conducted by Sir Norman Williams. The review recommended that the independent regulator of health and social care providers – the Care Quality Commission – investigate the broader 'system context' in which a suspected case of gross negligence manslaughter occurred.[1] It appears, then, that the review considers greater regulatory involvement, in the form of an investigation, to be part of the solution to the problem raised by gross negligence manslaughter convictions (ie, the problem of there being excessive focus on individual blame and not enough account being taken of the systemic environment in which the defendant found him or herself). The recommendation of the review underscores the author's conclusion that adverse health care events have a tremendous ability to resonate as moments of power application and political performance. Chapter 4 argued that political power is mobilised at specific moments of power application (eg, regulation). Adverse events become an occasion for the political system to assume more responsibility for the welfare of society, in the form of bureaucracy enlargement (ie, political performance). Whether it is a patient homicide or an instance of gross negligence manslaughter in a hospital, politics comes to the fore in the form of greater accountability for events that occur within the domain of the welfare state (ie, the NHS). Events trigger regulatory response. There is a greater drive towards more investigation of health services. Huge amounts of resource are committed by the government. Moreover, reputations, jobs and power hang in the balance. The mass media construct the event as a story to tell over many weeks and months. The governance space gets busy.

The same review into gross negligence manslaughter went as far as to recommend that the right of the General Medical Council (GMC) to appeal the decisions of the Medical Practitioners Tribunal Service (MPTS) to the High Court should be removed[2] as the procedure 'is inconsistent with other healthcare professional regulators'. Indeed, the review commented that the MPTS is a statutory subcommittee of the GMC and hence still part of it:[3] 'This has led to the perception that the GMC is in effect appealing against itself', with the review panel hearing 'evidence that this perception has led to fear in the medical community and a lack of confidence in the GMC'.[4] Risk and fear, yet again, acquire traction in the health care governance space. Compounding these concerns is the recent Court of Appeal decision *General Medical Council v Bawa Garba*.[5] Bawa Garba, a doctor, was convicted of gross negligence manslaughter in 2016 and was suspended from medical practice by the MPTS for 12 months in a separate fitness-to-practice procedure. The GMC disagreed with the Tribunal's decision and appealed it on

[1] N Williams, *Gross Negligence Manslaughter in Healthcare: The Report of a Rapid Policy Review* (London, Crown, 2018) 28.

[2] ibid 50.

[3] ibid 38.

[4] ibid.

[5] *General Medical Council v Bawa Garba* [2018] EWCA Civ 1879.

the basis that the doctor's conduct justified complete removal from the medical practice register. The media reported widely on the saga and the GMC exercised its powers of appeal vigorously. It lost the appeal in the end. The GMC has since received much criticism, with unease being directed at its regulatory compass during the whole affair.[6] The GMC is now in the midst of a backlash that it originally wanted to avoid. Williams' recommendation for the right of appeal to be removed from the GMC is telling because it exemplifies what is at stake: reputation and power. The saga has mired doctors and regulators in conflict. The risk and fear of regulatory reprisal for 'innocent' errors appears, therefore, to have engulfed the medical profession, according to some reports. *Mental Health Homicide and Society: Understanding Health Care Governance* is a book that provides a highly original theoretical blueprint for understanding the maelstrom of communications that make up the adverse event governance space generally, beyond the locus of homicides committed by mental health patients. The systems of law, politics, medicine, economics, morality, protest and love all resonate within and around the governance of adverse events, with the result that there is objection, regret, disagreement, unintended consequence, protest and talking at cross-purposes. The present work, therefore, provides a novel framework that research in other areas may recruit for the purpose of conducting a precise, comprehensive and rigorous analysis of complex regulatory governance dynamics.

Some readers may conclude that the observations made in previous chapters fail to add much to what is already known about homicide and health care. It perhaps comes as no surprise that patient homicides resonate in society. They occupy the focus of media reports, police investigations, clinical reviews, interest group campaigns and litigation. However, the argument that homicide and health care are communicational self-constructs in society's function systems enables a new way of thinking about the patient homicide governance space to emerge. The book's thesis opens up a unique opportunity to assess the ambitions of policy makers without subscribing to the foundational precepts that underpin those ambitions.

Michael King and Anton Schütz describe the ambitious modesty of Luhmann's work: 'What Luhmann offers is a theory of society, a "grand theory" in the European tradition, but one which runs directly contrary to the claims for universal competence and exhaustive accounts of reality associated with "grand theories"'.[7] For Luhmann, the importance of observation must displace the primacy of explanation and prediction in academic study. Independent investigations after patient homicide and the governance space they animate are managed and commonly understood as methods of explanation and prediction, albeit to varying degrees, but a task of the present book is to displace these common approaches and to

[6] A Samanta and J Samanta, 'Gross Negligence Manslaughter and Doctors: Ethical Concerns Following the case of Dr Bawa-Garba' (2019) 45(1) *Journal of Medical Ethics* 10.

[7] M King and A Schütz, 'The Ambitious Modesty of Niklas Luhmann' (1994) 21(3) *Journal of Law and Society* 261, 261.

'deal with failures in explaining and predicting' within an anti-humanist concept of society.[8]

Policy architects are eager to learn lessons and establish successful change to complex areas of regulation and governance, pursuant to predefined goals. They forge ahead with their objectives, despite the disappointments, inertia and objections that resonate on a regular basis. Responses to patient homicide are typified by these approaches. Suggestions have long been made to replace independent investigations with auditing regimes. According to Eastman, an audit would assess the risk assessment skills of mental health professionals employed by the NHS Trust on whose watch the homicide took place. An audit would also require mental health professionals to demonstrate their skills and demand local criteria for the admission of patients in the 'severe violent risk' category to be agreed under protocols for risk assessment and management.[9] It is interesting that, back in 1996, Eastman called for issues of causation and culpability to be separated, with independent investigations being limited to the investigation of the former.[10] Buchanan similarly suggests that investigations should sharpen their focus,[11] but the tenor of the author's work here may be summarised thus: whether or not a proposal or suggestion is advanced, it is bound to have its 'blind spots' and originate in first-order observation.

The author enlisted a highly rigorous theoretical framework for the purposes of recognising that policy efforts to explain and predict patient homicides are problematic and that an anti-humanist theory of society (ie, systems theory) is well placed to analyse and evaluate these efforts accurately. A unique examination of the governance space emerges as a result. As a self-constructed space of social communication, there is a telling absence of harmony, agreement and causality in how patient homicides are understood and addressed. The assumptions of policy makers and some investigators that universal lessons can be learned become questionable if Luhmann's theory is recruited as a theoretical framework for understanding them. In recruiting Luhmann for theoretical guidance, the book encourages policy approaches to moderate the taken-for-granted assumptions around lesson learning and safety improvements. It encourages policy makers to adopt new ways of approaching adverse events and patient homicides in particular.

There is academic reticence among some systems theorists regarding the suitability of systems theory for effecting normative change. In contrast, some regard systems theory as having an 'inability … to come up with any answers to regulatory problems'.[12] Luhmann contends that observing the codes of social systems is,

[8] ibid 262.

[9] N Eastman, 'Inquiries into Homicides by Psychiatric Patients: Systematic Audit Should Replace Mandatory Inquiries' (1996) 313(7064) *British Medical Journal* 1069, 1070.

[10] ibid.

[11] A Buchanan, 'Independent Inquiries into Homicide: Should Share Common Methods and Be Integrated into New Quality Systems' (1999) 318 *British Medical Journal* 1089, 1090.

[12] J Paterson, 'Reflecting on Reflexive Law' in M King and C Thornhill (eds), *Luhmann and Law and Politics: Critical Appraisals and Applications* (Oxford, Hart Publishing, 2006) 42, 45.

ultimately, an empirical exercise rather than a normative judgement about how those codes should be applied. Indeed, to make a judgement on how a code of a function system should be applied would be to re-introduce first-order observation and endorse the belief that society is amenable to steering. Moreover, systems theory itself is not 'the' answer to society's problems. For those hoping to locate a 'higher code' within systems theory itself for the purpose of directing legal, political, medical, economic or cultural change will be disappointed. Luhmann's theory embraces paradox. There is no one code that can inform a single meaningful reality for society generally.[13] The focus for systems theory is, rather, identifying how responses to society's problems germinate in oversimplified conceptions of what society is. Indeed, these conceptions have dominated problem-solving approaches taken by society's elites (eg, economists, regulators, judges, politicians) for centuries. They are, of course, visible in the present book's assessment of the patient homicide governance space.

It is, admittedly, difficult for abstract social theories to 'speak to' policy makers:

> Where social theories are too abstract or general, too remote from accepted ways of seeing the world, or too complex to be simply transformed into decisions, practising lawyers, politicians or civil servants are quite capable of ignoring them and proceeding with their business as if they had never been formulated.[14]

Concerns over the inability of systems theory to produce answers to regulatory problems reinforce the difficulty. King forcefully argues that systems theory is too different to be of any use to law and policy makers. The notion of systems theory being used to modify law and policy is tantamount to imposing one virtual reality steeped in research methods and publishing onto another virtual reality that is steeped in the practicalities of administration and procedure.[15] Both are radically different species. The latter rarely has time for the former. They are unable to communicate *with* each other. They are only able to communicate *about* each other, in accordance with their internal logics. An interesting alternative is to contend that systems theory has 'nothing to do with the instrumental manipulation of actors or systems'.[16] The importance of systems theory, rather, lies 'in its analysis of the way new and unexpected worlds of meaning emerge by processes which create their own reality'.[17] King, however, claims that such an alternative view trivialises systems theory.[18] Yet, policy makers may find that the 'unexpected worlds of meaning' that emerge out of an application of systems theory might

[13] M King, 'What's the Use of Luhmann's Theory?' in M King and C Thornhill (eds) *Luhmann and Law and Politics: Critical Appraisals and Applications* (Oxford, Hart Publishing, 2006) 45. King follows Luhmann by claiming that law cannot be 'reflexive'.

[14] ibid 38.

[15] ibid 40.

[16] G Teubner et al, 'The Autopoiesis of Law: An Introduction to Legal Autopoiesis' in J Penner et al (eds), *Introduction to Jurisprudence and Legal Theory* (London, Butterworths, 2002) 925.

[17] ibid.

[18] King, 'What's the Use of Luhmann's Theory?' (n 13) 50.

prompt a new look at where the limitations of policy making lie. Systems theory may help produce practical options; an experimentation using different ways of approaching a problem and adjusting their use over a period of time. At the very least, in conducting a series of interviews, the author makes an original effort to bring systems theory closer to the 'real world' of patient and homicide governance while preserving the need to avoid underestimating society's complexity of society. After all, Luhmann argues that a theory 'richer in content … achieves greater complexity' and becomes 'more capable of dealing with social phenomena'.[19]

[19] N Luhmann, *Social Systems* (Stanford, Stanford University Press, 1984/1995) 5.

BIBLIOGRAPHY

Adshead, G, 'Root Cause Analysis' (2005) 29(2) *The Psychiatrist* 71.

Appleby L, Kapur, N, Shaw, J, Hunt, IM, Ibrahim, S, Gianatsi, M, Rodway, C, Williams, A, Tham, SG and Raphael, J, *National Confidential Inquiry into Suicide and Homicide by People with Mental Illness, Annual Report 2017: England, Northern Ireland, Scotland and Wales* (Manchester, University of Manchester, 2017).

Aristotle, *Poetics* (London, Penguin Books, 1996).

Arnoldi, J, 'Niklas Luhmann: An Introduction' (2001) 18(1) *Theory, Culture & Society* 1.

Baecker, D, 'Why Systems?' (2001) 18(1) *Theory, Culture & Society* 59.

Bailey, KD, 'Towards Unifying Science: Applying Concepts Across Disciplinary Boundaries (2001) 18(1) *Systems Research and Behavioural Science* 52.

Baker, E, 'The Introduction of Supervision Registers in England and Wales: A Risk Communication Analysis' (1997) 8(1) *The Journal of Forensic Psychiatry* 15.

Baldwin, R, Cave, M and Lodge, M (eds), *The Oxford Handbook of Regulation* (Oxford, Oxford University Press, 2010).

Baraldi, C, 'Structural Coupling: Simultaneity and Difference Between Communication and Thought' (1993) 3(2) *Communication Theory* 112.

Barbesino, P and Salvaggio, SA, 'How Is a Sociology of Sociological Knowledge Possible?' (1996) 35 *Social Science Information* 341.

Baruch Bush, RA, 'Between Two Worlds: The Shift From Individual to Group Responsibility in the Law of Causation of Injury' (1986) 33 *UCLA Law Review* 147.

Beatson, J, 'Should Judges Conduct Public Inquiries?' (2005) 121 *Law Quarterly Review* 221.

Beck, U, *Risk Society: Towards a New Modernity* (London, Sage Publications, 1992/2005).

Beer, J, *Public Inquiries* (Oxford, Oxford University Press, 2006).

Bernstein, P, *Against the Gods: The Remarkable Story of Risk* (New York, Wiley, 1998).

von Bertalanffy, L, *General Systems Theory* (New York, G Braziller, 1988).

Black, J, 'Critical Reflections on Regulation' (2002) 27 *Australian Journal of Legal Philosophy* 1.

—— 'Decentering Regulation: Understanding the Role of Regulation and Self-Regulation in a "Post-Regulatory World"' (2002) 54 *Current Legal Problems* 103.

—— 'Regulatory Conversations' (2002) 29 *Journal of Law and Society* 163.

—— 'Tensions in the Regulatory State' (2007) (Spring) *Public Law* 58.

Blom-Cooper, L, Grounds, A, Guinan, P, Parker, A and Taylor, M, *The Case of Jason Mitchell: Report of the Independent Panel of Inquiry* (London, Duckworth, 1996).

—— and Hally, H, *The Falling Shadow: One Patient's Mental Health Care, 1978–1993: Report of the Committee of Inquiry Into the Events Leading Up to and Surrounding the Fatal Incident at the Edith Morgan Centre, Torbay, on 1 September 1993* (London, Duckworth, 1995).

Blühdorn, I 'Self-description, Self-deception, Simulation: A Systems-theoretical Perspective on Contemporary Discourses of Radical Change' (2007) 6(1) *Social Movement Studies* 1.

Bovens, M, 'Analysing and Assessing Accountability: A Conceptual Framework' (2007) 13(4) *European Law Journal* 447.

Bowen, GA, 'Naturalistic Inquiry and the Saturation Concept: A Research Note' (2008) 8 *Qualitative Research* 137.

Brans, M and Rossbach, S, 'The Autopoiesis of Administrative Systems: Niklas Luhmann on Public Administration and Public Policy (2002) 75(3) *Public Administration* 417.

Braun, V and Clarke, V, 'Using Thematic Analysis in Psychology' (2006) 3 *Qualitative Research in Psychology* 77.

Brinkerhoff, DW, 'Accountability and Health Systems: Toward Conceptual Clarity and Policy Relevance' (2004) 19(6) *Health Policy and Planning* 371.

Brown, GS, *Laws of Form* (London, George Allen and Unwin Ltd, 1969).

Brown, M and Pratt, J, *Dangerous Offenders: Punishment and Social Order* (London, Routledge, 2000).

Buchanan, A, 'Independent Inquiries Into Homicide: Should Share Common Methods and Be Integrated into New Quality Systems' (1999) 318 *British Medical Journal* 1089.

Burchell, G, Gordon, C and Miller, P (eds), *The Foucault Effect: Studies in Governmentality* (Chicago, IL, University of Chicago Press, 1991).

Burris, S, Drahos, P and Shearing, C, 'Nodal Governance' (2005) 30 *Australian Journal of Legal Philosophy* 30.

Bynoe, I, 'The Falling Shadow: A Lawyer's View' (1995) 6(3) *The Journal of Forensic Psychiatry* 588.

Campbell, D, 'Luhmann Without Tears: Complex Economic Regulation and the Erosion of the Market Sphere' (2013) 33(1) *Legal Studies* 162.

Chevalier-Watts, J, 'Effective Investigations under Article 2 of the European Convention on Human Rights: Securing the Right to Life or an Onerous Burden on a State? (2010) 21(3) *European Journal of International Law* 701.

Chiswick, D, 'The Falling Shadow: A Psychiatrist's View' (1995) 6(3) *The Journal of Forensic Psychiatry* 594.

Cornell, D, 'The Relevance of Time to the Relationship between the Philosophy of Limit and Systems Theory' (1992) 13(5) *Cardozo Law Review* 1579.

Crichton, JHM, 'A Review of Published Independent Inquiries in England into Psychiatric Patient Homicide, 1995–2010' (2011) 22(6) *The Journal of Forensic Psychiatry & Psychology* 761.

Davies, ACL, 'This Time It's For Real: The Health and Social Care Act 2012' (2013) 76(3) *Modern Law Review* 564.

Davies, JP, Heyman, B, Godin, PM, Shaw, MP and, Reynolds, L, 'The Problems of Offenders with Mental Disorders: A Plurality of Perspectives within a Single Mental Health Care Organisation' (2006) 63 *Social Science and Medicine* 1097.

Denby, S, *An Independent Investigation into the Care and Treatment of a Mental Health Service User Mr S in TEWV and BHFT* (Niche Health & Social Care Consulting Ltd, November 2017).

Department of Health, *Guidance on the Discharge of Mentally Disordered People and Their Continuing Care in the Community* (NHS Executive, HSG(94)27).

—— *Independent Investigation into Adverse Events in Mental Health Services* (Department of Health, 2005).

—— 'Chief Executive's Report to the NHS' (London, Department of Health, December 2005).

—— *Department of Health: Annual Report and Accounts 2016–17* (London, HMSO, 2017).

Diamond, S, 'Autopoiesis in America' (1992) 13(5) *Cardozo Law Review* 1763.

Dineen, M, Maden, A, Chase, J and Smith, S, *Independent Investigation into SUI 2006/8119*, (NHS Yorkshire and the Humber, Consequence UK, November 2009).

—— Nixon, J, Jolley, T and Lawrence, J, *Independent Investigation into the Care and Treatment Provided to SU* (NHS London Strategic Health Authority, Consequence UK, February 2012).

Domingues, JM, 'Sociological Theory and the Space-Time Dimension of Social Systems' (1995) 4 *Time & Society* 233.

Douglas, M, *Risk and Blame: Essays in Cultural Theory* (London, Routledge, 1992).

Downham, G and Lingham, R, 'Learning Lessons: Using Inquiries for Change' (2009) 57 *Journal of Mental Health Law* 57.

Durkheim, E, *The Division of Labour in Society* (New York, The Free Press, 1964).

Eastman, N, 'Inquiries into Homicides by Psychiatric Patients: Systematic Audit Should Replace Mandatory Inquiries' (1996) 313(7064) *British Medical Journal* 1069.

—— 'Ethical and Legal Applications' (2006) 11(1) *Criminal Behaviour and Mental Health* 124.

—— and, Peay, J, *Law without Enforcement: Integrating Mental Health and Justice* (Oxford, Hart Publishing, 1999).

Elias, N, *Time: An Essay* (Oxford, Blackwell, 1992).
Emanuel, EJ and Emanuel, LL, 'What is Accountability in Health Care?' (1996) 124 *Annals of Internal Medicine* 229.
Foucault, M, *The Order of Things: An Archaeology of the Human Sciences* (London, Routledge, 1966/2004).
—— *Discipline and Punish* (London, Penguin, 1977/1991).
—— *Madness and Civilisation* (London, Routledge, 1971/2008).
—— 'Subject and Power' (1982) 8 *Critical Inquiry* 777.
Fraser, JT and Lawrence, N (eds), *The Study of Time II* (Berlin, Springer, 1975).
Freeman, M and Hepple, B (eds), *Current Legal Problems, Vol. 46, Part II, Collected Papers* (Oxford, Oxford University Press, 1993).
Francis, R, Higgins J and and Cassam, E, *Report of the independent inquiry into the care and treatment of Michael Stone* (South East Coast Strategic Health Authority, Kent County Council, Kent Probation Area 2006).
Francis, R, *Report of the Mid Staffordshire NHS Foundation Trust Public Inquiry* (London, The Stationery Office, 2013).
Fuchs, C 'The Self-Organization of Social Movements' (2006) 19(1) *Systemic Practice and Action Research* 101.
Fuchs, S, 'Niklas Luhmann' (1999) 17(1) *Sociological Theory* 117.
Fujigaki, Y, 'Filling the Gap Between Discussions on Science and Scientists' Everyday Activities: Applying the Autopoiesis System Theory to Scientific Knowledge' (1998) 37(1) *Social Science Information* 5.
Galanter, M. 'The Turn Against Law: The Recoil Against Expanding Accountability' (2002) 81(1) *Texas Law Review* 285.
Giddens, A, *The Constitution of Society: Outline of the Structuration Theory* (Cambridge, Polity, 1984).
Gordon, C (ed), *Power/Knowledge: Selected Interviews and Other Writings 1972–1977* (Sussex, The Harvester Press, 1980).
Gregory, MJ, 'Managing the Homicide-suicide Inquest the Practices of Coroners in One Region of England and Wales' (2014) 42(3) *International Journal of Law, Crime and Justice* 237.
Grounds, A, 'Commentary on "Inquiries: Who Needs Them?"' (1997) 21 *Psychiatric Bulletin* 134.
Hacking, I, *Mad Travelers: Reflections on Transient Mental Illness* (Richmond, VA, University of Virginia Press, 1998).
Hallam, A, 'Media Influences on Mental Health Policy: Long-term Effects of the Clunis and Silcock Cases' (2002) 14(1) *International Review of Psychiatry* 26.
Hancher, L and Moran, M (eds), *Capitalism, Culture and Regulation* (Oxford, Clarendon Press, 1989).
Harrington, J, 'Time as a Dimension of Medical Law' (2012) 20(4) *Medical Law Review* 491.
Hernes, T and Bakken, T, 'Implications of Self-Reference: Niklas Luhmann's Autopoiesis and Organization Theory' (2003) 24 *Organization Studies* 1511.
Hier, SP, 'Risk and Panic in Late Modernity: Implications of the Converging Sites of Social Anxiety' (2003) 54 *British Journal of Sociology* 3.
HM Treasury, *Public Expenditure: Statistical Analyses 2018* (London, HMSO, Cmnd 9648, 2018).
Hobbs, P, 'Inquiries – High Costs, Unacceptable Side Effects and Low Effectiveness: Time for Revision' (2001) 9(2) *Australasian Psychiatry* 156.
Hood, C and Jones, DKC (eds), *Accident and Design: Contemporary Debates in Risk Management* (London, UCL Press Limited, 1996).
Horton, DP, 'Tackling Elder Abuse and Neglect: Adult Safeguarding under the Care Act 2014' (2016) 4 *Elder Law Journal* 333.
—— and Lynch-Wood, G, 'Rhetoric and Reality: User Engagement and Health Care Reform in England' (2018) 26(1) *Medical Law Review* 27.
—— and Lynch-Wood, G, 'Technocracy, the Market and the Governance of England's National Health Service' (2018) *Regulation & Governance* (forthcoming).
House of Lords Select Committee on the Inquiries Act 2005, *The Inquiries Act 2005: Postlegislative scrutiny* (House of Lords, HMSO, 2014).

Hunter, D and Cheeseman, P, *Domestic Homicide Review Incorporating an NHS Independent Investigation [Mental Health] Overview Report Post Quality Assurance Panel: 'Nina' and 'Jenny'* (Sefton Safer Communities Partnership, November 2017).

Hussain, T, Ewart, E and Ramsay, R, *An Investigation into the Care and Treatment of Service User Y*, NHS London SHA (Verita, 2012).

Hutchison, JS 'Scandals in Health-care: Their Impact on Health Policy and Nursing' (2016) 23(1) *Nursing Inquiry* 32.

Hutter, B and Dodd, N, 'Social Systems Failure? Trust and the Credit Crunch' (2008) *Risk & Regulation* 4.

Hyde-Bales, K and Ewart, E, *An Independent Investigation into the Care and Treatment of Mr J* (Verita, November 2017).

Ibbs, N, *An Independent Investigation into the Care and Treatment of a Mental Health Service User (Mr L) in London* (Niche Health and Social Care Consulting, August 2017).

—— *An Independent Investigation into the Care and Treatment of a Mental Health Service User (Mr H) in Sussex* (Niche Health & Social Care Consulting, September 2017).

Iedema, RAM, Jorm, C, Long, D, Braithwaite, J, Travaglia, J, Westbrook, M, 'Turning the Medical Gaze In Upon Itself: Root Cause Analysis and the Investigation of Error' (2006) 62(7) *Social Science & Medicine* 1605.

Iodem, *Independent Investigation into the Care and Treatment of Mr S* (Iodem, June 2017).

—— *Independent Investigation into the Care and Treatment of Ms Z* (Iodem, June 2017).

Illich, I, *Limits to Medicine: Medical Nemesis, the Expropriation of Health* (London, Penguin, 1990).

Jalava, J, *Trust as a Decision: The Problems and Functions of Trust in Luhmannian Systems Theory* (Helsinki, University of Helsinki, 2006).

Jenkins, G and Moor, N, *An Independent Investigation into the Care and Treatment of P in the West Midlands* (Niche Health & Social Care Consulting Ltd, June 2017).

Johnstone, A, *Independent Investigation into the Care and Treatment of Mr X by the Lincolnshire Partnership NHS Foundation Trust and the Avon and Wiltshire Mental Health Partnership NHS Trust* (NHS South West SHA and East Midlands SHA, Health and Social Care Advisory Service (undated)).

Kay, R, 'Are Organisations Autopoietic? A Call for New Debate' (2001) 18 *Systems Research and Behavioural Science* 461.

Keywood, K, 'Rethinking the Anorexic Body: How English Law and Psychiatry "Think"' (2003) 26 *International Journal of Law and Psychiatry* 599.

Kihlström, A, 'Luhmann's System Theory in Social Work: Criticism and Reflections' (2012) 12(3) *Journal of Social Work* 287.

King, M, 'Child Welfare Within Law: The Emergence of a Hybrid Discourse' (1991) 18(3) *Journal of Law and Society* 303.

—— 'The "Truth" About Autopoiesis' (1993) 20(2) *Journal of Law and Society* 218.

—— 'Psychology and the Legal Process: Is Science and Law an Impossible Marriage?' (1995) 7 *Current Issues in Criminal Justice* 20.

—— 'Future Uncertainty as a Challenge to Law's Programmes: the Dilemma of Parental Disputes' (2000) 63(4) *Modern Law Review* 523.

—— 'An Autopoietic Approach to "Parental Alienation Syndrome"' (2002) 13(3) *The Journal of Forensic Psychiatry* 609.

—— 'Children and the Legal Process: Views From a Mental Health Clinic' (2008) 13(4) *Journal of Social Welfare and Family Law* 269.

—— and King, D, 'How the Law Defines the Special Educational Needs of Autistic Children' (2006) 18 *Child and Family Law Quarterly* 23.

—— and Piper, C, *How the Law Thinks About Children*, 2nd edn (Aldershot, Arena/Ashgate Publishing, 1995).

—— and Schütz, A, The Ambitious Modesty of Niklas Luhmann' (1994) 21(3) *Journal of Law and Society* 261.

—— and Thornhill, C, *Niklas Luhmann's Theory of Politics and Law* (Basingstoke, Palgrave Macmillan, 2005).

—— and Thornhill, C (eds), *Luhmann and Law and Politics: Critical Appraisals and Applications* (Oxford, Hart Publishing, 2006).

Kramar, KJ and Watson, WD, 'The Insanities of Reproduction: Medico-Legal Knowledge and the Development of Infanticide Law' (2006) 15(2) *Social & Legal Studies* 237.

Lawson, G, 'The Rise and Rise of the Administrative State' (1994) 107(6) *Harvard Law Review* 1231.

Lee, DE, 'The Society of Society: The Grand Finale of Niklas Luhmann' (2000) 18(2) *Sociological Theory* 320.

Luhmann, N, 'The Future Cannot Begin: Temporal Structures in Modern Society' (1976) 43(1) *Social Research* 130.

—— *A Sociological Theory of Law* (London, Routledge & Kegan Paul, 1985).

—— *Social Systems* (Stanford, Stanford University Press, 1984/1995).

—— *Love as Passion: The Codification of Intimacy* (Cambridge, MA, Harvard University Press, 1986).

—— *Ecological Communication* (Cambridge, Polity Press, 1989).

—— *Essays on Self Reference* (New York, Columbia University Press, 1990).

—— *Political Theory in the Welfare State* (Berlin and New York, de Gruyter, 1990).

—— 'Technology, Environment and Social Risk: A Systems Perspective' (1990) 4 *Industrial Crisis Quarterly* 223.

—— 'Operational Closure and Structural Coupling: The Differentiation of the Legal System' (1991–1992) 13 *Cardozo Law Review* 1419.

—— 'The Code of the Moral' (1992) 14(4) *Cardozo Law Review* 995.

—— *Law as a Social System* (Oxford, Oxford University Press, 1993/2008).

—— 'Ecological Communication: Coping with the Unknown' (1993) 6(5) *Systems Practice* 527.

—— *Risk: A Sociological Theory* (New Brunswick, Aldine Transaction, 1993/2008).

—— *The Reality of the Mass Media* (Cambridge, Polity Press, 1995).

—— *Protest: Systemtheorie und soziale Bewegungen* (Frankfurt, Suhrkamp, 1996).

—— *Theory of Society, Volume 1* (Stanford, Stanford University Press, 1997/2013).

—— *Die Politik der Gesellschaft* (Frankfurt, Suhrkamp, 2002).

—— *Introduction to Systems Theory* (Cambridge, Polity Press, 2013).

—— *Theory of Society, Volume 2* (Stanford, Stanford University Press, 1997/2013).

Maden, A, *Treating Violence: A Guide to Risk Management in Mental Health* (Oxford, Oxford University Press, 2008).

Maden, T, 'The Falling Shadow' (1995) 167(6) *The British Journal of Psychiatry* 827.

Majone, GD, 'From the Positive to the Regulatory State: Causes and Consequences of Changes in the Mode of Governance' (1997) 17(2) *Journal of Public Policy* 139.

McGrath M, and Oyebode, F 'Characteristics of Perpetrators of Homicide in Independent Inquiries' (2005) 45(3) *Medicine, Science and the Law* 233.

Michailkis, D, 'A Systems Theory Concept of Disability: One Is Not Born Disabled, One Is Observed To Be One' (2003) 18 *Disability & Society* 209.

Mingers, J, *Self-Producing Systems: Implications and Applications of Autopoiesis* (London, Plenum, 1994).

—— 'Can Social Systems Be Autopoietic?' (2002) 50 *The Sociological Review* 278.

Moeller, HG, *Luhmann Explained: From Souls to Systems* (Chicago, IL, Open Court, 2006).

—— *The Radical Luhmann* (New York, Columbia University Press, 2011).

Moor, N, *An Independent Investigation into the Care and Treatment of Mental Health Service Users (F and Maureen) in County Durham* (Niche Health and Social Care Consulting, September 2017).

Morse, JM, 'Determining Sample Size' (2000) 10 *Qualitative Health Research* 3.

Mulgan, R, 'The Processes of Accountability' (1997) 56(1) *Australian Journal of Public Administration* 25.

—— '"Accountability": An Ever-expanding Concept?' (2000) 78(3) *Public Administration* 555.

Münch, R., 'Autopoiesis by Definition' (1991–1992) 13 *Cardozo Law Review* 1463.

Munro, E, 'Mental Health Tragedies: Investigating Beyond Human Error' (2004) 15(3) *Journal of Forensic Psychiatry & Psychology* 475.
—— and Hubbard, A, 'A Systems Approach to Evaluating Organisational Change in Children's Social Care' (2011) 41 *British Journal of Social Work* 726.
Munro, P, 'Privacy v. Publication: Homicide Inquiries in the Balance' (2007) 15(1) *Medical Law Review* 109.
Nassehi, A, 'Organizations as Decision Machines: Niklas Luhmann's Theory of Organized Social Systems' (2005) 53(1) *The Sociological Review* 178.
Neal, LA, Watson, D, Hicks, T, Porter, M and Hill, D, 'Root Cause Analysis Applied to the Investigation of Serious Untoward Incidents in Mental Health Services' (2004) 28 *Psychiatric Bulletin* 75.
Neves, M, 'From the Autopoiesis to the Allopoiesis of Law' (2001) 28(2) *Journal of Law and Society* 242.
NHS England, *Serious Incident Framework* (London, NHS England Patient Safety Domain, 2015).
NHS Improvement, *A Just Culture Guide* (NHS Improvement, 2018).
Niche Patient Safety, *Safeguarding Adults Review and a Mental Healthcare Related Homicide Independent Investigation into the Care and Treatment of B and A* (Niche Patient Safety, 2017).
Nobles, R and Schiff, D, 'A Story of Miscarriage: Law in the Media' (2004) 31(2) *Journal of Law and Society* 221.
—— and —— *Observing Law Through Systems Theory* (London, Hart Publishing, 2012).
Novella, EJ, 'Mental Health Care and the Politics of Inclusion: A Social Systems Account of Psychiatric Deinstutionalization' (2010) 31(6) *Theoretical Medicine and Bioethics* 411.
Nowotny, H, 'Time and Social Theory: Towards a Social Theory of Time' (1992) 1(3) *Time & Society* 421.
O'Mahony, P (ed), *Nature, Risk and Responsibility* (London, Palgrave Macmillan, 1999).
O'Malley, P, 'Uncertain Subjects: Risks, Liberalism and Contracts' (2000) 29(4) *Economy and Society* 460.
Paterson, J, *Behind the Mask: Regulating Health and Safety in Britain's Offshore Oil and Gas Industry* (Aldershot, Ashgate, 2000).
—— Trans-Science, Trans-Law and Proceduralization' (2003) 12(4) *Social & Legal Studies* 525.
Packer, H, *The Limits of the Criminal Sanction* (Stanford, Stanford University Press, 1968/1999).
Parker, C and McCulloch, A, *Key Issues in Homicide Inquiries* (London, MIND, 1999).
Pawlson, LG and O'Kane, ME, 'Professionalism, Regulation, and the Market: Impact of Accountability for Quality of Care' (2002) 21(3) *Health Affairs* 200
Peay, J, *Tribunals on Trial: A Study of Decision Making Under the Mental Health Act 1983* (Oxford, Clarendon Press, 1989).
—— (ed), *Inquiries After Homicide* (London, Duckworth & Co, 1996).
—— 'Clinicians and Inquiries: Demons, Drones and Demigods? (1997) 9 *International Review of Psychiatry* 171.
—— *Decisions and Dilemmas: Working with Mental Health Law* (Oxford, Hart Publishing, 2003).
—— 'Working with Concepts of "Dangerousness" in the Context of Mental Health Law' (2003) 51(1) *Criminal Justice Matters* 18.
—— 'Decision Making in Mental Health Law: Can Past Experience Predict Future Practice' (2005) *Journal of Mental Health Law* 41.
Penner, J, Schiff, D and Nobles, R (eds), *Introduction to Jurisprudence and Legal Theory* (London, Butterworths, 2002).
Perron, A, Rudge, T and Holmes, D, 'Citizen Minds, Citizen Bodies: The Citizenship Experience and the Government of Mentally Ill Persons' (2010) 11(2) *Nursing Philosophy* 100.
Petch, E and Bradley, C, 'Learning the Lessons from Homicide Tragedies: Adding Insult to Injury?' (1997) 8(1) *The Journal of Forensic Psychiatry* 161.
Philippopoulos-Mihalopoulos, A, *Absent Environments* (Oxford, Routledge-Cavendish, 2007).
Pitman, AL, Hunt, IM, McDonnell, SJ, Appleby, L and Kapur, N, 'Support for Relatives Bereaved by Psychiatric Patient Suicide: National Confidential Inquiry into Suicide and Homicide Findings' (2016) 68(4) *Psychiatric Services* 33.

Pollock, A, *NHS Plc* (London, Verso Books, 2004).

Popper, K, *The Logic of Scientific Discovery* (London, Hutchison, 1972).

Porter, R, *A Social History of Madness* (London, Weidenfeld and Nicholson, 1987).

Prasser, S, 'Public Inquiries in Australia: An Overview' (1985) 44(1) *Australian Journal of Public Administration* 1.

Prins, H, 'Half a Century of Madness and Badness: Some Diverse Recollections (2008) 19(4) *The Journal of Forensic Psychiatry and Psychology* 431.

Rae, M, Robinson, C and Georgiou, N, *Report of the Independent Investigation into the Circumstances Surrounding the Care and Treatment of Mr A* (NHS London Strategic Health Authority, Caring Solutions UK, February 2012).

Reiss, D, 'Counterfactuals and Inquiries After Homicide' (2001) 12(1) *The Journal of Forensic Psychiatry* 177.

Reith, M, 'Can We Learn Anything About Personality Disorder from Mental Health Inquiries' (1999) 37 *Criminal Justice Matters* 55.

Ritchie, JH, et al, *The Report of the Inquiry into the Care and Treatment of Christopher Clunis* (London, HMSO, 1994).

Roberts, G, Moor, N, Gaskell, C and Mikhail, S, *An Independent Investigation into the Care and Treatment of Mr R* (Niche Health & Social Care Consulting, February 2012).

Roberts, J, 'The Possibilities of Accountability' (1991) 16(4) *Accounting, Organizations and Society* 355.

Romzek, BS and Dubnik, MJ, 'Accountability in the Public Sector: Lessons from the Challenger Tragedy' (1987) 47 *Public Administration Review* 227.

Rooney, C, *An Independent Investigation into the Care and Treatment of a Mental Health Service User (B) in Greater Manchester: Executive Summary* (Niche Health & Social Care Consulting Ltd, March 2017).

—— *An Independent Investigation into the Care and Treatment of a Mental Health Service User (S) in Liverpool* (Niche Patient Safety, July 2017).

—— *An Independent Investigation into the Care and Treatment of a Mental Health Service User (Miss B) in Rotherham* (Niche Health & Social Care Consulting Ltd, October 2017).

Rooney, JL and Heuvel, LNV, 'Root Cause Analysis for Beginners' [2004] *Quality Basics* 45.

Rose, N, *Governing the Soul* (London, Free Association Books, 1989/1999).

—— 'Psychiatry as a Political Science: Advanced Liberalism and the Administration of Risk' (1996) 9(2) *History of the Human Sciences* 1.

Rumgay, J and Munro, E, 'The Lion's Den: Professional Defences in the Treatment of Dangerous Patients' (2001) 12(2) *The Journal of Forensic Psychiatry* 357.

Samanta, A and Samanta, J, 'Gross Negligence Manslaughter and Doctors: Ethical Concerns Following the Case of Dr Bawa-Garba' (2019) 45(1) *Journal of Medical Ethics* 10.

Schiltz, M, 'Space is the Place: The Laws of Form and Social Systems' (2007) 88(8) *Thesis Eleven* 8.

Scott, C, 'Accountability in the Regulatory State' (2000) 27(1) *Journal of Law and Society* 38.

Scott, R, 'Procedures at Inquiries – the Duty To Be Fair' (1995) 111 *Law Quarterly Review* 596.

Scull, A, 'The Domestication of Madness' (1983) 27(3) *Medical History* 233.

Seddon, T, 'Dangerous Liaisons' (2008) 10(3) *Punishment & Society* 301.

Sevanen, E, 'Art as an Autopoietic Sub-System of Modern Society: A Critical Analysis of the Concepts of Art and Autopoietic Systems in Luhmann's Late Production' (2001) 18(1) *Theory, Culture & Society* 75.

Shaw, J, Hunt, IM, Flynn, S, Amos, T., Meehan, J, Robinson, J and Kapur, N, 'The Role of Alcohol and Drugs in Homicides in England and Wales' (2006) 101(8) *Addiction* 1117.

Sheppard, D, *Learning the Lessons: Mental Health Inquiry Reports Published in England and Wales Between 1969–1994 and Their Recommendations for Improving Practice* (London, Zito Trust, 1996).

Sinclair, A, 'The Chameleon of Accountability: Forms and Discourses'" 20 (1995) 20(2/3) *Accounting, Organizations and Society* 219.

Sinclair, MBW, 'Autopoiesis: Who Needs It?' (1992) 16(1) *Legal Studies Forum* 81.

Smith, B and Hague, DC (eds), *The Dilemma of Accountability in Modern Government: Independence Versus Control* (London, Macmillan, 1971).
Stanley, N and Manthorpe, J, 'Reading Mental Health Inquiries: Messages for Social Work' (2001) 1(1) *Journal of Social Work* 77.
—— and —— (eds), *The Age of the Inquiry: Learning and Blaming in Health and Social Care* (London, Routledge, 2004).
Stirton, L, 'Back to the Future? Lessons on the Pro-competitive Regulation of Health Services' (2014) 22(2) *Medical Law Review* 180.
Stone, B, 'Administrative Accountability in the "Westminster" Democracies: Towards a New Conceptual Framework' (1995) 8(4) *Governance* 505.
Szmukler, G, 'Homicide Inquiries: What Sense Do They Make? (2000) 24 *Psychiatric Bulletin* 6.
Tabboni, S, 'The Idea of Social Time in Norbert Elias' (2001) 10 *Time & Society* 5.
Tada, M, 'Time as Sociology's Basic Concept: A Perspective from Alfred Schutz's Phenomenological Sociology and Niklas Luhmann's Social Systems Theory' (2018) *Time & Society* at 9 (forthcoming).
Taylor, PJ 'Decline of the English inquiry?' (2007) 17(2) *Criminal Behaviour and Mental Health* 69.
—— 'Psychosis and Violence: Stories, Fears, and Reality' (2008) 53(10) *The Canadian Journal of Psychiatry* 647.
Teplin LA (ed), *Mental Health and Criminal Justice* (California, Sage, 1984).
Tetlock, PE and Belkin, A (eds), *Counterfactual Thought Experiments in World Politics: Logical, Methodological and Psychological Perspectives* (Chichester, Princeton University Press, 1996).
Teubner, G, 'Substantive and Reflexive Elements in Modern Law' (1983) 17(2) *Law and Society Review* 239.
—— (ed), *Autopoietic Law: A New Approach to Law and Society* (New York, de Gruyter, 1987).
—— 'How the Law Thinks: Toward a Constructivist Epistemology of Law' (1989) 23 *Law & Society Review* 727.
—— 'The Two Faces of Janus: Rethinking Legal Pluralism' (1992) 13 *Cardozo Law Review* 1443.
—— *Law as an Autopoietic System* (Oxford, Blackwell Publishers, 1993).
Thompson T, Clifton, M and Rosenberg, M, *An Independent Investigation into the Care and Treatment of a Mental Health Service User (Mr EF) Provided by Barnet, Enfield and Haringey NHS Trust* (Caring Solutions (UK) Ltd, August 2017).
Tidmarsh, D., 'Psychiatric Risk, Safety Cultures and Homicide Inquiries' (1997) 8(1) *The Journal of Forensic Psychiatry* 138.
Tucker, P, *Unelected Power: The Quest for Legitimacy in Central Banking and the Regulatory State* (Princeton, NJ, Princeton University Press, 2018).
Verschraegen, G, 'Human Rights and Modern Society: A Sociological Analysis from the Perspective of System Theory' (2002) 29(2) *Journal of Law and Society* 258.
Vibert, F, *Rise of the Unelected* (Cambridge, Cambridge University Press, 2007).
Waldock, H, Rowland, L and Johnstone, A. and Allured, I, *Independent Investigation into the Care and Treatment provided to Mr Y by the Cornwall Partnership NHS Foundation Trust, Cornwall Council and Avon and Wiltshire Mental Health Partnership NHS Trust* (NHS South West SHA (Health and Social Care Advisory Service, undated).
——, Chenery, L and Irons, A, *Independent Investigation into the Care and Treatment provided to Mr AT* (NHS South West SHA, Health and Social Care Advisory Service, November 2009).
Walshe, K and Higgins, J, 'The Use and Impact of Inquiries in the NHS' (2002) 325 *British Medical Journal* 895.
—— and Shortell, SM, 'When Things Go Wrong: How Health Care Organizations Deal with Major Failures' (2004) 23(3) *Health Affairs* 103.
Ward, T, 'The Sad Subject of Infanticide: Law, Medicine and Child Murder, 1860–1938' (1999) 8(2) *Social & Legal Studies* 163.
Warner, J, 'Inquiry Reports as Active Texts and Their Function in Relation to Professional Practice in Mental Health' (2006) 8(3) *Health, Risk & Society* 223.
Webb, D and Harris R (eds), *Mentally Disordered Offenders: Managing People Nobody Owns* (London, Routledge, 1999).

Weinberg, AM, 'Science and Trans-Science' (1972) 10(2) *Minerva* 209.
Wigmore, J, *An Independent Investigation into the Care and Treatment of T, a Mental Health Service User in Camden* (Niche Health & Social Care Consulting Ltd, July 2017).
Williams M and Kevern P, 'The Role and Impact of Recommendations from NHS Inquiries: A Critical Discourse Analysis' (2016) 2(2) *Journal of New Writing in Health and Social Care* 1.
Williams, N, *Gross Negligence Manslaughter in Healthcare: The Report of a Rapid Policy Review* (London, Crown, 2018).
Wilson, L and Wicks, S, *An Independent Investigation into the Care and Treatment of JMcF* (Niche Health & Social Care Consulting Ltd, October 2011).
Wirth, JV, 'The Function of Social Work' (2009) 9(4) *Journal of Social Work*, 405.
Wistrich, AJ, 'The Evolving Temporality of Lawmaking' (2012) 44 *Connecticut Law Review* 757.
Wolfe, A, 'Sociological Theory in the Absence of People: The Limits of Luhmann's Systems Theory' (1992) 13(5) *Cardozo Law Review* 1729.
Wolff, N, 'Interactions Between Mental Health and Law Enforcement Systems: Problems and Prospects for Cooperation' (1998) 23(1) *Journal of Health Politics, Policy and Law* 133.
—— 'Risk, Response and Mental Health Policy: Learning from the Experience of the United Kingdom' (2002) 27(5) *Journal of Health Politics, Policy and Law* 801.
Zinn, JO (ed), *Social Theories of Risk and Uncertainty: An Introduction* (Oxford, Blackwell, 2008).

INDEX

www.ingramcontent.com/pod-product-compliance
Ingram Content Group UK Ltd.
Pitfield, Milton Keynes, MK11 3LW, UK
UKHW020806290926
15470UKWH00003B/981